Preface

The word Environment is derived from the French word 'Environ' meaning 'surroundings'. Each and everything around us is called as environment. Every organism is surrounded by materials and forces which constitute its environment from which it must derive its needs. Environment creates favourable conditions for the existence and deployment of living organisms. Environment is the concern of mankind. We all wish to have a clean environment but very few of us are aware and much less feel genuinely concerned about it.

Environment is the sum total of substances and forces around any organisms, affecting its very existence. Environmental education refers to organized efforts to teach about how natural environments function and particularly, how human beings can manage their behaviour and eco-systems in order to live sustainably. Related disciplines include outdoor education and experimental education. Environmental education is a learning process that increases people's knowledge and awareness about the environment and associated challenges, develops the necessary skills and expertise to address the challenges and fosters attitudes, motivations and commitments to make informed decisions and take responsible action. Environmental awareness may be defined as to help the social groups and individuals to gain a variety of experience in and acquire a basic understanding of Environment and its associated problems. Environment Awareness is the ABC of Environmental Literacy Environmental Education Environmental Issues Environmental Programmes and so on. It is the First step of the Ladder to Environmental Security for Sustainable development. Environment is closely linked to human beings and hence influences their health and quality of life. As such improving our environment by environmental awareness and education will improve human health and well being of all awareness. Environmental education has been considered an additional or elective subject in much of traditional curriculum. At the elementary school level, environmental education can take the form of science enrichment curriculum, natural history field trips, community service projects and participation in outdoor science schools. Environmental education policies assist schools and organisations in developing and improving environmental education programmes that provide citizens with an in-depth understanding of the environment. School related Environmental education policies focus on three main components: curricula, green facilities and training. The originality of this edition owes to the contributors. As an editor I acknowledged all the contributors.

Dr. S.K. Panneer Selvam

Contents

PART–III : AWARENESS ON TRAFFIC RULES AMONG STUDENT TEACHERS

PART—I

Awareness on Environmental Education

Chapter 1

Introduction

Education

Education for all children is a prime goal of our Indian democracy. Education is a basic request for responsible citizenship, maintenance of our life and for successful entry into today's complex world of work. In our country, Education is freely available, yet an alarmingly large number of intellectually capable children leave school education. They are wasting their mental capacities dissipating their opportunities and circumscribing their chances for a better life.

Schooling is the major task of the adolescent just as earning. In the present system of Education, it is the elementary stage which is the most crucial stage of education as it lays the foundation for the personality attitudes, self-confidence labia, learning skills and to scope with the difficulties of real life situations secondary education is also more valuable and it is the platform to foster and develop economical and societal growth. A major challenge is to given better and quality education.

The progress of a nation in the world of today is more than ever dependent upon the quantity and quality of education reviewed by people. From the point of view of Education, as a human need, emphasis has to be placed on the mastery of the spoken word as a medium of communication and socialization the acquisition of universal literacy, its capitalization, the acquisition of universal elementary and secondary education on a part time are full time basis and as a life long activity. Education as a basic human need, therefore, opens unlimited possibilities calling for responses that are constructive, creative and challenging.

In most of the countries, there is widespread acceptance of the principle that Education is fundamental human rights. Education is fundamental to all rural development of human potential, material and spirit, thus furthering the goal of socialism, secularism and democracy enshrined in our constitution. Education develops manpower for different levels of economy and empowers the poor masses to become self reliant enough to participate in the process of national development. Education is thus an instrument for developing an economically prosperous society and for ensuring security and social justice.

Education is the soul of human civilization and development which is lacking among the people. To complete with general communities, it is necessary to equip them educationally. As per general perception, the schooling system offers the children and opportunity. On equal terms with others to gain knowledge and enable them to rise in socio-economic status.

Education is to be complete must have five Principal aspects relating to the five principal activities of human beings. The physical the mental, the social, the emotional and the spiritual. Usually these phases of education succeed each other in a chronological order following the growth of the individual.

The term 'education', as a learning process implies acquiring knowledge. Education cannot "Modification of human behavior" or "drawing out the best in man" and it is a lifelong process which cannot be confined only to four walls of the schools or colleges. Education aims at the total and wholesome or harmonious development of the personality of the child: it should afford opportunities to the individual to develop physically, mentally, intellectually, morally and socially education makes man rational. Self-reliant, self-conscious, civilized, sociable and harmonious. It inculcates good habits in man and makes his life systematic, develops aspirations ambitions and desires in him, makes him powerful and paves the way for his development.

Importance of Education

(*a*) Education is the special manifestation of men.

(*b*) It is the treasure which can be preserved without fear of loss.

(*c*) It secures materials pleasure, happiness.

(*d*) It secures honor at the hands of state not money.

(*e*) Learning is an excellence of wealth that none destroy to man. To man naught else affords reality of joy.

(*f*) The fundamental purpose of education is the same of all times and in all places.

(*g*) Education is a preparation for a living and life.

Environmental Education

The word Environment is derived from the French word 'Environ' meaning 'surroundings'. Each and everything around us is called as environment. Every organism is surrounded by materials and forces which constitute its environment from which it must derive its needs. Environment creates favorable conditions for the existence and deployment of living organisms.

Environment is the concern of mankind. We all wish to have a clean environment but very few of us are aware and much less feel genuinely concerned about it. Environment is the sum total of substances and forces around any organisms, affecting its very existence.

Environmental education refers to organized efforts to teach about how natural environments function and, particularly, how human beings can manage their behavior and ecosystems in order to live sustainably. The term is often used to imply education within the school system, from primary to post-secondary. However, it is sometimes used more broadly to include all efforts to educate the public and other audiences, including print materials, websites, media campaigns, etc. Related disciplines include outdoor education and experiential education. Environmental education is a learning process that increases people's knowledge and awareness about the environment and associated challenges, develops the necessary skills and expertise to address the challenges, and fosters attitudes, motivations, and commitments to make informed decisions and take responsible action.

Environmental education has two components via Environment and education. Education involves Knowledge, understanding and application of facts and concepts pertaining to a discipline and forming desirable believes, attitude, disposition, value as well as inculcation of interests pertaining to that discipline.

The purpose of environmental education is to improve the quality of environment, to create awareness among the people on environment problems and conservation. Therefore, the objectives of the environmental education are to generate awareness, Knowledge, attitude, Skills, evaluation ability and participation to help social groups and individuals.

Focuses of Environmental Education

(*a*) Awareness and sensitivity about the environment and environmental challenges.

(*b*) Knowledge and understanding about the environment and environmental challenges.

(*c*) Attitude concern for the environment and help to maintain environmental quality.

(*d*) Skills to mitigate the environmental problems.

(*e*) Participation for exercising existing knowledge and environmental related programs.

Environmental Awareness

"The Environment is everything that affects the individual except his genes". The term Environment refers to the surroundings of an organism, which includes both living and non living components. The components of Environment is viewed in different ways with different angles by different groups of people but it may be safely argued that environment is an inseparable whole and is constituted by the interacting systems of physical, biological and cultural elements which are interrelated individually as well as collectively in myriad ways.

The International Union for Conservation of Nature and Nature Resources defines Environmental Education as "the process of recognizing values and clarifying concepts in order to develop the skills and appreciate the interrelated among man, his culture and his biophysical surroundings".

Environmental awareness may be defined as to help the social groups and individuals to gain a variety of experience in and acquire a basic understanding of Environment and its associated problems. The concern of a small group of scientists and naturalists has become the focus of the society as a whole. Our survival depends both directly and indirectly upon the presence of stable eco-systems and stable cultivated eco-systems.

Environment Awareness is the ABC of Environmental Literacy Environmental Education Environmental Issues Environmental Programs and so on. It is the First step of the

Ladder to Environmental Security for Sustainable development. Environment is closely linked to human beings and hence influences their health and quality of life. As such improving our environment by environmental awareness and education will improve human health and well being of all awareness.

Environmental education has been considered an additional or elective subject in much of traditional curriculum. At the elementary school level, environmental education can take the form of science enrichment curriculum, natural history field trips, community service projects, and participation in outdoor science schools. Environmental education policies assist schools and organizations in developing and improving environmental education programs that provide citizens with an in-depth understanding of the environment. School related Environmental education policies focus on three main components: curricula, green facilities, and training.

Schools can integrate environmental education into their curricula with sufficient funding from Environmental education policies. This approach is known as using the "environment as an integrating context" for learning inserts environmental education into the core subjects and thus environmental education does not take time away from other important subjects, such as art, gym, or music. In addition to finding environmental curricula in the classroom, environmental education policies allot the financial resources for hands-on, outdoor learning. These activities and lessons help address and mitigate "nature deficit disorder", as well as encourage healthier lifestyles.

Green schools, or green facility promotion, are another main component of environmental education policies. Greening school facilities cost, on average, a little less than 2 per cent more than creating a traditional school, but payback from these energy efficient buildings occur within only a few years. Environmental education policies help reduce the relatively small burden of the initial start-up costs for green schools. Green school policies also provide grants for modernization, renovation, or repair of older school facilities. Additionally, healthy food options are also a central aspect of green schools. These policies specifically focus on bringing freshly prepared food, made from high-quality, locally grown ingredients into schools.

In secondary school, environmental curriculum can be a focused subject within the sciences or is a part of student interest groups or clubs. At the undergraduate and graduate level, it can be considered its own field within education, environmental studies, environmental science and policy, ecology, or human/cultural ecology programs.

Environmental education is not restricted to in-class lesson plans. There are numerous ways children can learn about the environment in which they live. From experiential lessons in the school yard and field trips to national parks to after-school green clubs and school wide sustainability projects, the environment is a topic which is readily and easily accessible. Furthermore, celebration of Earth Day or participation in EE week (run through the National Environmental Education Foundation) is a great way to dedicate your lessons to environmental education. To be most effective, promote a holistic approach and lead by example, using sustainable practices in the classroom and school grounds and encouraging students and parents to bring environmental education into their home.

The final aspect of environmental education policies, but certainly not least important, is training individuals to thrive in a sustainable society. In addition to building a strong relationship with nature, American citizens must have the skills and knowledge to succeed in a 21st century workforce. Thus, environmental education policies fund both teacher training and worker training initiatives. Teachers must be trained to effectively teach and incorporate environmental studies in their curricula. On the other hand, the current workforce must be trained or re-trained so that they can adapt to the new green economy. Environmental education policies that fund training programs are critical in educating citizens to prosper in a sustainable society.

Related Disciplines

Environmental education has crossover with the disciplines of outdoor education and experiential education. Both disciplines complement environmental education yet have unique philosophies.

1. Outdoor education means learning "in" and "for" the outdoors. It is a means of curriculum extension and enrichment through outdoor experiences. Environmental education is often taught or enhanced through outdoor experiences. The out of doors experience, while not strictly environmental in nature, often contain elements of teaching about the environment.
2. Experiential education is a process through which a learner constructs knowledge, skill, and value from direct experiences experiential education can be viewed as both a process and method to deliver the ideas and skills associated with environmental education.

While each of these disciplines has their own objectives, there are points where both disciplines overlap with the intentions and philosophy of environmental education. Paraphrasing Webster collegiate Dictionary awareness implies vigilance in observing something or experience and alertness in drawing inferences from what one observes. Awareness in a personal development sense is a consciousness of which you are being and the impact that you are having on others. Heighten your awareness by imagining a small creature on your shoulder who watches over what you think and what you do and whispers what he observes in your ear.

The following guidelines should be considered to inculcate Environmental Education at school level:

1. Environmental education at school level should aim at creating environmental awareness.
2. Environment concept should be integrated in existing courses in physical, natural and social sciences.
3. Students should be exposed to the concepts of nature education and the experience of participating in nature conservation programmes.
4. Various educational bodies should reorient early education curriculum to include environmental issues.
5. Extracurricular environmental programs for school children are a powerful tool for imparting environmental education to children and should be increasingly encouraged.
6. Several techniques for providing extracurricular environmental education to school children are available. These include sending out by mail by mail or distributing in the classroom entertaining children's magazines on environment, organization of nature and science clubs, visits to exhibitions and museums, organizing painting and essay competitions and exhibitions, participation in community environmental action program and using songs, plays folktales, puppet shows and environmental games and puzzles.
7. At the higher school level, it would be more purposeful to involve youth in seeking and finding solutions to environmental problems and thus indicate a positive environmental attitude.
8. Environmental magazines for the use of and teachers are brought out.
9. Periodical workshops and seminars on environmental topics should be arranged for teachers by organizations.

10. Besides text books, other kinds of teaching aids for environmental education such as guides, hand-books, slide shows, film models etc. should be developed.
11. Parent–Teachers associations should discuss environmental education strategies critically and evolve appropriate school-home integration for infusing the right attitude to environment in the children,
12. Program suited for non-school going and drop-out children should also be developed.

Environmental Education and Awareness

Public Education and awareness are the key factors in any attempt to maintain a proper balance and ensure sustainable development. Recognizing the potential of Environmental Education is an Effective instrument in preventing environmental crises and as an essential element of sustainable development Indian Environmental society has been engaged in spearheading Environmental Education and awareness from the very beginning. Indian Environmental society has undertaken a few new projects on environmental Education and is also continuing with some of the ongoing programs.

Education and Environment

Environment influences one's education. The intersection between education and environment can be described as follows:

1. Education creates the urge for a clean environment.
2. It inculcates in the young minds the basic principles of sanitation and hygiene.
3. It helps pupils and students appreciate the need for conservation of our multifaceted heritage.
4. It teaches newer and environmentally safe technologies.

Environmental Education should start from the school level to pass on to Posterity our rich heritage. "The nation behaves well if it treats the natural resources as assets which it must turnover to the next generation increased and got impaired in Value"

Objectives for Teaching Environmental Education

The Belgrade charter has suggested the following

1. **Awareness:** To help individuals and social groups, acquire an awareness and sensitivity to the social environment and its associated problems.
2. **Knowledge:** To help individuals and social groups, acquire basic understanding of the total environment, its associated problems and humanity's critically responsible presence and role it.,
3. **Attitude:** To help individuals and social groups, acquire social values, strong feelings of concern for the environment and motivation to actively participate in its protection and improvement.
4. **Skills:** To help individuals and social groups, acquire the knowledge and skills of solving environmental problems.
5. **Evaluation ability:** To help individuals and social groups, evaluate environmental measure and educational programmes in term of ecological, political, economical, social, aesthetic and educational factors.
6. **Participation:** To help individuals and social groups, develop a sense of responsibility and urgency, regarding environmental problems to ensure appropriate action for solving the problems.

Environmental Education Curriculum and Different Approaches

In order to achieve the objectives of the environmental education, the curriculum should be continuous, life-long and inter-disciplinary in its approach. The curriculum should be planned horizontally, embracing all the related subjects vertically dealing with one packing. The learners should receive insights into the environmental issues in the bio-physical, bio-chemical, bio-geological and bio-technological areas. The interdisciplinary approach may be in terms of drawing on the specific contents of each discipline in making possible a holistic and balance perspective. The Disciplines such as social sciences and environmental sciences should not be studied in isolation. The curriculum should be so flexible, that the material can be presented according to the background, needs and aspiration of the learners. It should be learner–oriented. They should create a learning environment, and assist learners as they search for information.

As the environmental education is concerned with man's life, it should include environment in its natural totality and built-up. In this connection, the environmental education should not be viewed as one or more subjects added to the already heavy-loaded into the curricular programs for all the learners, whatever be their age group and level of learning.

Approach For Environmental Education

Newman (1981) described a 3-fold classification based on the disciplines.

1. **Environmental Studies:** This is concerned with the case of environmental disturbances and minimization of their import through social change (Social Sciences).
2. **Environmental Sciences:** This deals with the study of the processors in water, air, soil and organism, which lead to "pollution" or environmental damage and to find out a scientific basis for establishing a standard and healthy natural ecosystem.
3. **Environmental Engineering:** This deals with the study of the technical process, which can be used

to minimize pollution and environmental impact. The objectives of environmental education are:

(*a*) To improve the quality of environment.

(*b*) To create an awareness among the people on environmental problems and conservation.

(*c*) To develop skills to solve the environmental problems.

(*d*) To create the necessary atmosphere to make it possible for citizens to participate in decision making and to develop the capabilities to evaluate the development programs.

Perspective on Environment Education

Environmental Education enhances public awareness and knowledge of environmental issues and challenges to civilization. Teachers are the backbone of a society. They play a crucial role in highlighting crucial environmental issues and implementing practical solutions to current local environmental problems in order to reduce the global environmental impact.

Environmental Education is a permanent process in which individuals gain awareness of their environment and acquire the knowledge, values, skills, experiences, and also the determination which will enable them to act individually and collectively to solve present and future environmental problems in order to meet their needs without compromising those of future generations.

Therefore, rather than defining a subject area, environmental education is a learning process featuring awareness of environment, acquiring knowledge, skills, values, experiences, and technical expertise to solve present and future environmental problems by acquiring holistic understanding of environmental problems. The Environmental Education may be summarized based on the following components:

(*a*) Earth is finite,

(*b*) All forms of life are important ,

(*c*) Everything is dynamic, interconnected and independent,

(*d*) Everything must go somewhere,

(*e*) Nature is not a gift from our forefathers but it is a loan from our grandchildren.

Environmental Issues

Environmental education is vast and diverse by nature covering multidisciplinary areas. The principal goals of the teaching of Environmental Education are listed below:

1. Helping people to develop a clear understanding about environment and its relationship with all human activities.
2. Understanding the concept of the inter relationship between natural, socioeconomic and political systems from the grassroots to the global levels as well as activities affecting the environment and major environment issues, such as pollution, occupational hazards, climate change, etc. The best example of it may be the global warming.
3. Designing and running development and production processes from resources extraction to waste disposal in a holistic manner keeping understanding the need for incorporating environmental safeguards in industrial developmental projects and appreciating the need for obtaining environmental clearances.
4. Developing the concept of Biodiversity.
5. Developing Knowledge and skills for identifying and solving immediate local environmental problems, and maintaining on eco-friendly work environment.

6. Understanding the concept of stewardship and motivation critical thinking, reflection and decision making that is reflected in personal life styles.

Awareness of the School Students by the Use of Various Models of Teaching

Emergence of environmental education as a compulsory component of curriculum at school level is a welcome step. India, a developing country, can restore environmental and natural processes by proper awareness on such issues among its citizens. It is a new field and not much canvassing is being done by the public media. Teaching of environmental education is the most burning problem of the country; for this the role of the teacher and his by/her methodology of teaching crucial. Teachers quantum of Knowledge and understanding of Environment is directly related with the objectives and problem of Environmental Education. Since the need of hour is environmentally oriented citizens, the teachers being the national builders have the responsibility to produce such conscious citizens. If we want secure the future of Environment; we have to create awareness about the environment and an attitude for caring and sharing of natural resource among children who are the feature citizen of our nation as rightly said by Pandit Jawaharlal Nehru, The first prime minister of Independent India that "feature of India is shaped in her class rooms" where students are the foundations and teachers are the pillars of development.

One important purpose of education is to provide an understanding of the world environment from physical, biological, social, economical, and political point of view. This understanding also requires the study of the in numerable problems which the man kind faces today. An understanding of environmental problems can be developed by first creating awareness than developing appropriate solution for the Environment. These problems have resulted in a global effort to include aspects of Environmental Education in school curriculum at all levels in on appropriate manner. However, the objective of Environmental Education cannot be realized simply by infusing Environmental concept into the existing curriculum. The effective infusing of Environmental Education curriculum into school programs is possible only when teachers possess the knowledge, and skills and effective attributes which they will impart to the students. The Teachers should use proper methods to transfer Knowledge skills to pupils.

In spite of International efforts, the progress of Environmental Education in world scene does not present a very satisfying picture. It seems that Environmental education has been more accepted than actuated particularly in developing countries.

Environmental Activity

Environmental Activity was done by the students to have direct experience of the Environment in the real life under the supervising of teacher.

Educational Implications

Environment Education is broad based and is strongly related with basic principles of general Education. The various models of teaching Environmental Education have been useful improving the quality of Education through different subject in different classes especially at higher secondary level. Environmental education helps to produce citizens who are environmentally knowledgeable skilled. It leads them towards maintaining a dynamic equilibrium between quality of life and the quality of the Environment.

Need for the Study

Human beings have always exploited the resources available in their natural surroundings for their benefit. Air, Water, land, the Atmosphere living organisms—each of these elements is of important in some form or other to human beings. However technological advancement has made human beings rapacious in their exploitation of natural resources.

India faces environmental challenges on two fronts: Poverty as well as economic development. Poverty and Population pressure clearly result in overuse of land, water forests and other resources without thought of future for who wants to think of coming generations when it is so difficult to survive today? Uncontrolled economic development overuse of groundwater systems and population of natural resources has become the order of the day. So it is the need of the hour to implement Environmental education in full swing. Education is the only way to Environmental Awareness.

Environmental Education would have to aim at producing a citizenry creating a constituency of environmentally oriented people that is knowledgeable regarding the biophysical and manmade environment and its problems and motivated enough to work towards their solution. Such a challenge has to be taken up by the educational institutions, and among these, universities and colleges will have to show the leadership.

It is to effectively educate man regarding his relationship to the total environment the relationship which based on the mutually of respect rather than on superior subordinate relationship. Hence major goals of environmental education should be to help individuals acquire:

(*a*) A Clear understanding that man is an in separable part of the biosphere which consists of man and his built in environment the excising bio physical environment and the substances of the ecological balance.

The basic responsibility of the society and government to work for solving environmental problems.

(*b*) Development of Environmental ethics which will motivate people to participate in the decision making process and to demand protection of the environment so as to advance human welfare and dignity.

(c) Environmental Education should aim to provide factual information to students which will lead to the understanding of the intricate system of ecological balance and man's place in it. To foster Environmental Education awareness is one of the main factors of awareness and concern about economic, social, political and ecological interdependence in urban and rural areas. Tuticorin Educational District is situated in the southern coast of Tamil Nadu. It is an Industrial area. This induced the investigator to make an attempt to study the awareness on environmental education among the Higher Secondary Students at Salem Educational District.

Objectives of the Study

The Following Objectives were formulated for the present Study. To find out the environmental awareness of higher secondary school students in Salem Educational District.

To find out the significant difference in the environmental awareness of:

1. Gender
2. Student locality
3. Types of school
4. Parent occupation
5. School locality

Statement of the Problem

Environmental Awareness is necessary to know the importance of keeping the environment clean and protecting the earth. So the study focuses on the topic entitled:

"A Study on Environmental Awareness of Standard XI Students in Salem District".

Hypotheses of the Study

1. There is no significant difference between aided boys & Aided girls towards awareness on environmental education among Higher Secondary students at Salem District.
2. There is no significant difference between boys and girls towards awareness on environmental education among Higher Secondary Students at Salem District.
3. There is no significant difference between rural and urban students towards awareness on environmental education among Higher Secondary students at Salem District.
4. There is no significant difference between rural and urban schools towards awareness on environmental education among Higher Secondary students at Salem District.
5. There is no significant difference between Government and Private Parents Occupation towards awareness on environmental education among Higher Secondary students at Salem District.
6. There is no significant difference between Government Boys and girls towards awareness on environmental education among Higher Secondary students at Salem District.

Scope of Environmental Studies

Environmental Study is an important tool to educate the people for preserving quality environment. The main scope of environmental studies includes.

1. To get an awareness and sensitivity to the total environment and its related problems.
2. To motivate the active participation in environmental protection and Improvement.

3. To develop skills for identifying and solving environmental problems.
4. To know the necessity of conservation of natural resources.
5. To Evaluate Environmental Programs in terms of social economic ecological and aesthetic factors

About Higher Secondary Students

After the Completion of the High School level of education students enter the secondary level i.e. in Standard XI in Higher Secondary School. Now they attain the adolescence stage as teenagers.

Salem District

Since Salem is a growing industrialized town it is apt for the study and also special for steel and the mango.

Delimitation of the Study

1. The study has been limited to Salem District only.
2. The study has been restricted to the Higher Secondary students only.
3. This study adopted survey method using questionnaires to collect data from respondents.
4. A purposive stratified random sample was used to choose the subject to be included in the study.
5. This study is focused mainly on the variables, gender, and students locality, types of the school, parents occupation, and school locality.

Organization of the Thesis

The first chapter gives introduction, definitions of the terms, statement of problem, objectives and limitation of the study.

Second chapter deals with the review of related literature which are done in India and abroad related to this problem.

Third chapter gives a detailed account of research procedures and methodology used in this problem.

Fourth chapter deals with the tabulation of analysis and the interpretation of the data in detail.

Fifth chapter describes the findings, conclusion and certain recommendations about the problem.

Chapter 2

Review of Related Literature

Introduction

"A good thesis is one that me how to replicate or extend the previous work with improvements to reduce bias, eliminate flaws consider pertinent variables, settle unsolved issues to check contradictory or uncertain finding".

The aim of this chapter is to record briefly a survey of literature related to the problems under study. It is necessary to enter on any research project. This will help in understanding the various aspects of the problem.

The research worker must be acquainted with up-to-date information about what has been thought and done in the specific area from which he intends to take up a problem of research.

A review of related literature gives the scholar an understanding of the previous work that has been done in the area, it enables him to know the means of getting to the frontier in the field of his problems, methods and limitations and it enables him to locate comparative data useful in the interpretation of results.

Review of Related Literature

A review of related literature is a direction of find out the reality and the beneficial nature and the reliability of a work undertaken, keeping in mind the material that are available in connection with the topic. A review will give the investigator a vivid idea of what he should do and how he should go about his investigation. Clarke, D.H. and Clarke, H.H. (1970) gave the importance of review of related literature as that of before completing a plan for a research understanding, the investigator needs to conduct a literature search in the area of the proposed investigations.

The review of related literature is an instrument in the selection of the topic formulation of hypothesis and defective reasoning leading to the problem. It helps to get a clear idea and supports the findings with regard to the problem under study (Tirumalai Swamy 1995).

The research scholar had come across several books, periodicals, journals, internet and unpublished thesis while searching for relevant facts and findings that are related to this present study. Such of these facts are given below for a better understanding and to justify his study.

Purpose of Review Literature

The phrase Review of literature consists of two words Review and Literature of a particular are of any discipline which includes theoretical practical and its research studies.

The literature in any field forms the foundation upon which all future work will be build. If we fail to build foundations of knowledge provided by the review of literature one work is likely to be shadow and that has already done better by someone else.

A search for knowledge cannot yield something meaningful if this relation with the existing knowledge has not been examined. A research study is never conducted in a vacuum. Hence an attempt was made, as far as possible, to find out what has already been done. A review of literature gives both thematic as well as methodological direction. In a rare case a study may justify accomplishment of a new knowledge without paying attention to what has been done carrier. In an age where we already find vast store of knowledge, it is necessary to examine what has been done before we boast of a new achievement (Barotia and Sharma, 1999). Hence, a brief review of the studies related to the present problem is described in this chapter.

The following are the some of the purposes of the review of literature:

1. It provides ideas, theories, explanations or hypothesis valuable in formulation the problem.
2. To avoid the risk of duplicating some of the studies already undertaken.
3. To suggest methods or research methodology appropriate to the problem.
4. It suggests valuable basis for hypothesis.
5. It helps delimit the problem.
6. It helps the investigator not to allow the mistake (or) pit fall which occurred in the previous findings.
7. To locate comparative data useful in the interpretation of results.
8. It contributes to the investigator for the general scholarship.

Studies Conducted in India

Arundhati Vishvasrao, Various ideas have been introduced for teaching environmental sciences through formal education. These attempts have created environmental awareness, but Environmental Education has still not been achieved. For bridging the gap between environmental awareness and education three important changes are proposed:

1. The focus of science education must change from creationism to a naturalistic view, right from school.

2. The learner must remain the focus and must develop a holistic understanding of his environment.
3. Environment friendly habits must be developed from school days, wherein teachers become role models in the formal education system.

Awareness leads to understanding and understanding to action. Awareness leads to information', which develops an understanding of the 'science' and leads to action, which is culture (ethics). Ancient Indian culture allowed the population to put environmental ethics into practice. This was achieved through role models. The Gurukul system practiced in India at that time is a very good example of this.

Ehsan [1985] examined the nature and scope of the environmental studies programs in the primary schools of Bangladesh in terms of their objectives, content and teaching learning strategies his findings were treat.

1. The objectives of teaching environmental science were not explicitly stated in the program.
2. The contents of topics included in the programme were up-to-date and suitable to learner's needs, interests and abilities.
3. The teaching learning strategies suggested in the programme were feasible and practicable for use by teachers in the class-room.

Guptha [1986] in his study attempted to develop a tool which can measure the attitude of teachers towards environmental education the data for his study were collected from150 teachers working in primary and secondary schools and junior colleges. The study showed that the teachers had favorable attitude towards environmental education. But the degree of favorableness was the highest among .college teachers .the study identified that crowded class room's lack of time for proper planning of activities and loss of interest in the absence of follow up actions as stumbling blocks to the implementation of environmental education program.

Rath N.C. Mohanthy [1992] jointly conducted a study to assess the awareness of adolescents on Environmental pollution.

1. It was found that 59 per cent of the school going adolescents had medium level of awareness while19 percent and 22 per cent of them had high and low level of awareness on environmental pollution, respectively. Among the non school adolescents, it was observed that 68 per cent of them had medium level of awareness while 17 per cent and 15 per cent of them had high and low level of Awareness on environmental pollution respectively.
2. It was presumed that education has got definite impact on the awareness of environmental pollution. The more an individual becomes educated, the higher will be his or her awareness on environmental pollution.
3. It was revealed that out of the total respondents 1153 and 36 per cent were having low, high medium exposure, to media respectively. The 'r' value indicated exposure, to different media and the awareness towards environmental pollution only in the case of school going, adolescents. In the case of nonschool going adolescents .also, the relationship between exposure to media and awareness existed but it was weak and statistically in significant.

Reddy [1992] studied the use of environ mental mode in teaching primary classes the study revealed that the use of environment was effective in teaching. By making effective use of this device pupils can be helped to become active learners. It creates class room more interesting and attracts the pupils to come to schools .It improves the enrollment reduces dropouts. Thus use of environment helps in achieving universalization of elementary education.

According to singh and singh [1992] environmental education is an investment in future the environmental education in children is likely to result in greater consciousness about global issues, an improved healthful loving and greater prosperity due to more judicious use of natural resources. Environmental education creates personal commitment to, or acceptance of responsibility for the proper maintenance of the environment. Benefits from the environmental education will always be positive whatever be the expenditure involved

Swatantra Devi [1992] identified a few strategies for the teaching of environmental education. She suggested a few activities to facilitate teaching and learning process of environmental knowledge to secondary school students. She suggested that problem solving Approach, use of visual aids and follow up in terms of class discussions were effective strategies. She delineated the benefits and risks involved in sticking to single strategy.

Sundararajan. S and Rajashekar.S [1993] conducted a study on "Environmental awareness among higher secondary students. The study revealed that the environmental awareness of the higher secondary students in Tamil Nadu had not been influenced by the locality to which they belong or by their sex similarly no significant difference existed between student's environmental awareness and there, socio-economic, background or their special subject of study .

V.M. Galushin [1994] noted that there are three kinds of approaches to school environmental education.

1. Environmental topics may is dispersed throughout the entire curriculum by insertions at appropriate places in the syllabi of various, disciplines.
2. A specially designed lesson on nature, conservancy may be inserted as a unit, within the framework, of one of the existing school subjects.
3. An integrated course of environmental education may be offered as a separate discipline on par with other school subjects.

He felt that three approaches may be used in successive stages, rather than as alternatives.

Irmeli Palmberg [2000] Mostly students describe Environmental issues as increasing problems and horrible disasters as presented in mass media. Only a small minority of students has more optimistic views and trust in time, changes in man's environmental attitude and lifestyle for they simply put their trust in new technology.

K. Durga Malathi [2002] found that there is a significant difference between rural and urban regions and gender difference in the environmental awareness.

G.C. Pradhan [2002] show that the teachers teaching science had significantly higher awareness compared to teachers of social science and languages.

M. Selvam, G. Anto Boopalrajan, B. William Dharma Raja [2003] Another study revealed that teacher trainees had significant difference in terms of age.

Joanne [2004] A study suggested combining Environmental Education and artwork in the primary grade for sustainability day.

M. Balamurugan [2005] Association could be seen between environmental awareness and fathers' occupations as skilled workers. Some findings showed significant difference in environmental awareness, and religious groups and school types.

P. Dharani [2005] A study on student's perception on 'Disaster Management' found that there is a correlation of perception of school students between the natural and manmade disaster management.

Fishman, Lianne [2005] Some international investigations revealed promoting of opportunities for children to experience nature first hand on the way to school, the promotion of children's awareness of nature in their daily lives and the promotion of interest and tolerance of local plants and animals.

Mercy Abraham, Arjunan NK [2005]: Another study found that there is no significant difference between girls and boys in secondary classes with record to their pre-environmental.

R.Sahaya mary, I. Paul Raj [2005]: Studies showed that boys especially from urban area have more awareness than girls. Some studies revealed that science students have more awareness of biodiversity and conservation than non-science students.

Sandhya Gihar [2006]: Finding of another study revealed that male students and scientific background students were having higher environmental responsibility behavior than their counterparts.

Ami Mat & Yahaya, Nurizon & Ahmadun, Fakhrul-Razi [2007]: Findings show that environmental awareness had raised the consciousness of students but was rather im effective in changing action and behavior patterns.

Dr. R. Gnanadevan [2007]: Findings revealed that environmental awareness of Hr. Sec students is high.

Shobeiri, S.M., Omidvar B and Prahallada N.N. [2007]: A comparative study revealed that there are significant differences in Indian and Iranian students in their environmental Awareness.

Chandrasekar [2008]: from the review of journals, it could be observed that some investigation had been conducted to find out the level of environmental awareness among tenth standard high school students of Hyderabad city. Findings concluded that environmental awareness of high school students is moderate.

An analysis of level of environmental awareness: the case of prospective teachers (2010) G.Ekambaram, B.Nagaraja: In this study, the investigators among other things found that the level of environmental awareness differs among science and non-science teachers with science teachers having a higher level of environmental awareness.

Objectives of the Study Were

Though the study in general aims at an analysis of awareness among under-training teachers, it specifically aims at the following objectives:

1. To analyze the levels of awareness about environment among prospective teachers.
2. To compare and contrast the attitude of science and non-science prospective teacher with regard to environmental awareness, and
3. To evaluate the impact of gender, age and social status of the prospective teachers on the level of environmental awareness.

Sample Size

Keeping the objectives in view, a total of 200 prospective teachers, who are under B Entraining in Tirupati College were selected at random, consisting of 112 Science trainee-teachers and 88 non-science trainee teachers in Chittoor district of Andhra Pradesh.

Summary of Findings

The analysis of level of awareness of 200 sample prospective teachers consisting of Science and Non-Science, male and female, different age groups and social groups indicate that;

1. The level of awareness differs in Science and Non-Science teachers. Science teachers were found with higher level of environmental awareness compared to Non-Science teachers.
2. Gender difference also was found in the level of awareness. The results of the analysis show that level of environmental awareness was higher among female sample teachers compared to male sample teachers.
3. An exercise is also made to know the impact of some selected social variables like age and social status. The age-wise analysis of the level of aware-

ness reveals that there is statistically significant difference in the sample teachers who are in the age groups of below 23 years and above 23 years.

4. The social status wise analysis of the level of awareness revealed that there is statically significant difference in the level of awareness between the sample teacher representing other classes and SC and ST social group. The sample teachers belonging to other classes had higher level of awareness compared to SC and ST teachers.
5. No statistically significant difference was found in the level of awareness between the sample teachers belonging to backward classes and others forward classes and also between backward classes and scheduled caste and schedule tribes.

Studies Conducted in ABROAD

Madduma Bandara C.M. [1989] examines the need to increase awareness of the interactions between human activity and environmental change based on the HDGC (Human Dimension of Global Change Programme) perspective. In addition to that, the whole issue is referred to various international conferences regarding the impacts global environmental education has on the poorest and weaker groups in developing countries. This reading also talks about the target groups for these educational initiatives but also notes what he calls "a continuing need to reach out to the unconverted groups in most developing Countries".

Although international environmental education has a global perspective, the author identifies "special" target groups with special problems. Mainly populations in rural areas form these groups. Most people in these zones are among the poorest and most ill educated on the plane. They are subject to numerous factors that don't facilitate the implementation of sustainable management plans, factors that relate to simple survival needs, which are more important to their lives than environmental concerns.

Environmental awareness in vulnerable communities in developing countries can be improved through both formal and non-formal education. Mass media, art, and traditional knowledge, are elements that can greatly contribute to the encouragement of environmental awareness in developing countries.

Filho [1995] also notes that in the relatively short history of "the environment" as a social problem, public concern has been cyclical and so has the media coverage of environmental news.

Leal Filho [1995] declares; "to ensure didactic potential of the media for environmental information and for environmental education is fully used, there are a number of items, which need to be considered. Some of these are:

1. *Diversity of information:* newspaper articles, as well as television and radio programs may be used as resource materials for classroom-based lessons provided that due guidance are given and that the issues discussed may be closely related to curricular themes.
2. *Time relevance:* the use of printed or broadcast materials ought to provide a supply of recent information with up-to-date details.
3. *Accuracy:* Teachers and others using the media for environmental education should be aware of this reality and try to carefully select materials prior to use, so that misunderstanding and misinformation may be prevented."

Tilbury [1995] argues that Environmental Education for Sustainability differs from previous environmental Education approaches in that it focuses more sharply on developing closer links between environmental quality, ecology and socio-economic and the political threads which underlie it. Its basis is the creation of a more holistic outlook on problems, requiring a deeper integration between the study of environment and development problems.

Although there is a great deal of work required to develop meaningful and workable definitions of Environmental Education for Sustainability, the following elements are important:

1. Ethical awareness
2. Shaping values and attitudes
3. Skills and behavior consistent with sustainable development
4. Effective public participation in decision making
5. Making decisions and taking action
6. Consideration of future generations.

Of the indicators used in the mapping process, a sub-set of 36 specifically pertaining to environmental education for sustainability were also used to further evaluate and rate course content in relation to the above elements.

As Smyth [1995] Environmental education is a cross curriculum topic promoting global awareness, sustainable living and active citizenship. It involves a structured and planned process that seeks the implementation of environmental curriculum at educational institutions at different levels. Cross-cutting subjects that are integrated in a global perspective but that can be learned and applied locally should implement this curriculum.

Based on these principles we might assert that Environmental education should be multilevel and continuous. A first educational level should target special programs for non-formal adult and community-based audiences. The second level focuses on secondary school. It involves teaching the main disciplines within an environmental context. The third level focuses on obtaining environment based professional skills within the different professional disciplines. An urgent need to educate humankind on conservation and sustainable uses of natural resources through environmental education has been accepted as a global necessity. The concept of environmental education gained great momentum at the UN conference in Stockholm in 1972. In

Agenda 21 a holistic view of Environmental education was adopted and acknowledged by 175 countries at the first UN Earth summit in Rio de Janeiro on environment and development. The now famous "Agenda 21" identifies education as a vital aid to support all the needed changes for sustainability to take place. Signatory nations agreed to pursue actions to include environment sustainable development as a cross cutting matter in curriculum at different levels of education, and also to ensure it reaches different audiences, including those located at remote communities .

As Smyth (1995) lays it out, "Agenda 21 signals the need for a clear lead from the top and for facilitation of collaboration between the main interests concerned, in national and local government, government agencies, formal education, the business sector, cultural, community and youth organizations and the voluntary sector. All of these are concerned in different ways with direct educational activity and services, whether formal or informal, with staff training and with exemplary environmental practice and there is an often unrealized potential for collaborative programs."

The main goal of Agenda 21 is that all signatory countries incorporate Environmental education into their educational systems at all levels. Norway and Malta represent two examples of countries that are trying to implement environmental curricula in their educational systems. They have both experienced difficulties but they have also made progress. Their efforts deserve analysis because they demonstrate many positive aspects that can be applied elsewhere if locally adapted.

It is obvious there is a need to tackle environmental problems globally by means of a systematic process that requires changes in traditional education schemes. The entire scientific community is reasonably responsible for getting involved in adequate public relations efforts that enable communication of its research, concerns and uncertainties, to the institutions, organizations and governing bodies responsible for education. Similarly establishments responsible for education should make efforts that direct to the public information received from scientists in effective and understandable ways.

As Pace notes [1997], elementary school curricula are essentially fragmented and mono-disciplinary, making interdisciplinary learning hard to apply. Even though environmental topics have become much more relevant in recent years in secondary schools, it is also fragmentary.

While environmental education is not a national Maltese priority, at least there is a growing awareness phase by government and other organizations where the need to incorporate environmental topics into their educational system is being recognized. Different organizations have included environmental education in their agendas. However, they have been forced to work in an uncoordinated way due mainly to a lack of official support and organization.

As Pace (1997) declares, "In an attempt to improve the situation the Education Division, the Environment Secretariat, the faculty of education and some nongovernmental organizations jointly organized the Second National Training Workshop on Environmental Education in Malta (May 1995). The goal of the event was that of getting all those involved in environmental education together to; become aware of the state of environmental education in the region, identify the problems, needs and support required for the successful implementation of environmental education initiatives and, to discuss the possibility of coordinating these initiatives so as to improve their effectiveness".

While Malta has a long way to go before a national environmental education strategy can be fully implemented in their educational system, the country has at least recognized the intention of incorporating environmental education into their education system and some efforts in this direction are being produced.

Benedict [1999] points out "The goal of the Ministry of Education's strategy was that all pupils should receive environmental education in line with the UNESCO goals, including knowledge, attitudes, capabilities and behavior. A rather large group of teachers, researchers and organizations was involved in developing the strategy, which went through several stages of revision and is still being periodically revised. Thus, the Ministry of Education itself has taken a leading role in initiating change. Staffing (one full-time position) and a substantial budget were allocated to this work, which was led by the Ministry of Education."

According to Benedict's study (1999) the goals of the Norwegian strategy were oriented toward the system as a whole, not individual schools or programs.

Goals

1. Clarify the goals and contents of environmental education.
2. Contribute to organizational development in schools.
3. Ensure that the strategy is implemented.
4. Clarify and coordinate efforts in environmental education between the school system and its cooperative partners.
5. Evaluation.

These goals touch on three of the four 'Cs': commitment and responsibility, and on the part of the Ministry of Education, competence and cooperation. Curriculum was being dealt with in a general curriculum reform so it did not appear in the strategy goals.

According to Benedict (1999) the most important lessons learned from the Norwegian case are, "First, shortcuts don't work. Teachers who struggle to implement systemic environmental education within the framework of an educational system that isn't made for it may succeed in the classroom in the short term, but their efforts are usually not sustainable. Teachers cannot succeed without support from the higher levels and the Ministry of Education cannot do well in conducting educational development without full cooperation from teachers and principals.

A second is that the process of bringing about systemic changes in priorities, competence, curricula and patterns of cooperation and communication is a long term process. Experiences in Norway indicate that raising teacher's competence in environmental education will require much more than short in-service training courses, although these kinds of courses can be effective in initial awareness rising. Understanding the cross-cutting elements between natural and human systems is intellectually challenging and requires openness to a wide range of disciplinary paradigms, from history, anthropology and literature to economics, biology and political science.

A third is that structural changes in communication and cooperation require patience, goodwill and commitment. Vertical communication between the Ministry of Education and local bodies such as municipal school directors and schools is full of tensions. Some sort of compromise by both parts and understanding of the roles and responsibilities must be reached if change is to be possible."

Cooperation between the Ministry of Education and Ministry of the Environment in Norway is also a sensitive subject. They can easily step on the other's "territory" and put at risk vital mutual aid. Cooperation and network building between the school and external players is fundamental to efficient environmental education.

As Allen [2001] says; "Scientists and journalists have had plenty of positive interactions. Yet despite the idealistic motivations of scientists and professional journalists, chaos and hard feelings sometimes characterize the interactions between them. Such discord is largely the result of a clash of two cultures, science and the newsroom. Framed simply, science is the world of labs, publications, peer review, and acceptance according to the values and norms of science.

Journalism's task is to inform the public speedily, to detail history on the run."

Nkosi [2002] carried out a community oriented education program on biological diversity, conservation and sustainability in Swaziland. It emphasized the need for a public education program. This program was intended to be seen as an investment in the people by teaching them a self-regulating culture that would help raise awareness of the role biodiversity and conservation can play in sustainable development among the most vulnerable communities in the developing world.

De Lorme et al. [2003] reviewed the connection between human growth, development and water resources in central Florida. By including six focal groups, the report was based on the importance input from the community had in contributing to the preproduction stages of a public educational campaign in the region. The groups recommended five messages and five key delivery options that could be included in the campaign.

Messages

1. Make clear to homeowners the financial advantages of long-term water management practices.
2. Promote self-efficacy at home.
3. Make evident the association between quality of water and quality of life.

4. Recognize the demographic characteristics of the region.
5. Keep the messages straightforward and brief.

Delivery

1. Water resource information could be delivered through direct mail in utility bills.
2. Messages could be delivered through public service announcements and stories on local television programs.
3. The use of websites and electronic newsletters can be positive.
4. Messages and information could be distributed through educational programs in the school system where parents are able to participate.
5. Information kits could be delivered through homeowner's associations.

Vaughan [2003], Environmental education and community conservation needs should be viewed in a continuous and progressive perspective. A study conducted during a 4-week period in the town of Quebrada Ganado, Costa Rica by Vaughan revealed that if Environmental Education programs for children are guided in a proper way, parents and other adults could also benefit from them. Knowledge gain passed on from children to parents (and other adults) indicates that awareness can be delivered in a consecutive way from the classroom to the community.

Analogy

Out of total thirty four studies identified, the investigator found twenty three studies conducted in India and eleven studies conducted in abroad. Majority of the studies belongs to survey studies and few of them are experimental studies.

Most of the studies followed random sampling technique in the collection of data and the size of the selected samples range from to samples. In majority of the studies the questionnaire, Opionnarrie rating scale developed by the investigator was utilized as a tool. Since all the reviewed studies were related to awareness on Environmental Education. In majority of the studies of the data was collected only from the school students and no standardized tool was catalyzed. Mean, standard deviation and 't' test were the statistical technique followed in the majority of the study.

Durga Malathi K. [2002] states that there is a significant difference between rural and urban regions and gender difference in the environmental awareness. This finding is related to the present study.

Ehsan [1985], Sundararajan.S and Rajashekar.S [1993], GalushinV.M. [1994], Pradhan G.C. [2002], Dr. R. Gnanadevan [2007] states that states about environmental education . This finding is related to the present study. The following chapter deals with the methodology of the present study.

Chapter 3

Methodology of the Study

Overview

The Methodology followed in the present study is described in this Chapter. The present study is a Normative Survey Research which aimed to measures the Awareness on Environmental Education among Higher Secondary Students. The Design of the study, construction of the Tool, Pilot Study, Validity and Reliability, Size of the Sample, Selection of the Sample, Administering the Tool among the Students, Scoring Methods, Statistical Techniques utilized etc., have been reported in detailed manner in this present Chapter and ends with the Limitations of the study.

Design of the Study

Research design is a plan, a structure and a strategy of investigation conceived to obtain answers to various issues in research. The object of research design is to test the research hypotheses. The research design, therefore, is built in the principle of maximization of the results of the study, minimization of variance. A research design however, is not a highly specific plan to be followed without direction. Rather, it is series of guideposts to keep right direction. Thus, research design is the process of planning a research, choosing methods and procedures that can be expected to yield meaningful and most interpretable results.

Table 3.1 : Schematic Representation of the Research Design

Sl.No.	Type	Sources
1.	Nature of the research	Normative Survey Research
2.	Tools Developed	Awareness on Environmental Education among Higher Secondary Students (AEEHSS)
3.	Variables	Students
4.	Demographic Variables	1. Gender 2. Student's Locality 3. Types of School 4. Parent Occupation 5. School Locality
5.	Sampling Technique	Stratified Random Sampling Technique.
6.	Size of the Sample	Students-150 Boys-72 Girls-78
7.	Statistical Techniques used	Mean, Standard Deviation, 't' test

The present study belongs to Normative Survey Research. In this, Demographic Variables like Gender, Students Locality, Types of School, Parent Occupation and School Locality are used. The Tool use in the Study is Awareness on Environmental Education among Higher Secondary Students at Salem District, along with a Personal Data Sheet to know the background of the Students; Random Sampling technique was followed in this study. Data were collected from 150 Students in different locations of Salem District. The Statistical Techniques were used Mean, S.D. and 't' Test.

Objective of the Study

1. To find out the level of significant different between Aided boys and Aided girls towards awareness on Environmental education among Higher Secondary students at Salem district.

2. To find out the level of significant different between boys and girls towards awareness on Environmental education among Higher Secondary students at Salem district.

3. To find out the level of significant different between rural and urban students towards awareness on Environmental education among Higher Secondary students at Salem district.

4. To find out the level of significant different between rural and urban school's towards awareness on Environmental education among Higher Secondary students at Salem district.

5. To find out the level of significant different government and private parents occupation towards awareness on Environmental education among Higher Secondary students at Salem district.

6. To find out the level of significant different government boys and government girls towards awareness on Environmental education among Higher Secondary students at Salem district.

Hypotheses of the Study

1. There is no significant difference between aided boys & Aided girls towards awareness on environmental education among Higher Secondary students at Salem District.

2. There is no significant difference between boys and girls towards awareness on environmental education among Higher Secondary Students at Salem District.

3. There is no significant difference between rural and urban students towards awareness on environmental education among Higher Secondary students at Salem District.

4. There is no significant difference between rural and urban schools towards awareness on environmental education among Higher Secondary students at Salem District.

5. There is no significant difference between Government and Private Parents Occupation towards awareness on environmental education among Higher Secondary students at Salem District.

6. There is no significant difference between Government Boys and girls towards awareness on environmental education among Higher Secondary students at Salem District.

Tool Used for the Study

To access the awareness on Environmental Education among Higher Secondary Students in Salem District with three types of Four Point Rating Scale was developed under the objective of the study. In the type of tool, with the options such as Strongly Agree, Agree, Disagree and Strongly Disagree were utilized.

Preliminary Draft of the Tool

The investigator being a Teacher Educator was going on to write appropriate statements related to the objectives of the study and reflect the aim of the study. The steps on the different issues based on the experience of Teachers and other aspects the investigator refine the written statements in all the Opinonnairre. After the corrections, the Opinonnairre had 50 Statements only. Then it was administered as a Pilot Study.

Pilot Study

The above Opinonnairre was neatly typed and administered among the 40 Students, their respective our College Staffs and our College B.Ed Students in the time of Pilot Study the two Opinonnairre had 50 statements for students. After completion of the pilot study, gathered valuable suggestions, corrections and deleting of some statements were taken by the investigator and refine the Opinonnairre.

Finally the tool AEEHSS was consists of 50 statements, the above the tools were used to a study on finding the Awareness on Environmental Education among Higher secondary Students at Salem District.

Table 3.2 : Distribution of Positive and Negative Statements of ASEBS

S.No.	Students		Total
	Positive Items	Negative Items	
1.	1, 3, 5, 6, 8, 9, 10, 12, 15, 18, 19, 21, 22, 24, 25, 26, 28, 29, 30, 32, 34, 37, 39, 40, 42, 43, 45, 46, 50.	2, 4, 7, 11, 13, 14, 16, 17, 20, 23, 27, 31, 33, 35, 36, 38, 41, 44, 48, 49	
	30	20	50

The above table 3.2 shows the student Opinonnairre to access the students awareness on Environmental education this tool AEEHSS consists of 4 point scale with 30 positive and 20 negative statements.

Reliability

A reliable scale agrees with itself and measure consistently that which it is supposed to measure. The same yard stick applied to the same individual or subject should yield the same value from moment to the moment, provided the thing measured has itself not changed.

The reliability of a scale may be determined in four different ways.

(*i*) The test-retest method

(*ii*) Alternate or parallel from method

(*iii*) The spilt half method

(*iv*) National equivalence

The spilt half method is regarded as the best of the methods. The main advantages in this method is the fact of that data for calculating reliability are got upon one instance, so that the variations brought about by differences between the two testing situations are eliminated considering these the investigator preferred this method for computing reliability.

The useful procedure is to spilt the whole list into two halves, odd numbered illustrated in the table 5, taking two groups one along the '*x*' axis the other along the '*y*' axis. The pear son's product moment correlation was calculated by using the formula in this simplest form. Form the reliability of the half test, the self correlation of the to hole test was calculated using the spearmen brown prophecy formula where *r* testing is the reliability co efficient of the whole test and r is the reliability co efficient of the test. In this case the value of $r' = 0.71$ and applying the prophecy formula $r = 0.86$. this is highly significant

Validity

The problem of insuring validity in attitude scales is a particularly difficult one because attitudes can be measured only indirectly. Techniques for determining validity are ill-developed and poorly standardized.

A valid scale should be reliable also. But a reliable scale need not necessarily be valid. A valid scale measures that which it is supported to measure. Three methods are ordinarily used to test the validity of attitude scales. They are:

1. Logical test of validity-a scale is said to be valid if it does not violate any accepted theory by its measurement.
2. Pragmatic test-if the scores of the scale confirmed common sense observation and experience the scale is declared valid.
3. The verbal responses can be checked with has verbal behavior towards a particular thing or issue. The scores of the scale are correlated with one or more independent criteria of phenomena being measured.

Types of Validity

Broadly, five types of validity are discussed in the literature on testing. They are:

(*i*) Content validity

(*ii*) Criterion-related validity

(*a*) Con-current.

(*b*) Predictive.

(*iii*) Construct validity.

(*iv*) Face validity.

(*v*) Factorial validity.

Content validity

Content validity also means logical or curricular activity. Content validity is best considered in relation to achievement test. 'An Achievement test has content represents faithfully the objectives of a given instructional sequence and reflects the emphasis accorded to these objectives as the instruction was carried out thus, the content validity is determined by the fact that it adequately coves both the content and objectives of the subject matters unit on which the test is based. The test, in this sense, gives equal weight age to all the aspects'. The over all extent of agreement between the test and the instructional plan.

Prof. Lindeman sounds a point of warning. He says that 'an achievement test may have adequate content validity at a given time for a particular class and teacher but may not be equally valid for testing another group taught by a different teacher at a different time'. So, he suggests, "one should, however, keep in mind that the content validity of a test is not necessarily a fixed and changeless characteristics. It must be examined a new whenever the test is used with a different group or when the testing situation is altered".

Construct Validity

Construct validity of a test refers to the extent to which the test measures a particular characteristic of the individual. If a test is valid from the 'construct' point of view, it can indicate the individual's actual achievement of instructional objectives. High construct validity for a test may be ensured by having quality individual test items and by tricking a proper balance between easy and difficult items.

Construct validity may be ascertained by the method of factorial analysis. This validity has special references to the areas of abilities and personality. Expect working in these areas have demonstrated that each of the above areas may be reduced to statistical elements called factors, for example: Thurston's factorial approach to mental abilities. A test which correlates with may one of the factors (e=verbal, numerical, spatial, reasoning, etc.) would be said to have factorial validity. Construct validity is used in such tests as those of study habit skills, appreciations, understandings and interpretation of data.

Face Validity

Face validity means that the given test appears or seems to measure what it is to measure. This validity does not refer to what the test actually measure but refers to what the test seems to measure. After actual process, the test may or may not come out to be valid.

Predictive Validity

Predictive validity determines the future success of test. We need a test having high predictive validity when we which to use it for predicting the future status of an individual. The predictive validity of a test is determined on the basis of an established criterion. For this purpose, the given test scores are correlated with data collected at a future date. For example, a new entrant to a class is given a new test of academic ability. At the end of the first term, grades on this test are correlated with each student's average grades for the term. In this case, these first-term grades are called the criterion. This criterion becomes the measure of validity.

Concurrent Validity

Tests are said to have concurrent validity when they can distinguish between two or more groups of individuals whose status at the time of testing is different. For example, tests used to distinguish between persons with personality disorders and the Normal ones it successful, demonstrate concurrent validity. Such an example of a test is the Minnesota multiphase personality inventory.

Personal Data Sheet

To know the background of the Students, The investigator used personal data sheets along with the Developed Questionnaire. It asked for details of Gender, Students Locality, Types of School, Parent Occupation and School Locality. The students were asked to fill in all the particulars given in the personal data sheets. A specimen copy of the personal data sheet and Opinonnairre used in this study is given in the Appendix- I Tamil version was used for this study.

Size of the Sample

There are so many Schools' in Salem district among that the investigator select the 3 School's in random sampling method.

Table 3.3 : List of Male and Female samples

Sl.No.	Category	Students
1.	Male	72
2.	Female	78
	Total	**150**

The present study is done by Normative Survey Method. The Stratified Random Sampling Technique was followed. The size of the Sampling was 150 Students only.

Administering the Tool

The Opinonnairre were administered separately among the 150 Students, 72 Male Students and 78 female Students of the following Sampling School's in Salem District. The name of the sampling Schools in Salem District following

Table 3.4 : Name of the Sampling School's in Salem District from Which the Samples are Collected

Sl.No.	Name of the Schools	District
1.	Vedhha vikas Higher Secondary School	
2.	Government Higher Secondary School	Salem District
3.	Sri Saradha Ramakrishna Higher Secondary School	

The above table 3.4 shows the name and the district of the 3 School's from which the Samples are collected.

Scoring Key

The Opinonnairre consists of 30 Positive Statements and 20 Negative Statements. The Negative questions were scored as 1/2/3/4 and positive questions were scored as 4/3/2/1. They are Strongly Agree, Agree, Disagree and Strongly Disagree. The total maximum scores for the Tools were 150 and the total minimum scores to the same are 50 respectively.

Statistical Techniques

For the analysis of data following statistical technique were adopted.

They were,

1. Arithmetic Mean
2. Standard Deviation
3. 't'–test

Arithmetic Mean

$$M = \frac{\Sigma fx}{N}$$

f = Frequency of each class interval

x = Mid point of each class

N = Total number of scores.

Standard Deviation

$$S = \sqrt{\frac{\Sigma fx^2}{N} - \frac{(\Sigma fx)^2}{Xi}}$$

x = Deviation of each score from mean

N = Total number of score.

i = class interval

't'-test

$$t = \frac{m_1 - m_2}{\sqrt{\frac{SD_1^2}{N_1} + \frac{SD_2^2}{N_2}}}$$

m_1 = Mean of first sample

m_2 = Mean of second sample

SD_1 = Standard Deviation of first sample

SD_2 = Standard Deviation of second sample.

N_1 = Total Number of first sample

N_2 = Total Number of second sample

Delimitations of the Study

Broadly speaking, any study is impossible without limitation. Research studies is general will have delimitation due to many factors. This study too has some delimitations. It is the responsibility to the researches to see that the study is contacted with maximum care in ordered to be reliable

How ever, the following delimitations were unavoidable in the present study:

1. The study has been limited to Salem district only.

2. The study restricted to the higher secondary students only.
3. This study adopted survey method using Questionnaires to collect data from respondents.
4. A purposive stratified random sample was used to choose the subject to be included in the study.
5. This study is focused mainly on the variables, Gender, Students Locality, Types of School, Parent Occupation and School Locality.

Chapter

4 Analysis and Interpretation

Introduction

Any research work could be meaningful when the data were analyzed and interpreted properly. Therefore the researcher has given much important to this part. The data collected from the sample analyzed and interpreted in the following heads.

(*a*) Descriptive analysis

(*b*) Differential analysis

Descriptive Analysis

It includes comparison of measures of central tendency such as the mean and the measures of variability such as standard deviation. The calculated values are used to describe the properties of the different sub-samples.

150 students from Salem District constituted the sample. The variable studied in the present judgment was with reference to some selected variables like. Gender, Types of School's, Locality of students, Locality of School's, Parents occupation. After the data was collected, it was classified as the above mentioned variables.

Differential Analysis

It contains the determinations of the statistical significance of the difference between references to selected variables. It contains *'t'* test. A *'t'* test is a numerical procedure that takes into account the difference between the means of the sample present in the scores. Thus the *'t'* test is a technique to find out whether the difference the mean performance is significant or not.

Level of Significance

Experimenters and research workers choose several arbitrary standards for their convenience. These arbitrary standards are called level of significance. Most commonly used level of significance is 0.01 and 0.05 level. For the present investigation, the researcher has used 0.05 levels as significance to analyze the existence of various hypotheses.

Differential Analysis

From the above table 4.1. It shows calculated *'t'* value is less than the tabulated *'t'* value at 0.05 level of significance. We accept the null hypothesis .So there is no significant difference between Aided boys and Aided girls towards awareness on Environmental Education among Higher Secondary Students.

Table 4.1 : Significant difference between Aided boys and Aided girls towards awareness on Environmental Education among Higher Secondary Students

S.No.	Variables	N	Mean	Standard deviation	't' Value	Significant Level of 0.05
1.	Aided Boys	41	79.71	7.12	2.45*	1. 96
2.	Aided Girls	34	83.44	5.99		

*Significant **No Significant

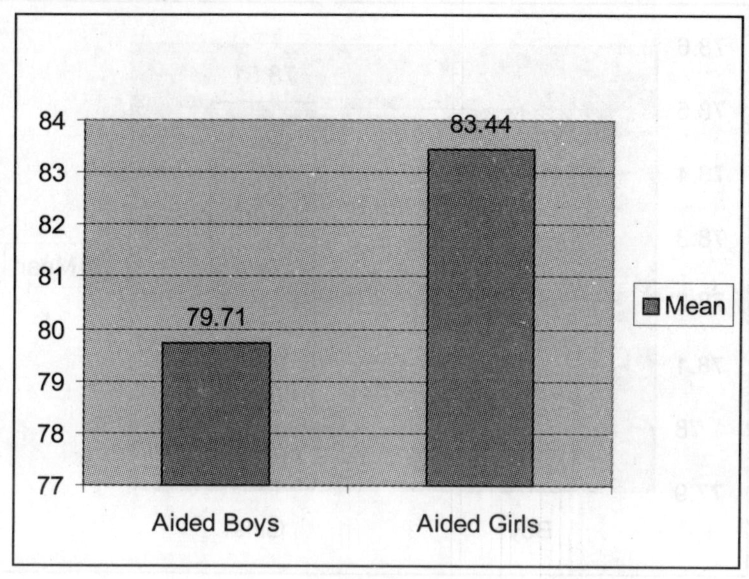

Fig. 4.1

Table 4.2 : Significant difference between boys and girls towards awareness on Environmental Education among Higher Secondary Students

S.No.	Variables	N	Mean	Standard deviation	't' Value	Significant Level of 0.05
1	Boys	72	78.138	7.904	0.28**	1. 96
2	Girls	78	78.51	8.148		

*Significant **No Significant

From the above table 4.2. It shows calculated *'t'* value is less than the tabulated *'t'* value at 0.05 level of significance. We accept the null hypothesis. So there is no significant different between boys and girls towards awareness on Environmental Education among Higher Secondary Students.

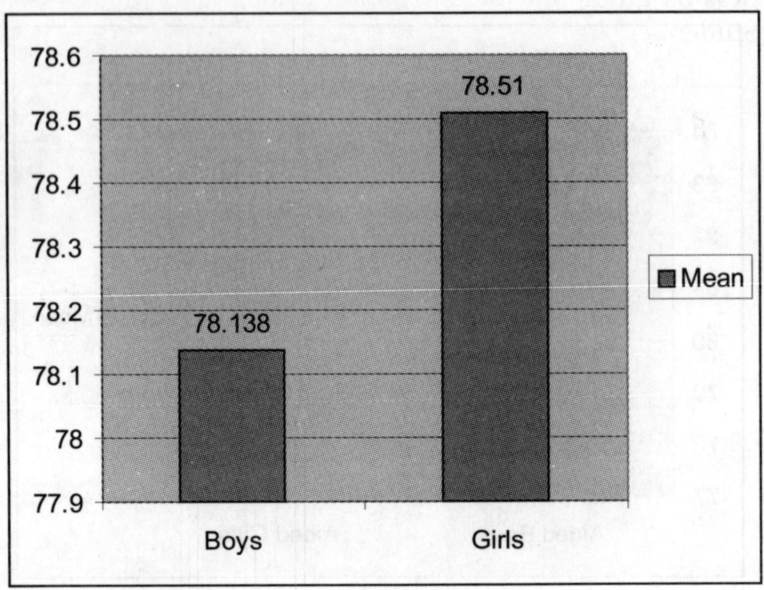

Fig. 4.2

Table 4.3 : Significant difference between Rural and Urban Students towards awareness on Environmental Education among Higher Secondary Students

S.No.	Variables	N	Mean	Standard deviation	't' Value	Significant Level of 0.05
1.	Rural Students	79	78.25	10.96	0.29**	1. 97
2.	Urban Students	71	78.7	7.884		

*Significant **No Significant

From the above table 4.3. It shows calculated *'t'* value is less than the tabulated *'t'* value at 0.05 level of significance. We accept the null hypothesis. So there is no significant different between Rural and Urban Students towards awareness on Environmental Education among Higher Secondary Students.

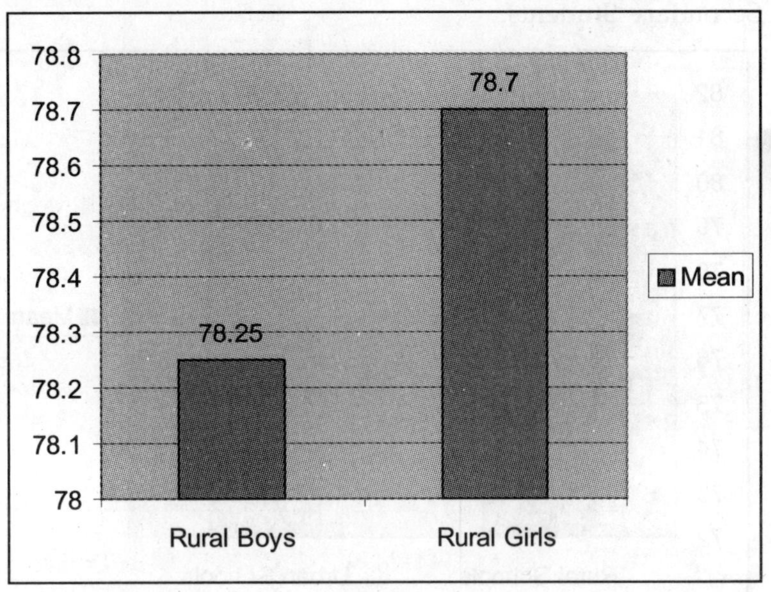

Fig. 4.3

Table 4.4 : Significant difference between Rural and Urban Schools towards awareness on Environmental Education among Higher Secondary Students

S.No.	Variables	N	Mean	Standard deviation	't' Value	Significant Level of 0.05
1.	Rural Schools	75	75.4	7.972	4.86*	1.97
2.	Urban Schools	75	81.33	6.847		

*Significant **No Significant

From the above table 4.4. It shows calculated *'t'* value is less than the tabulated *'t'* value at 0.05 level of significance .

We Reject the null hypothesis. So there is no significant different between Rural and Urban Schools towards awareness on Environmental Education among Higher Secondary Students.

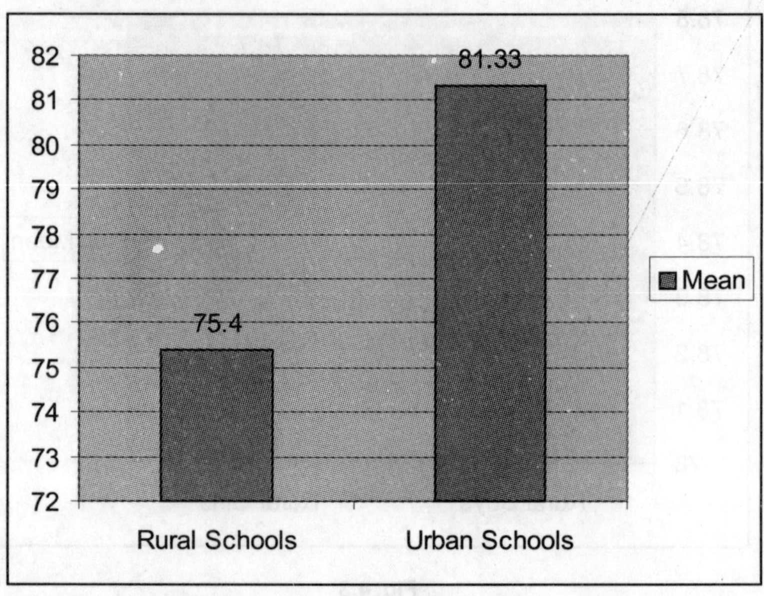

Fig. 4.4

Table 4.5 : Significant difference between Government and Private Parent's Occupation towards awareness on Environmental Education among Higher Secondary Students

S.No.	Variables	N	Mean	Standard deviation	't' Value	Significant Level of 0.05
1.	Government Parents Occupation	52	79.35	7.54	0.818*	1.96
2.	Private Parents Occupation	98	78.255	8.43		

*Significant **No Significant

From the above table 4.5. It shows calculated *'t'* value is grater then the tabulated *'t'* value at 0.05 level of significance. We accepted the null hypothesis. So there is significant different between Government and Private Parent's Occupation towards awareness on Environmental Education among Higher Secondary Students.

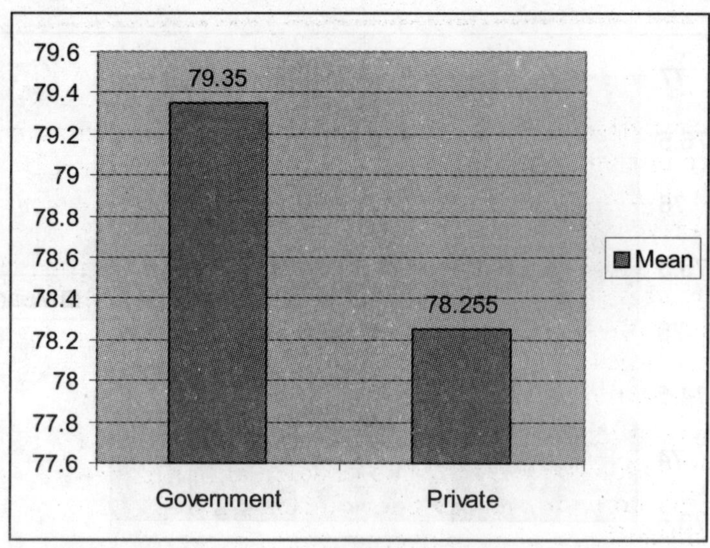

Fig. 4.5

Table 4.6 : Significant difference between Government Boys and Government Girls towards awareness on Environmental Education among Higher Secondary Students

S.No.	Variables	N	Mean	Standard deviation	't' Value	Significant Level of 0.05
1.	Government Boys	31	76.39	6.36	1.19**	1.96
2.	Government Girls	44	74.48	7.43		

*Significant **No Significant

From the above table 4.5. It shows calculated *'t'* value is grater then the tabulated *'t'* value at 0.05 level of significance. We accepted the null hypothesis. So there is significant different between Government Boys and Government Girls towards awareness on Environmental Education among Higher Secondary Students.

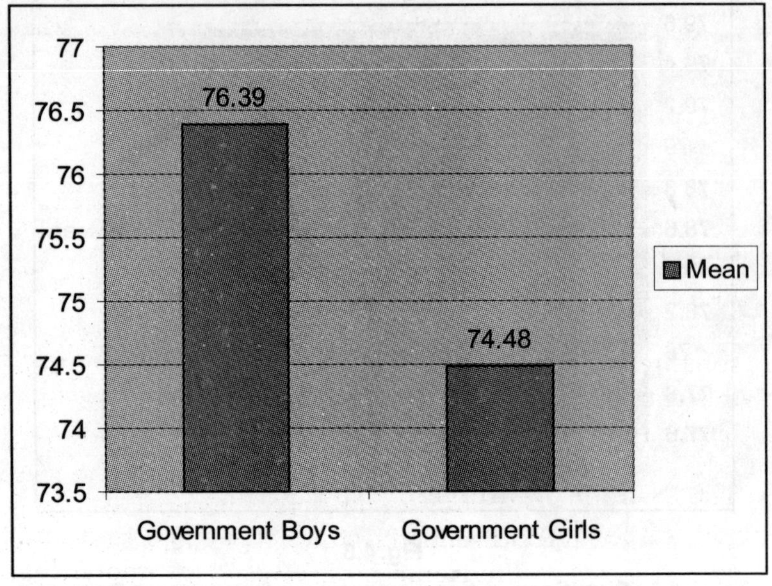

Fig. 4.6

Conclusion

Thus the analysis of the data generated by the administration of the tool on the sample of 150 higher Secondary School Students at Salem District has yielded many interesting results. Which are summarized in the succeeding the next.

Chapter 5

Findings, Conclusions and Recommendations

Introduction

In this chapter an attempt had been made to consolidate all the findings of the present study, the investigator also made some recommendation, which include the relevant area for this research and lastly the conclusion the findings are based on the result collected from the opinioned.

The Study in Restrospect

The aim of the present investigation was to find out the "Awareness on Environmental Education among higher secondary students at Salem District".

Methodology in Brief

For the present study normative survey method was adopted for the sample of the study, 150 students of Salem District were collected. The tool used for the collection of data is Environmental Education awareness scale.

Statement of the Study

The problem under the study is entitled as:

> "Awareness on Environmental Education among Higher Secondary Students at Salem District."

Objectives of the Study

The Major Objective of the study was to find out the level of Environmental Awareness. The Specific objectives are as follows.

Main Objectives

The first and foremost objective is to find out the Awareness on Environmental Education among Higher Secondary students at Salem District.

Specific Objectives

The specific objective is to find out the significant difference towards Awareness on Environmental Education among Higher secondary Students at Salem District is based on

1. Gender (Male/Female)
2. Student's Locality (Rural/Urban)
3. Types of school (Government/Aided)
4. Parent occupation (Government/Private)
5. School Locality (Rural/Urban)

The third Objectives are to find out the mean, Standard deviation on the various factors of the Awareness among Higher Secondary students.

Major Findings of the Study

From the present study the investigator came the following finding:

1. There is no significance difference between Aided boys and Aided girls towards awareness on Environmental education among Higher Secondary students.
2. There is no significance difference between Boys and Girls towards awareness on Environmental education among Higher Secondary students.

3. There is no significance difference between Rural and Urban students towards awareness on Environmental education among Higher Secondary students.
4. There is no significant different between Rural and Urban Schools towards awareness on Environmental education among Higher Secondary students.
5. There is significant different between Government and Private Parents Occupation towards awareness on Environmental education among Higher Secondary students.
6. There is significant different between Government Boys and Government Girls towards awareness on Environmental education among Higher Secondary students.

Conclusion of the Study

From the present study the investigator came to the following discussion and conclusion:

1. Aided boys and Aided girls have a similar awareness on Environmental Education. Because Tamil Nadu Education System add Environment study in science subject.
2. Boys and Girls also have a similar awareness on Environmental Education. Because Tamil Nadu Education System add Environment study in science subject.
3. Urban Locality School students have more awareness on Environmental Education than Rural Locality School students. Because the Urban area students communicate with the surroundings and have gather more information about Environmental Education through many mass media.

4. Parental occupation of government parents and private school parents also has the similar awareness on Environmental Education. Because awareness on Environmental Education is not based on parental occupation.
5. Urban school students and rural school have similar awareness on Environmental Education. Because the teachers asked their students to planning the plant is the school surroundings and develops the knowledge of importance of Environment in their life.
6. Government Boys and Government Girls also have a similar awareness on Environmental Education. Because Tamil Nadu Education System add Environment study in science subject.

Suggestions for Environmental Studies

1. The present study is limited to students studying in classes XI-XII. Similar studies can be conducted for students after secondary and senior secondary stage.
2. A similar study can be conducted to compare the environmental awareness of rural and urban students.
3. Present study has been conducted by using only three models of teaching. Similar studies can be undertaken by using many other models of teaching.
4. The present study confined only to the students. Similar studies can be extended to compare environmental awareness of teachers of different schools.
5. Studies can be conducted to find out the effectiveness of various models of teaching in different subjects in different schools and across different districts.

Education Implications of the Study

1. More measures are to the taken at rural and urban schools to create Environmental Education awareness.
2. More programmers related to Environmental Education awareness are to be conducted to the students.
3. The students may be trained to give some activist like quiz debit discussion, seminar, workshop etc., on Environmental Education awareness.
4. The teacher may be trained to teach their lesson linked with Environmental Education.
5. Government Should introduce and enrich awareness on Environmental Education programmers
6. The government has to modify the syllabus according the needs and mental level of students.

Areas of Research for the Future

Research is a chain activity. There purpose of any research in education is to find solutions for problems related to teachers, students, learning etc... But one problem always leaves many related research questions that can be investigated by other researchers, some of the areas for research in the future may be as follows:

(*a*) The present study can be repeated with wide sample.

(*b*) A similar study can be conducted on the professional school students.

(*c*) A Study can be conducted to find out the demographic and motivational variable associated with Environmental Education activities.

(*d*) A similar study can be conducted on the higher secondary school students.

(*e*) The present study could be undertaken at various states in India.

(*f*) A study can be conducted on the primary, secondary and Higher Secondary school teachers.

(*g*) The gender difference in Environmental Education awareness can be studied.

(*h*) Development of CA, package on the awareness on Environmental Education.

(*i*) A study on the modern techniques to develop the awareness on Environmental Education among the D.T.Ed training students.

(*j*) A comparative study on the awareness on Environmental Education among the students of different categories like secondary and higher secondary students.

(*k*) A critical on evolving strategies promoting the awareness on Environmental Education among the arts and science students.

Conclusion

Environmental Education among Higher Secondary students. The findings of the present study revel that the Higher Secondary students having awareness among Gender, Type of college, marital status, Locality, Challenged persons from the samples families, with respect to the questionnaire.

PART—II

Child Labour and School Student's Achievement in Science

Chapter 6

Introduction

Education

The concept of education like a diamond which appears to be of a different color when seen from angle:

"Education is a controlling grace to young, consolation to the old, wealth to the poor and ornament to the rich".

Education contributes significantly to national development. It is the main instrument of change, modernization and production. In modern times, science based technological education is successful in giving momentum to the process of economic development. Education helps to make the thinking, understanding and attitude of the citizens, comprehensive, wide, scientific and objective. It enables to solve multifarious problems and bear responsibilities as a healthy and cultured citizen.

Education is necessary for the society. Man cannot be conceived merely in terms of his biological existence. Education brings into focus the social aspect of man. Education signifies man's supreme position in society. An individual is made up of different entities. Education brings about the integration of these separate entities. Education is a sign of freedom. Epictetus had declared, "Only the educated are free". Education is an essential basis of good life. In short, "education is an essential concomitant of all human societies". "What sculpture is to a block of marble, education is to the soul", says Addison.

The word 'Education' has a very wide connection. It is difficult to define. There is no single objective which can cover the whole of life with its various manifestations. The concept of education is like a diamond which appears to be of a different colour when seen from a different angle.

Education is

Creation of a sound of whole man	.........Aristotle
Development of whole man	.........Comenius
Leading and Guiding for peace	.........Froebel
All round drawing out of best	.........Gandhi
Manifestation of the perfection all ready present in man	.........Vivekananda

Education creates integrated human being. Only, such for human beings are intelligent and capable of solving individual collective problems.

John Dewey says that "Education is not preparation for life, it is life itself". Edward says that "Education is transmission of life by the living to the living".

In the report of UNESCO, entitled learning to be, the idea as life-long education has been developed as "Human beings keep on learning and training themselves thought their lives, above all through the influence of the surrounding environments and through the experience which mould their behavior, their concept of life and the concept of their knowledge".

Meaning of the Child Labour

A generally valid definition of child labour is presently not available either in the national or international context. Any definition turns upon the precise meaning we attach two component of the term "Child labour". *i.e.,* "Child" in terms of his chronological age, and "Labour" in terms of its nature, quantum and income generation capacity. Child labour, however can broadly be defined as that segment of the child population which participates in work either paid or unpaid.

Magnitude of the Problem of Child Labour

The problem of child labour in India is also immense magnitude when one considers the number of children involved. According to the 1971 census, there were 10.74 million children working, representing 4.66 per cent of total population and 5.95 per cent of the total labour force. According to the 1981 census, workers in the age group below 14 years of the age (excluding Assam) where 13.59 million. And the basic of the National Sample (32nd Round). The numbers of the child workers us on 1st march, 1983 were 17.36 million. The working children mainly belong to the age group 5 – 14 years. Nearly 93 per cent of the total child labour force works in the rural areas and the rest in urban areas.

A great majority of these children work in agriculture and the unorganized sector like small commercial establishments and shops are quasi family undertakings. 79 per cent are employed as cultivators or agriculture labours, 8 per cent in livestock, Forestry, plantation, etc., 6 per cent in household and other services the rest in trade, commerce and transport various surveys conducted by the labour bureau rival that children are employed to do like job, such as helping in the field, in factories for packing, pasting of labels, etc., and in match factories, tea factories, tea estates, bidi manufacturers, printing, publishing, etc., unorganized sector employees a large number of children as domestic servants, works in hotels, restaurants, canteens, way side shops, news paper selling, coolies, shoe-sign boys, vendor, etc., though Indian laws prohibit the employment of children in cottage industries, family households restaurant, or in agriculture yet it is quite evident that the working conditions of the children in these small organizations is far inferior to those of large factories.

Global in Child Labour

Child labour problem is a global phenomenon. According to International Labour Organization's Bureau of Statistics (1998), there are 250-million child labourers in the age group 5-14 in the developing countries. Of them, 120 million children are working full time and are engaged in hazardous and exploitative occupations.

Child Labour in India

India continuous to host the largest number of child labours in the world today according to the 1981 census, the number of working children in age group of 5-4 in the country was 13.6 million which reduced to 11.3 million in 1991. However the number increased to 12.66 million in 2001. A closure look at census data in figure 6.1 reveals that there is marginalization of child labour in India. There is a decline in the absolute number as well as percentage of main workers in the age of 5-14 to total population in 2001. Despite the decline in the number of main workers from 9.08 million in 1991 to 5.78 million in 2001 the total number of children in the workforce increased due to rise in the number of marginal workers from 2.2 million in 1991 to 6.89 million 2001.

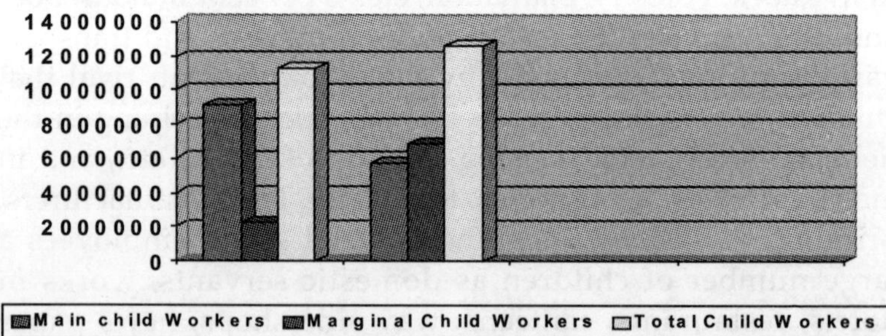

Fig. 6.1 : Child Workers in 5-14 Years of AgeWorkers aged 5-14 years (2001 vis-avis 1991) India1991-2001

Child workers are engaged primarily in agriculture and allied activities in rural areas and in a variety of industries and informal sector activities in the urban areas. Census 2001 reports that over half of the working children (54%) are in agriculture, and most others are employed either in construction (15.5%) or in house hold work (18%). About 5 per cent are in manufacturing jobs, and the remainder (about 8%) are scattered across other forms of employment. NSSO data (61st Round, 2004-2005) also have similar kind of findings and report that around 68 per cent children are engaged in agriculture and allied activities in India. This sector is followed by manufacturing sector which account for 16.55 per cent of the child employment. Considerable proportions of children with 8.45 per cent are engaged in trade, hotel and restaurants.

In 1970, Government formed the first committee called Gurupadswamy committee to study the issue of child labour and to suggest measures to tackle it. The committee observed that as long as poverty continued, it would be difficult to totally eliminate child labour and hence, any attempt to abolish it through legal resource would not be a practical proposition. The committee felt that in the circumstances, the only alternately left was to ban child labour in hazardous areas and to regulate and ameliorate the conditions of work in other areas. It recommended that a multiple policy approach was required in dealing with the problems of working children.

Following the recommendations of Gurupadswamy committee, the child labour (Prohibition & Regulation) Act was enacted in 1986. The act prohibits employment of children certain specified hazardous occupations and processes and regulates the conditions in others. The list of hazardous occupations and processes is regularly revised on the recommendation of Child Labour Technical Advisory Committee constituted under the Act.

In consonance with the above approach, a National Policy on Child Labour was formulated in 1987. The Action Plan outline in the Policy for tackling this problem included legislative Action Plan for strict enforcement of Child Labour Act and other labour laws to ensure that children are not employed in hazardous employments, and that the working conditions of children working in non hazardous areas are regulated in accordance with the provisions of the Child Labour Act. It also identified additional occupations and processes, which are detrimental to the health and safety of the children.

As poverty is the root cause of child labour, the action plan emphasizes the need to cover these children and their families also under various poverty alleviation and employment generation schemes of the government Project Based Plan of Action was made in areas of high concentration of child labour. Pursuant to this, in 1988, the National Child Labour Project (NCLP) Scheme was launched in 12 districts of high child labour concentration in the country. The coverage of the NCLP Scheme has increased from 12 districts in 1988 to 100 district in the 9th Plan to 250 districts during the 10th plan. The Scheme envisages running of special schools for child labour withdrawn from work. In the special schools, these children provided formal/nonformula education along with vocational training, a stipend of Rs.100 per month; supplementary nutrition and regular health checkups so as to prepare them to join regular mainstream schools. Under the Scheme, funds are given to the District Collectors for running special schools for child labour. Most of these schools are run by the NGOs in the district. The 10th Plan also recommended expanding the National Child Labour Projects to additional 150 districts. Linking the child labour elimination efforts with the Scheme of Sarva Shiksha Abhiyan of Ministry of Human Resource Development was also tried to ensure that children in the age group of 5-8 years get directly admitted to regular schools and that the older working children are mainstreamed to the formal education system through special schools functioning under the NCLP Scheme.

Even 25 years after having banned child labour in India, the country continues to be home to the largest number of child labourers in the world. As per the Government records, about 12 million children are engaged in child labour and are out of school.

In India the problem of child labour continues to be a challenge before the authorized. Government has been taking various actions to tackle this problem. However, considering the magnitude and extend of the problem and that it is essentially a socio-economic problem inextricably linked to poverty and illiteracy, it requires concerted efforts from all sections of the society to make a dent in the problem.

Tamil Nadu in Child Labour

In Tamil Nadu, according to 1991 census, there were 5.78 lakhs child workers. 48.2 per cent of them were male and 51.8 per cent were female child workers. The survey for the SSA (Sarva Shiksha Abhiyan—Education for all Programme) during the year 2001 has estimated child labour figure as 3.49 lakhs.

Occupational Classification of Working Children in Tamil Nadu

(Based on 1991 Census)

Category	Percentate of Male Child Workers	Percentate of Female Child Workers	Percentate of All Child Workers
Cultivators	18.78	14.46	16.70
Agricultural labourers	40.90	53.43	46.94
Manufacturing, Processing, Servicing & Repairing in Household Industry	4.64	8.74	6.62
Others*	35.68	23.37	29.74
Total	**100.00**	**100.00**	**100.00**

* Livestock, Mining, Manufacturing Processing, Servicing & Repairing in other than Household Industry Construction, Trade, Transport and other services

In Tamil Nadu about 64 per cent of the child work force is concentrated in agriculture and allied activities. Though agriculture is the predominant occupation where children are involved, employment of children in manufacturing and service sector is quite significant in Tamil Nadu with over 36 per cent of the working children.

Child Labour is widely prevalent in Shops, Hotels and Restaurants in all the Districts of Tamil Nadu, Child labour is prevalent in match and fireworks industries of Virudunagar, Tuticorin, Tirunelveli districts, in tanneries of Vellore and Dindugal districts, in Hosiery industry of Tiruppur and Coimbatore, in beedi industry of Tirunelvei and Vellore districts, Silver anklet manufacturing in Salem, Germ cutting in Trichy and in Pudukottai.

In 1995, a survey was conducted by the District Administration to identify children in child labour intensified district. Vellore, Trichirappalli, Pudukkotai, Salem, Coimbatore, Tirunelveli, Virdhunagar and Dharmapuri. The identified chiildren in the above districts were 2,45,796.

Special Schools for Child Labourers in Namakkal District

Under INDUS project of Child Labour, with the financial assistance both form Governtment of the India and the United States Department of Labour and the execution by international Labour Organisation, six special schools are being run in Pallipalayam and Momarapalayam areas where the textile industries concentrated in Namakkal District. The six Schools are catered to 262 child labourers in the following areas:

1. Subash Nagar, Pallipalayam.
2. Amman Nagar, Pallipalayam.
3. Avathipalayam, Pallipalayam.
4. Chinnayakatoor, Pallipalayam.
5. K.Olappalayam, Komarapalayam.
6. Perantharkadu, Komarapalayam.

The child labourers in the special schools are provided with nutritious lunch and they have been given intensive education at the transitional educational centers daily at par with the Tamilnadu Government Education syllabus. Apart from the educational input, the skilled teachers are teaching various skills on cultural, sports and games and fine arts.

Keeping in mind that poverty is the main cause of the child labour system in the society, the parents of the children are being motivated to form as self-reliance. It also paved a way to spur the rural economy at the village level. the efforts have been taken to enroll the child labourers who have got through the final examinations. Teaching various skills on cultural, sports and games and fine arts.

Education and Child Labour

Poverty is what forces children into the work place. Education is a way out. Therefore, improvement in education presents a possible solution for the child labour problem in India. The child labour and education is strongly inter-linked. According to National Human Rights Commission of India, Child labour can never be eradicated unless compulsory primary education up to the age of 14 is implemented. Highlighting how education can transform a child's life, Shantha Sinha, chairperson, National Commission for Production of Child Rights (NCPCR), said: "Going to school opens up new avenues and opportunities with children learning to think, explore, discover, question and acquire knowledge. Only is all working children are in school can it lead to equity and justice, further deepening the foundation of our democracy" (Sakshi Khattar, 2009). The importance of basic education for all children is expressed in the combined mandate of the convention on the Rights of the Child (CRC), the Child Labour Conventions 138 and 182 of the International Labour Organizations(ILO) and the Millennium Development goals (MDGs) aimed at the realization of basic education for all children (boys and girls) by the year 2015. Sarva Shiksha Abhiyan, under the flagship of government of India, also aims to provide useful and relevant elementary education for all children in the age group of 6 -14 years.

As per a survey conducted by Child Rights and You (CRY), in India there are 5 lakh formal schools for a population of 239 million; 14 per cent have no school building; 38 per cent have no blackboards; 30 per cent have only one teacher for the whole school; 58 per cent have no drinking water. As a result 4 out of 5 children do not even enter a school and 70 per cent of children drop out before they enter Class IV. Studies have shown that improvement in education leads to diminishing child labour. An example is found through comparing education vs. child labour in Kerala and Andhra Pradesh. In Kerala, where virtually all children attend school, exists the lowest incidence of child labour; in Andhra Pradesh, with one of the lowest school attendance percentages, the highest occurrences of child labour are found.

The act to ban child labour today covers only 15 per cent of the total child labour population in the country, according to Dipankar Majumdar, director, Child Rights and you (CRY). He said: "Sectors like commercial agriculture, unregulated factories and immediacies employ close to 80 per cent of the child labour, is not covered by the Child Labour (Prohibition and Regulation) Act 1986". (Sakshi Khattar, 2009)

Literacy Status and Child Labour

Literacy level of adults plays a major role in reducing child labour. The literate and educated adults understand the value of education and are aware about the health and welfare of the children. The studies have proved that high literacy results to low incidence of child labour. In this context, it has been tried to find the linkage between literacy level and the child workforce participation across different states of India.

Table 6.1 indicates that the states with high literacy have comparatively low proportion of child labour like Maharashtra, Tamil Nadu and Kerala with the exception of Himalacha Pradesh. States like Andhra Pradesh, Madhya Pradesh, Chattisgarh and Rajasthan have literacy rate in the range of 55 to 65 per cent, (< the all India level average), are having high percentage of child labour i.e., more than the national average. This shows that as the level of literacy goes up, the incidence of child labour comes down. In Himachal Pradesh the literacy levels have improved significantly for both the males and females between 1991 and 2001 and its impact on the reaction of incidents of the child labour may be witnessed in the new future.

Table 6.1 : Literacy Rate and Share of Workers in age group of 5-14 years in Various States/UTs of India (2001)

State/Union Territories	Total Population Literacy	Share of Workers In age group of 5-14 years(%)
Bihar	47.00	4.68
Jharkhand	53.56	5.47
Uttar Pradesh	56.27	4.08
Rajasthan	60.41	8.25
Andhra Pradesh	60.47	7.70
Orissa	63.08	4.37
Assam	63.25	5.07
Madhya Pradesh	63.74	6.71
Chattisgarh	64.66	6.96
Karnataka	66.64	6.91
Haryana	67.91	4.78
Gujarat	69.14	4.28
Punjab	69.56	3.23
Uttranchal	71.62	3,24
Tamil Nadu	73.45	3.61
Himachal Pradesh	76.48	8.14
Maharashtra	76.88	3.54
Kerala	90.86	0.47
Total	**65.4**	**5.00**

Source: Census of India 2001, selected educational statistics 2004-2005 Ministry of Human Resource Development, Government of India.

From the facts in the table below, it clearly emerges that it is not merely the economic advancement but the overall social development including education which provides the major explanation for the incidents of child labour. *i.e.*, why Kerala has lower incidents of the child labour than Punjab, Hariyana, Himachal Pradesh and several other states which have low poverty ratios as compared to Kerala.

Need for the Study

As a nation, India has always followed as proactive policy in the matter of eliminating child labour and making elementary education universal. The constitutional and statutory provisions combined with a range of development measures have been the cornerstone of our efforts to eliminate child labour and provide education to all children. However the goal of Universal Elementary Education (UEE) has still not been realized and child labour still persists.

Based on the data analysis presented above it is clear that the elimination of child labour and achievement of target of UEE are inextricably linked and one cannot be achieved without addressing the other issue. For ensuring the children to be in school and not in employment the governments need to adopt a holistic view and efforts need to be made to remove the demand and supply side constraints.

Child labour may not be tracked as a welfare issue but as a persisting social problem in the context of the existing inequalities and exploitative socio-economic structure in the county and as violation of a child's basic human rights. The laws eliminating child labour must be implemented in letter and spirit. It should be the Endeavour of the national government to establish an inextricable link between child labour and education and to create a coherent policy for the elimination of child labour.

Child labour is a challenging problem but, for several reasons, there is the potential to eliminate it. In 1996, Carol Bellamy, director of the United Nations Children's Fund, released the annual State of the Children report citing education as the single most important step in ending child labour. A solution to this predicament can be achieved through educational improvements which will therefore overcome the other factors influencing the India child labour crisis.

Statement of the Problem

The purpose of this paper is to analyze and compare the effect of child labour school students with the normal school student's science achievements. Its particular significance is that to analyze whether the child labour students give better performance than the normal school students. This is made possible by the achievement test to measure the science achievement for both the students in standard-V. The statistical techniques like Mean, Standard Deviation and "t" were taken for the analysis of the study. The results show that the Mean achievement of the child labour students is lower than the normal school students science achievement it's due to the children that work as well as going to school may find they less able to learn, as a result of exhaustion or insufficient time to complete homework.

Background of the Problem

Considering the grim reality of the problem of child labour, we can suggest a few measures to tackle the issue. Providing alternative employment opportunity to child labour-prone households, improving their working conditions, regulating the employment of child labourers in exploitative occupations through efficient supervisory machinery are some of the measures, which deserve urgent attention.

Definitions of Terms

Child Labour

The census of India treats persons below the age of fourteen as "Children" While making use of standard demographic data, social scientists include females in the age group of

15 to 19 years under the category of the "girl child". According to the constitution, no child below the age of 14 years shall be employed to work in any factory or mine or engaged in any other hazardous employment. The legal definition of "child" depends very much upon the specific legislation.

Achievement

Refer to performance in School or College in a Standardized series of educational test.

Achievement Test

Refer to test designed to measure the effects of specific teaching or training in an area of the curriculum.

Achievement Rating

Means comparing achieved performance and the ranking assigned to compare.

Achievement Quotient (AQ)

It is the ratio between the expected and actual measured performance level in a educational or training programme. Sometime called accomplishment quotient or educational ratio.

Science

The word science has its origin from a Latin word "'Science meaning 'to know'. Science in universal but has been defined in different ways for example,

"Science is a systematized body of knowledge."

"Science is nothing but organized common sense."

"Science is a heap of truth."

John Woodburn and E.O. Obourn consider science as that human endeavour that seeks to describe with even increasing accuracy, the event and circumstances which occur or exits within our natural environment.

The definition of the science found in report on Policies for Science Education is 'Science is a cumulative and endless series of empirical observation which result in the formation of concept and theories, with both concept and theories being subject to modification in light of further empirical observations. Science in both a body of knowledge and the process of accruing and refining knowledge'.

The science is simultaneously a body of knowledge and continuous self evaluate process of enquiry.

Science thus has two important approaches:

(*a*) Science as a product

(*b*) Science as a process

Whereas laws, theories, principals etc. or included in the category of science as a product where as scientific attitude, scientific method etc. from part science as a process though both aspects are important in their own way but to attain the aim of science education in school more emphasis will be placed on process approach.

Science is considered to be one of the most important subjects in school curriculum because it can play a vital role in the development of human resources. Progress in knowledge in Science is the key to progress in all walks of life. Every country develops its own system of Education to meet the challenges of the changing times. The progress, welfare and security of a nation largely depend on the scientific researches done on its laboratories. But it is a fact that no country can produce qualified person at higher levels of Education, all of a sudden without putting a firm base of Science Education right from the school level. The Education commission (1964-66) report rightly directed that "the science teaching can become meaningful and useful only if the methods of teaching are utilized and proper facilities are provided of the teaching of the subject". Science is essentially a practical subject and that the young pupils like doing something rather than simply listening. Even after sixty years of Independence, Science

Education in the schools seems to have serious drawbacks. The reasons for this type of situation can be traced to the inadequate and weak foundations of Science Education in the school system.

The Science curriculum must be used as an instrument for achieving social change in order to the divide based on economic class, gender, caste, religion and region. We must use textbooks of the primary instruments for equity. Since for a great majority of school going children, as also for their teachers, it is only accessible and affordable resource for Education. So it is not a simple task to communicate scientific knowledge in a comprehensive manner reflecting the true nature of science. Moreover, it is very important to think whether that minimum science education has been provided equally to the student's urban, rural and tribal localities. The establishment of the equal educational opportunities is to be ensured in the democratic country like India.

Primary Education

Education provided by a primary school or elementary school: The students at primary stage are in the age group 5-10 and so they are quite immature thus the be given only a formal education in science. At this stage it is desirable to develop the subject matter under the following heads;

1. Living things
2. Universe
3. Matter and energy

The curriculum must provide for some students activity in additional to the subject matter. Of the estimated hundred hours allotted to teaching of science in a class about 20 hours be spent on exclusions and visits, about 50 hours on projects and other activities and the remaining 30 hours be given to class room teaching.

Kothari Commission (1966) recommended under:

(*i*) In lower primary classes, the focus should be on the child's environment—social, physical and biological.

(*ii*) In classes I and II accent should be on: (*a*) cleanliness; (*b*) Formulation of healthy habits; (*c*) development of lower of observation.

(*iii*) In addition to emphasizing the above qualities in class III and IV the information be provided about: (*a*) Personal hygiene; (*b*) Sanitation; (*c*) Plants and animals in surroundings of the child; (*d*) Air; (*e*) Water; (*f*) Weather; (g) Earth; (*h*)Simple machines; (*i*) Care of body; (*j*) Heavenly bodies.

(*iv*) To provide direct and valuable experiences of natural phenomenon it is recommended that school gardening be encouraged.

Progressive Achievement Tests in Science (PAT Science)

The *Progressive Achievement Tests in Science (PAT)* is a thoroughly researched and nationally normed test to assess student achievement in scientific understanding from Years 3 to 10. The test questions are designed to assess science knowledge, scientific literacy and understanding of scientific principles, as well as their application.

Key Features

1. Test booklets that target a specific year level and cover a wide range of year levels to cater for differing abilities.
2. Short-answer questions and marking guides to provide more diagnostic information about a student's ability.
3. A common scale for all eight tests, giving teachers the ability to compare different students using different tests and monitor development over time

4. National norms to allow for comparisons between student performances and the Australian reference group for each year level.
5. Comprehensive norm, diagnostic and descriptive individual and group reports.
6. A CD containing copy masters of administration instructions, score keys and a range of report formats.

Benefits

1. Track students' progress in science from Year 3 to Year 10.
2. Identify students' strengths and weaknesses using the optional short-answer questions.
3. Use results to help report students' progress to parents.

Achievement Test

As a teacher one is involved directly in the evaluation of the learner. The theory that you have learnt will have to be applied by you as a teacher in the classroom situation. The present block Learner's Evaluation' in general and this unit in particular is concerned wid1 this very important activity of teachers.

Teachers teach and help the learners to learn. The learning that takes place is assessed or evaluated not only for the learner's benefit but also for the teacher to evaluate his/her own work. At the end of a lesson or a group of lessons, the teacher needs to get feedback on wile the learner has achieved, as a result of the teacher's efforts and also, indirectly to assess his her own, Achievement as a teacher. This feedback comes with the help of a tool, generally an achievement test. An achievement test is designed to evaluate a unit during the teaching-learning process. The unit of teaching-learning may be, as has already been mentioned, one lesson or a group of lessons transacted in a particular time period. You have already read about achievement tests in the previous unit. In this unit we will discuss the same in detail.

Objectives of Achievement Tests

- Discuss the purpose of achievement tests.
- Describe the steps involved in construct the achievement test.
- Explain/illustrate how the design and blueprint of an achievement Lest are prepared.
- A write a variety of questions - objective, short answer and essay.
- A prepare a sample achievement test with a marking scheme.
- Describe how an achievement test should be administered.
- Mark/score an achievement test and interpret test scores.
- Discuss the different types of grading and their purpose.

Purpose of Achievement Tests

Achievement tests are universally used in classroom mainly for the following purposes:

1. To measure whether students possess the pre-requisite skills needed to succeed in any unit or whether the students have achieved the objective of the planned instruction.
2. To monitor students' learning and to provide ongoing feedback to both students and teachers during the teaching-leaning process.
3. To identify the students' learning difficulties-whether persistent or recurring.
4. To assigns grades.

Construction of Achievement Tests

There are several steps involved in the construction of Achievement Tests. We will now discuss these in detail one by one.

Instructional Objectives

The first and the most important step in planning a test are to identify the instructional objectives. Each subject has a different set of instructional objectives. In the subjects of Science, Social Sciences, and Mathematics the major objectives are categorized as knowledge, understanding, application and skill, while in languages the major objectives are categorized as knowledge, comprehension and expression. Knowledge objective is considered to be the lowest level of learning whereas, understanding, application of knowledge in sciences or behavioral sciences is considered higher levels of learning.

Design

The second step in planning a test is to make the "Design". The Design specifies weight ages to different: (*a*) instructional objectives; (*b*) types (or forms) of questions; (*c*) units and sub-units of the course content; (*d*) levels of difficulty. It also indicates as to whether there are any options in the question paper, and if so, what their nature is.

The design, in fact, is termed as an instrument which reflects major policy decisions of the examining agency, whether it is a Board or an individual. A sample format for presenting design of a test is given on the next page.

Blueprint

The third step is to prepare the "Blueprint". The policy decisions, as reflected in the design of the question paper, are translated into action through the Blueprint. It is at this stage that the paper setter decides as to how many questions are to be set for different objectives. Further him/her & decides under which unit/topic a particular question is to be set. Furthermore, he/she packs up various forms of questions.

Thereafter, the paper setter decides how all the questionnaire to be distributed over different objectives and content areas so as to obtain the weight ages decided in the Design. The three dimensions of the blueprint consist of content areas in horizontal rows and objectives and forms of questions in vertical columns. Once the blue prints prepared, the paper setter can write/select the items and prepare the question paper.

Objectives

1. To find out the level of Achievement in science among the Vth std Normal Students and Child Labour Students.
2. To find out the level of significant difference on the achievement in science among the Vth std normal students and child labour students.
3. To find out the level of significant difference on the achievement in science among male between normal students and child labour students in Vth std.
4. To find out the level of significant difference on the achievement in science among female between normal students and child labour students in Vth std.
5. To find out the level of significant difference on the achievement in science among Illiterate parents of normal students and child labour students in Vth std.
6. To find out the level of significant difference on the achievement in science among Literate parents of normal students and child labour students in Vth std.

Hypotheses

1. There is no significant difference on the achievement in science between normal students and child labour students.

2. There is no significant difference on the achievement in science among the Vth STD normal students and child labour students.
3. There is no significant difference on the achievement in science among male between normal students and child labour students of Vth std.
4. There is no significant difference on the achievement in science among female between normal students and child labour students of Vth std.
5. There is no significant difference on the achievement in science among Illiterate parents of normal students and child labour students of Vth std.
6. There is no significant difference on the achievement in science among literate parents of normal students and child labour students of Vth std.

Scope of the Study

The topic is an investigation of the Achievement in science among the students of child labor school and normal school. Since this is the survey study. The investigator attempt to know the Achievement in science among the student of child labor school and Normal School.

This study will be of great help for the educationists particularly for the teachers since the concept of education has been changing from time to time.

The Achievement may differ child labor students and normal students. One can learn and do anything with involvement only when he had a better involvement only when he had a better achievement towards it. If we compel anybody to do any work in which one does not have good Achievement, then it may be root cause for many problems. It may give a lot of mental and physical fatigue to child labors students. Thus he can't do it effectively. In this content investigator attempt to study the child labour student and normal students of science Achievement in Vth STD student in various categories.

Delimitation of the Study

Broadly speaking, any study is impossible without limitation. Research studies is general will have delimitation due to many factors. This study too has some delimitations. It is the responsibility to the researches to see that the study is contacted with maximum care in ordered to be reliable. However, the following delimitations were unavoidable in the present study:

1. The study has been limited to Tamilnadu only.
2. The study has been restricted to the normal students and child labour only.
3. The Study has been restricted to the Vth Std students only.
4. This study adopted survey method using questio-nnaires to collect data from respondents.
5. In this study examination marks were considered as achievement.
6. A purposive stratified random sample was used to choose the subject to be included in the study.
7. This study is focused mainly on the variables Illiterate, Literate, Male, Female, Father and Mother.
8. The ensuring chapter deals with the Data Analysis of the study.

Organisation of the Thesis

The report of the thesis will be presented according to the following sequences.

The first chapter gives introduction definitions of terms, statement of problem, objectives and limitations of the study.

Second chapter deals with the review of related literature which are done in India and abroad related to this problem.

Third chapter gives a detailed accountant of research procedures and methodology used in this problem.

Fourth chapter deals with the tabulation of analysis and the interpretations of the data in detail.

Fifth chapter describes the findings, conclusion and certain recommendations about the problem.

This is followed by the bibliography and appendices which consist of the tools used for the problem and the related matters.

Chapter 7

Review of Related Literature

Introduction

Survey of related literature provides valuable help to the development of knowledge of research project. It helps the investigator to gain insight into various aspects of the problem area that is formulating a framework for the study, developing methodology, constructing the tool for the data collection and planning the analysis of data.

Good, Barr and *Scates* (1935) analyse the purpose of review of literature as:

To show the evidence already available to solve the problem adequately without further investigation and thus to avoid the risk of duplication.

To provide ideas, theories, explanation or hypothesis valuable in formulating the problem.

To suggest methods of research appropriate to the problem.

To locate comparative data useful in the interpretation of results.

To contribute to the general scholarship of the investigator.

Effective research is based on the past knowledge. The search for related literature is one of the first steps in the research process. This step helps to eliminate the duplication of what has been done and provides useful hypotheses and helpful suggestion for significant investigation.

Research is not an isolated activity, but of an ongoing and concentrated effort to attain and understand the reality. Thus, every attempt to unearth truth is connected with all such endeavors of the past and elsewhere. Therefore, it is imperative that the researches tales pain to find what his fellow researchers in other parts of the world have done in the field of his research.

It is indispensable part in the solution of any research problem. The survey of related literature is crucial aspect of the planning of the study. It involves the critical study of existing research work. Since, effecting research is based upon past knowledge, the review of literature helps to eliminate the duplication of what has been done and provides useful hypothesis and helpful suggestions for scientific investigation.

Overview of the Literature in Child Labour

There are numerous researches and studies on child labour. The coverage of these studies ranges from the estimation of the nature of child labour in specific area or industry or occupation, causes of child labour and forms of child labour to the impact of various governmental, non-governmental and international interventions towards combating the problem of child labour. The issue of child labour comes to sharper focus particularly in the period following the adoption of structural adjustment programmes and macro adjustment measures in 1991.

Indeed the conclusions of the Uruguay round of GATT and consequently the formation of World Trade Organization (WTO) in 1995 and linking up of the trade issues to the issue of the labour standards has led to several attempts in the developing countries to counter the arguments of social clauses as stated in the WTO.

Thus studies on child labour have been done by the organizations such as the World Bank, Population Reference Bureau, International Labour Organisation and UNICEFF since the Declaration of International Year of Child in 1979 in India the studies on the problems of child labour are undertaken at the maro level were undertaken in the Report of National Commission on the Lanour(1969), the Labour Bureau, Ministry of Labour, Delhi, In 'Child Labour in India' (1954), S.C. Pant's 'India labour Problem's(1965).

However, it is imperative to present a detailed survey of literature in order to trace out the gap that exists in literature and the need for the present study in the light of that. Hence a review of such studies has been outlined below.

Indian Studies Related on Child Labour

Labov (1970) stated that the compensatory education is designed to repair the child rather than the school. Failure in school is not caused by the child but by the school itself. Implies that the school should change ensure that the child does not fail. The theory and practice of compensatory education is of significant consequences. It rationalizes prejudices of the teachers, educational administrators and the public against the lower class children. Rosenthal and Jacobson (1968) stated that an unfavorable social relation between the teacher and taught damages 'The self concept' of the child and is counterproductive to the self fulfilling prophecies in the class room and contribute to the failure of learning. According to Saini Debi, S. (1994), it is not only the availability of the schooling system to retain the student by making the environment interesting based on child psychology will have a casting impact on school going children.

Rath (1974) established close relationship between low aspiration levels and income among the backward classes. Positive correlation was observed between educational level, economic status and job aspiration of the school going children of the backward classes. Lack of determination on the part of parents about their children's education and other developmental programmers is resulting into school dropouts. In some communities, the need for education was not felt due to indifference caused by culture of poverty.

Pichholia (1980) found that the educational level of an average child worker is only fifth standard *Kitchulu (1987)* and *Singh (1992)* in their studies observed that more than 50 per cent of working children discontinued their studies just after primary level of formal schooling. Jha, S.M. (1997) observed that illiteracy caused by non availability of relevant and quality education is the major factor for the incidence of child labour.

A recent study conducted by centre for Media Studies (CMS), government of India reported that poor economic condition of the household is only a contributing factor, but not the primary reason for child labour. Environment within the family, impact of teachers at, school and general social conditions affect the thinking of a child infavour of or against education. In spite of the educational facilities available in the urban centers, due to lack of interest on the part of parents and indifferent attitude of teachers in the schools run be local bodies, the formal schooling in the public sector has become through failure in attracting and retaining the children of low income groups, who could not afford private schools.

Ghosh (1984) study also revealed that majority (50.42 per cent) of the child workers had only primary level of education. The bi-variate correlation coefficient between education levels of parents and their children proved that higher the parental education, the more will be educational level of their children. Among the different efficiency of the present education system. Especially people who are having hand to mouth existence are flot interested in investing their children's education.

Juyal (1985) has studied the in human exploitation inflicted upon child laboures. He has remarked that, "child labourers rescued in the famous Bilwaria incident bore visible marks of physical torture, such as branding with hot iron, bruises and lathi blows. They were severely beaten with iron rods if they were slow at work, made mistakes in the weaving, asked for adequate food or even they went to ease themselves without master's permission. At night they were all locked up in a small room. This happened to them daily. But "once they were caught in the act of escaping, their feet were tied together and they were slung upside down from the branch of the tree and then, to 'properly' drive the lesson home, they were branded with hot irons".

Juyal, Sudarshan Kumari and Chandola (1985) have studied the problem of child labour in Varanasi. They have made a study of child labour engaged as domestic servants, manufacturing activities etc. They have made a study of child labour engaged as domestic servants, sweepers, construction sector, dairy units, hotels and restaurants, manufacturing activities etc. They have observed that, "Child labour is certainly a tragic phenomenon. Beyond the travail of hard work, often of manual kind, for long hours, in the city slums and densely crowded localities. What is even more distressing to see is that the child themselves becomes commodity, rather than their labour, being commodity? Most of them are literally put to work by their parents. It is generally found that the parents themselves become indifferent to the physical and psychological exploitation of the children. Thus the child labour is the target of exploitation by the employers as well as the patriarchal family. Such is the depth of dehumanization."

The character of industries like carpet manufacturing, silk textile manufacturing, repair services etc. consume abundant child labour in Varanasi. There is also 'feudal' element manifested in such manufacturing industries. There is continuous stranglehold of merchant capital over the household or family units of production.

Fernandes. Burra and Anand (1986) in their report on Child Labour unfold that 80 per cent of all child labourers belong to the scheduled caste and scheduled tribes. They have been exploited and marginalized in India for centuries. A major consequent upward mobility. Thus the child labour becomes a mode of perpetuating an unjust social system and of ensuring the continued availability of subsequent, unskilled illiterate, labourers who do not have the bargaining power to question the system that marginalize them and deprives them of their right to human."

Many equally hazardous operations like brassware and glass making have been omitted. Bidies are cheap cigarettes and their manufacturing has long been by children's hands, which come much cheaper than machinery. Engaged for long hours of work child labourers suffer permanent physical deformation as well as contracting chronic bronchitis and T.B. In the carpet weaving, child labourers work in rows behind the looms, in pits dug in the floor of the loom sheds. The atmosphere is stuffy, full of wool guff, which gets in to their lungs. One study shows, nearly 60 per cent of them suffer from asthma and TB. Weaving and wool cleaning have the same effect, and dyes are often toxic, causing further distress.

In precious stone industries, and in working with substances like mica, eyes are particularly vulnerable to both injury and disease.

Two hundred kilometers from Agra, is located Firozabad, the fiery furnaces manufactures glasses form bottles and beakers to bangles and beads-all glass work are manufactured but ironically free from any regulations. It has ah a high proportion of child labour since about 50,000 who lead pitiable life due to heat and dangers associated in such industry.

Accidents and death are common in construction sector where child labourers are employed. Perhaps the most horrific and dangerous of all these trades to employ children is that found in Sivakasi.

"The incentive to keep filling the frame must have been so great that most of them scarcely looked up and even when they did, their hands mechanically continued their activity. The children were pain 15 paisa for filling each frame and they earned, depending on their day's output, between Rs. 2 and Rs. 5".

Illiteracy or low level of education among parents was manifested as the contributory factors for child labours. Congestation, poor ventilation, long hours of work, piece wage payments, hazardous occupation, Sub-human living conditions etc., are some of the bleak features of the child labour in March factory. Children are exposed to certain health hazardous like respiratory disease and eye infection.

They mostly suffer from T.B., malnutrition, gastro intestine disorders, skin diseases and body injuries etc. the problem of abject poverty and adult unemployment are factors resulting in the problem of high incidence of child lanbour.

The situation of working children has been examined by *Patil (1988).* The urban working children in Bangalore have been studied and the findings were compared with the slums of working children in Delhi and Mumbai. It was inferred that economic compulsions were the strong motivating forces influencing children to indulge in wage employment (46.33).

Tripathy (1989) studied the problem of bounded labourer in Indian states with special reference to Orissa and its tribal districts. The field study brought to the lights that in the tribal regions of Kondhmal district of Orissa indebtedness and bondage have led to distressed and deplorable living conditions of children.

George (1990), studies the widely accepted view that children should not be an art of workforce and concludes that children should be allowed to work in environment and conditions suitable or favorable to their growth and development. To him in the US agricultural sector there are children engaged in between 1.5 million t 2 million. He suggests that all efforts against child labour should be unanimous for children all over the globe.

Joda and Sing (1991), studying the child labour in dry agricultural lands in India concluded that the average productive period, when the farmers reap the maximum benefits usually extends 3 to 4 months of the monsoon season. During this period in order to accelerate overall incomes of the family, children did not attend schools and were found engaged in agricultural operations. In dry season children were found involved in various informal works like animal grazing and harvesting minor crops for family consumption etc.

Thus, the education and schooling of children were severely affected resulting thereby the final dropouts.

Weiner(1991) examined the reason for children's presence in labour force and not in schools in India, resulting thereby the illiteracy, an acute problem. He strongly advocates for compulsory education as the key to regulate the problem of child labour. He suggested that compulsory education is an absolute necessity for completely abolishing child labour as it has been historically proved.

Tripathy (1991) examines the problem of child labour in a tribal district of Orissa and highlighted that land alienation over the years has been the most significant cause of backwardness of the tribal people of Phulbani district. Decline in the forest area due to "podu" or shifting cultivation, restrictions imposed by the government on the use of forests by the tribal people, decline in the agricultural falls, frequent crop failures-all these entangle the tribal, uncertain rain falls, frequent crop failurews-all these entangle the tribal in misery. A family size of 4 to 6 members has been manifested among 83 per cent of sample scheduled caste families.

The study further reveals that 56 per cent of total sample households constitute landless families. The incidence of child labour falls more progressively upon lower castes with poor economic status. In the 35 scheduled caste and scheduled tribe sample labour households, there are 29 dependents, which comes to 82.85 per cent. The fact is that there is 78 per cent of child lanourers belong to the age of 14 and below that age. There is high level of dropouts and illiteracy among the child labour sample households.

The child workers are asked to work for long hours without any weekly offs. About 60 per cent of the child workers get only Rs. 2 per day. The study unfolds that 54 per cent of the loans are incurred mainly for pressing consumption needs. Only 20 per cent of the sample child labour households possess only one room and 30 per cent have no rooms to live in. the food taken by sample household is mango kernel, wild roots, jawar and maize, which are far from being satisfactory.

Thus the study made by Dr. Tripathy reveals that the problem of child labour in tribal areas seems to be a product of such factors as the customs, traditional attitude, lack of education or reluctance of parents to send their children to school coupled with mass poverty.

The economic role of children in developed and developing countries have been revealed by *Dnenovsky (1992).* He assessed the children's labour force of 70 developed and underdeveloped countries. Under the framework of dependency theory, Commodity concentration in exports in 1970 and multinational corporation penetration in 1973 were taken to exhibit dependency. As independent variables, urban population growth and women's labour participation were used. It was found that there was positive correlation between urban growth and child labour.

Burra (1992) focused that on an average children are paid Rs. 50 a month after an initial period of unpaid apprenticeship in lock industry of Aligarh. A child works 10 to 14 hours a day. Some works like polishing is hazardous. The children engaged in spray painting units are exposed to lung cancer. The inhale unacceptable large dusts of paints; paint thinners etc. these cause severe chest disorders, breathlessness, fever and T.B. bronchitis, asthma and pneumoconiosis. These are some of health hazards caused by the employment of children in lock industry. It is deplorable to note that there is no limit to working hours, conditions of work, well-being and living standards of child laboures. Piece wage and below living wage is paid to child workers in lock industry.

Panicker and Nangi (1992) have focused on the living conditions of the working and street children in Delhi. The study illustrates that migration comprise more than two-third of working children. They have migrated mainly from the nearby Hindi speaking areas of Uttar Pradesh, rajasthan, Bihar and Madhya Pradesh etc. Some children have come across the border from Bangladesh, Pakistan and Tibet, where political disturbances forced them to migrate.

Most of those who migrated from Bangladesh and Pakistan are found working as rag pickers, from Tibet as sales boys and girls and those who are migrated from Nepal are working as domestic and shop servants. The children migrated from Nepal are owing to their poverty which is due to low productivity. They have migrated to India because they found that India provides better job opportunities for them in cojmparison to their own motherland.

However the search for jobs and the availability of better job opportunities in Delhi are main reasons for the migration of children.

Pandey (1993) outlined the problem of street children. In the management of workers, boys outstrip the girls. Working street children are employed in unstable casual work, which are informal and unorganized.

They are paid poor wages without any bargaining power. They work for full time and even beyond that of the adult workers and the girls do not have sufficient clothing. Educational facilities or vocational training is grossly inadequate for street children. The community exhibits lukewarm attitudes towards the street children.

Study conducted by *Rita and Kalpana (1993)*, portrays that the children responsibilities at the tender age of 8. Most part of their childhood is wasted in performing various jobs both within and outside the housed. Children are discriminated on the basis of sex. As girls are overburdened with works while boys are allowed to enjoy the freedom. In the matter of health and nutrition, girls are neglected.

Meera and Neeta (1993), attempts to touch upon certain aspects of girl child labour in India. According to them, several economic and social factors are responsible for the prevalence of large-scale female child labourers in India. Poverty is probably the most important cause of the prevalence of child labour particularly female child labour in India. The untimely death of father or mother or both the parents, large size of family and ill-habituated father are found to be the other reasons forcing female child to become labourer in India.

Old traditions, social customs and prejudices are also contributing to the injustice due to the female child in India. It is aptly remarked that existence of female child labourer is an index of underdevelopment of the India society.

Dr. Sahoo's study (1995), illuminates the factors and conditions of child labour in two advanced village under changing agrarian production process. In the context of dire poverty and bondedness, the poor peasants, agricultural labourers, and artisans being unable to survive on the meager land with them with the irregular wage employment in rural settings, seasonally migrate to urban centres and get them employed in the insecure, unorganized, informal sectors. This is evident from both agriculturally developed as well as underdeveloped districts. The only difference is that from the backward districts, labour contractors, for unskilled low paid and strenuous jobs mostly recruit them.

The sample village study of *Dr. Sahoo* reveals that nearly 85 per cent of the child labourers belong to farm workers and small peasant families of labour caste and tribes. During the last decade, one f-fifth of these families have sold their tiny pieces of land. Moreover 83 per cent are indebted mostly moneylenders. To repay the debt 28 per cent of these families were employed. Obviously poverty illiteracy, low social and economic position, perpetual indebtedness etc, forced them to employ their children to eke out a living.

In brief, Dr. Sahoo's study concludes, "advancement of agriculture, instead of declining the employment of tin y workers, has in fact made them more vulneranel to economic and social classes and status groups, the continuance of the small holdings too necessitated the utilization of children in the farming. The future of the under-aged workforce, if any, has been rendered bleak. Intervention of democratic institutions and processes may perhaps case the situation, but as yet here is nothing in sight".

Burra (1995) highlights that the work of girl child is invisible. This invisibility has serious negative consequence in terms of her status within the family, which in turn determines her role in the family as well as in the society. In rural area, bulk of female working child population is manifested. With regard to the works in agricultural sector, household and the unorganized industry, there is division on the basis of sex, as 'male works' and 'female works'. Girls are employed in low-paid, unskilled jobs and thus, skill formation is obstructed.

In the journey of life, the destination of female child in marriage. Minimum wages are not guaranteed to the parents of the child labourer. Therefore the parents could not finance the needs of the children. The study observes, "where the child is a girl, (it) results in the child being prevented from going to school, leading to the inevitable cycle of no education, low skills and low earning capacity, thus perpetuating home work with its exploitatively low wage".

Gangrade (1995) endeavoured to study the position of the girl child and meaning of social development. With reference to girl child and her social development, it largely depends on education. The neglect of education in India has made our country as one of the largest adult illiterates.

Kumar and Rani (1996) analyzed various offensesagainst children and observed that, child prostitution stems from child labourer in India. The researchers pointed out that most of the children have been compelled in to prostitution due to poverty and utter destitution.

Mehtas and Jaswal (1996) made a study in child labour in various tea-stalls, sweet shops and found that children are employed in all sorts of works. Most of the children received a wage below Rs. 950 per month. They do not have facilities of entertainment and put hart labour working of 8 to 15 hours in a day with non-stop work.

Tripathy (1997) portrays the problem of child labour in Indian states with special reference to migrant tribal children of the Boloangir district of Orissa state. The study brought to light that migrant child labourers are mainly from the drought prone, poverty stricken scheduled caste and tribe families. The contribution of child labour to the family income is substantial as they contributed at par with the adult members. Child labour constitutes more than 38 per cent of total labour force among the brick-kiln labourers of Bolangir migrating to Ganjam district. Work environment of the brick-kiln child labourers is grim and they usually victimized by health hazards of T.B., eye and hand injuries. Most of the migrant labourers of Bolangir are illiterate and they constitute more than 85 per cent of the migrant child labour households.

Sekhar (1998) viewed that the poverty gap is to be reduced in order to reduce the incidence of child labour. This is because there is a strong correlation between poverty and child labour. The enforcement of child labour laws must be supplemented by the implementation of welfare measures to have the desire effects. Further, the protection of child labour becomes a reality only by protecting the entire household from which child labour originates. Improvement in the living conditions of child labour prone households can eliminate the exploitation and employment of child labour.

Savyasachi (1999) suggests that a holistic approach is needed to eliminate child labour. They are to be supported by promoting community development awareness building and advocacy activities lured with effective policies and legislation. The elimination of child labour needs multe-dimensional approach.

Ankaer, Barge, Rajgopal and Joseph (1999) examined the economics of child labour in six industries, namely carpet, glass, diamond, gem and mosaic chips and limestone. The book is pioneering in the sense that it has attempted to assess the employment of children in these industries from the demand side as against the earlier studies seeking and explanation of the problem of child labour mainly from the supply side.

The issue of employment of children in these hazardous industries has been sought to be explained on the basis of the industrial structures in the process of contracting and sub-contracting.

Prof. Desai (2000) in his study focused on the nature of child labour in diamond industry of Surat. The study highlights three important dimensions of the issue of child labour, viz. demand side factors and the state of education. The demand side includes some structural and other related information pertaining to industry. The supply side factors include, first macro level profile of the area and, secondly, the household level information. In all information from 750 households of child labourers and 250 households who are sending children to school were gathered and analysed.

Misra (2000) has made an in-depth study of the problem of child labour. He states that the child labour in the country from generally families of agricultural labourers, share croppers, families of rural artisans, fishermen and women, those of inter-state migrant workmen, beedi workers, weavers, leather workers, brick-kiln and stone quarry workers and those of collectors of minor forest produce in tribal areas.

The authors hold that every child is a human being: and, childhood is a stage in the evolution and growth of human life. He finds it essential that the consciousness of all sections of the society be awakened at least the task should remain half done. They include opinion molders, policy-makers and programmed implementers. The study focuses light on employment of child labour in various hazardous occupations in different states of India long with the role played by NGOs and international bodies to tackle the problem.

A study conducted by *Davuluri Venkateswarly in Andra Pradesh (2001)* has brought to light that children work on long-term contract basis, with less wages and long duration of working seed producers (more often it is thrust upon them) and thus are forced to live in a debt trap for years. If the local supply of child labourers is found insufficient, the seed producers bring children from neighboring areas.

These children are put in the camps and are given food. The child labourers both male and female children are paid wages approximately half or 50 per cent of the adult male wage rates.

It has been estimated that about 4 lakh girl children, in the age group of 7 to 14 years, are employed in cottonseed fields, in which Andhra Pradesh alone accounted for 2.5 lakhs. The number is far greater than the number of children employed in the carpet, glass bangle, gem polishing, and limestone industries put together in India. Child labour in these industries did not exceed 25 per cent, with a majority of children being boys, whereas in cottonseed, girl's child labour constitutes 90 per cent of the labour force. Cottonseed production is concentrated in Mahabubnagar, Rangareddy and Kurnool districts, which account for 90 per cent of production in the state and 62 per cent in India.

Foreign Studies Related on Child Labour

Levison and Moe (1998), Peru: This study estimates work and school equations, where the sample is restricted to girls, and work refers to hours allocated to household chores. As in the evidence reviewed in the previous section, it is possible to compare coefficients for the same variables in the two equations. Six were significant in both, and all of them were oppositely signed.

Akabayashi and Psacharopoulos (1999), Tanzania: These authors provide the most direct evidence concerning the relationship between hours of work and hours of study, where the latter are understood to be in addition to regular school time. The sample was drawn from the Tanga region 200 km north of Dar es Salaam in 1993-94. 542 children maintained time use logs; their reading and math skills were also estimated by their parents, information that will be considered later in this review. The researchers estimated equations for hours of study and hours of work, taking into consideration that these are jointly determined. They found that nearly all explanatory variables with a positive effect on one had a negative effect on the other, confirming that studying and working compete for children's time allocation. Their work does not calibrate this trade-off, however, nor do the data permit a comparison of different types of work; all forms of work, market and non-market, economic and non-economic, were recorded without distinction.

Summing up this section, we are unable to avoid the conclusion that the evidence remains thin on the essential question of work hours and schooling. As generalizations, one can say that work hours compete with school hours beyond some threshold, but the threshold varies from one country to another. Work also competes with study at home, but little is known as yet about threshold effects. In addition, it appears that non-market work, including work outside the SNA boundary, ought to be considered in addition to market work, but these different types of work probably differ in their effect on schooling.

Graitcer and Lerer (2000), Egypt: As described previously, this study examined 78 children working in small enterprises in Cairo, along with a control group of 100 school children from the same neighbourhoods. All children were in the 10-14 age range. They found no significant difference in either height or weight measures, nor in a range of other health indicators (including back and joint pain).

Kassouf et al. (2001), Brazil: A sample of 4840 adults was drawn from the 1996/1997 Pesquisa de Padrões de Vida covering two regions. The mutual effects of early entry into the labour force, education and health were controlled sequentially; limited household controls were also employed. Income plays a mediating role between child labour and subsequent health, but the direct effect of early work is stronger in this study. There is no control for the endogeneity of child labour, however.

Admassie (2002), rural Pakistan: A wide range of variables predict school attendance; nearly all are inversely related to child labour in a model that permits joint choice of work, school, work and school or neither. An example is the adoption of more mechanized agricultural methods, controlling for household wealth.

As previously noted, *Ersado (2002)* examined schooling and child labour in Nepal, Peru and Zimbabwe. She found that having younger siblings has no effect on the school outcomes for girls in rural areas, but does for urban girls. This can be interpreted as evidence for the role of childcare as a work activity competing with school for these latter girls.

Ray and Lancaster (2003), seven countries: These authors began with the working assumption that the relationship between hours worked per week and educational outcomes would take the form of an inverted U, and their explicit purpose was to ascertain the switch point—the number of hours at which the relationship would switch from positive to negative. They examined three measures of educational performance and used three different estimation techniques. The dependent variables were school attendance/enrolment, number of years of education completed ("schooling"), and schooling for age (SAGE), defined as SAGE = (Years of schooling\Age"E) x 100 where E is the age at which students typically begin school in the country in question. The techniques were a four-equation model simultaneously estimating the likelihood of working only, attending school only, doing neither or doing both, ordinary least squares (OLS) and instrumental (IV) regression relating hours of work to educational outcomes, and a two equation instrumented model (3SLS) simultaneously estimating work hours and educational outcomes.

A different view is offered *in Kandel and Post (2003)* in their analysis of Mexican survey data. Children currently in school were asked about their expectations for continuing to a higher educational level. Children working for pay had lower expectations, but regression transferred this effect to other variables that are associated with the likelihood of working. On the other hand, after controlling for confounding factors, the authors found that children who work without pay for more than 14 hours per week are 30% more likely to anticipate further educational progress-a result that may be subject to the same endogeneity bias discussed earlier in the context of this study.

Assaad et al. (2003), Egypt: These researchers considered three definitions of child labour, market (the most restrictive), SNA (including all work encompassed under the System of National Accounts) and "Inclusive" (SNA work plus household chores). For each of these they used a cut-off of 14 hours per week to distinguish child labourers from non-labourers. They note, incidentally, that the measurement of household chores in the Egypt Labour Market Survey they employ is inexact: it is reported by adult respondents, and parents often under-report the number of hours due to their expectations of what girls should be doing. Instrumenting for their different measures of work, the authors find that work has no impact on schooling for boys, but does for girls only if the most inclusive measure is employed. Depending on the subgroup and model specification, working more than 14 hours per week in a combination of economic and household tasks reduces girls' probability of school attendance by 50-90%.

Ritchie et al. (2004), Guatemala, India, Kenya, Nicaragua, Pakistan, South Africa: They analyze time use data in one-hour increments gathered during these countries during the period 1996-2003, finding that girls, and particularly those not enrolled in school, worked far more hours when non-economic work (according to SNA) was taken into account.

Neri et al. (2005) drew on the Brazilian Pesquisa Mensal de Emprego for six cities over the period 1982-99. They were interested in what happened to children from households whose heads experienced a spell of unemployment; this means they followed transitions during the period subsequent to this initial loss of income. What they found was that these children were more likely to enter the labour force themselves and drop out of school. The average incremental effect on dropout rates was 24 per cent, and it was higher for households that earned lower incomes prior to the onset of unemployment; in the lowest income quintile the increase was 46 per cent. This is not just a matter of children working or not working. These researchers also found that, if a child both works and attends school at the time that parental unemployment begins, the likelihood of not advancing a grade also rises, by 30 per cent for the bottom quintile.

Phoumin and Fukui (2006), Cambodia: They instrumented for hours worked and estimated school attendance, finding that the relationship is an inverted-U, with school attendance increasing and then decreasing in hours worked per week. Using three different measures of school attendance, they locate the turning point, where additional work has a negative educational effect, from 15-16 hours. Unfortunately, they use only a dummy variable for gender, so the gendered impact of work time measurement cannot be ascertained.

Surveys may also ask adult respondents for the reason that children in their households have left school. Here the evidence is somewhat mixed, perhaps reflecting larger differences in the denominator. Thus Nielsen and Nielsen (1997) find that only 2 per cent of their samples of Zambian households give work as the primary reason for children leaving school, while 35 per cent of Ethiopian respondents in Cockburn (2001) and more than half in Cockburn and Dostie (2007) said that work was the main reason for failure to attend school. The corresponding figure was 37.7 per cent for a sample of Egyptian households in Graitcer and Lerer (2000).

Emerson and Souza (2007), Brazil: The object of study was the differential effect of household factors on school and work outcomes for boys and girls. Bivariate probit models were estimated separately by gender; with nine explanatory variables there were 18 possible pairs of effects (on school and work). In 11 instances a variable's coefficients were statistically significant in both the school and work equation, and in 10 of these they were oppositely signed.

A different estimation strategy employing the same data can be found in Duryea et al. (2007), who incorporated a wider range of household characteristics and distinguished between income shocks occurring during the school year and those arising over the summer. This latter distinction makes it possible to concentrate the analysis on those shocks that are potentially more relevant to schooling decisions. Thus, they find that, if household head experiences unemployment during the summer, school outcomes are unaltered. On the other hand, shocks during the school year appear to have even larger consequences for child labour, school attendance and grade advancement.

Cortez et al. (2007), Brazil: 2063 adults between the ages of 23-25 living in Ribeirao Preto were surveyed. They were divided into three groups depending on the age at which they had begun working, with the youngest bracket being less than 14. There was a raw negative correlation between sorting into this group and height, but this relationship did not survive a regression controlling for demographic, household and behavioural variables. The sample size had sufficient power to test for a height difference of 2 cm at .05 alpha and .20 beta. Drawbacks include no control for parental height and the predominance of service work (90%) in employment.

Indian Studies Related on Normal Students

Clark (1927) found that students whose parents had college education ranked higher in scholarship. *Shuttleworth (1927)* reported that the low-achieving group of students had strict religious home training.

Bear (1928) found that parental occupation was related to academic success. He reported that sons of farmers and businessmen ranked low in scholarship in comparison with those of artisans, salesmen and so on.

Steinzer (1944), Cattell (1945) and Thompson (1948) pointed out that over-achievers were characterized by good adjustment to school and greater awareness and responsiveness to environmental influence. Frankel (1960) found that over-achivers conforming to school regulations adjusted better to the academic situation. Christenson (1956), Popham and Moore (1960) and Roberts (1962) achievers differed significantly from under-achievers in their adjustment to college. French (1958) considers that lack of adjustment to college life in the freshman introduces extraneous influences on scholastic success.

The studies of *Zyve (1929), Berton and Perry (1975)* on predictive value of Stanford scientific aptitude Test found that the scientific aptitude can be employed for predicting science achievement.

Berger and Sutker (1956) observed that students with adequate personality adjustment achieved better in academic performance. Brown (1953), Wellingron (1965) and Graff (1957) demonstrated that high-achievers tend to be more stable and adjusted than low-achievers. Scott (1958) felt that only the best mode of adjustment maximize the chance of success.

Havighurst (1964) contrasted achievement test performance of middle-class and lower-class children in 21 Chicago school district. He found that 6th grade students in the seven districts with the highest average socio-economic status ranged from grade level to one year above socio-economic status districts, the score clustered around one year below grade level.

Satyanandam (1969) highlighted two sub-aspects of socio-economic status. Viz., educational level of parents and economic status of parents. According to him, the children of graduate parents performed far better than the children of matriculate parents.

Sreekumar (1972). Chatterji,et al. (1978) and Sujatha (1987) identified the positive relationship between scientific aptitude, science interest and science achievement.

General ability scientific aptitude/reasoning, problem solving ability were signifncantly responsible for the learning of science (pal.1982)

Menon(1973) found over-achievement and under-achievement are highly influenced by socio-economic status. *Anand (1973)* established relationship between socio-economic status and academic achievement even when the influence of intelligence of non-verbal and verbal type was partialled out. He also found that the impact of socio-economic environment was found to influence mental abilities and academic achievement.

Kuppuswamy (1974) informed that the achievement in school is closely related to the level of aspiration. *Shukla (1973)* observed that the level of aspiration determines the limits of academic achievement to some extent. *Hussain (1977)* concluded that the academic performance of the group showing moderated goal discrepancy was better than that of the groups showing either high or low goal discrepancy, implying a curvilinear relationship between the level of aspiration and academic performance.

Reddy (1974) found academic significantly related to the scholastic performance of secondary schools pupils, Soman (1977) also observed that personal adjustment variables had a considerable influence on achievement. Vashishtha (1991) found a positive relationship between adjustment and achievement.

Choudhari (1975) expressed an opinion based on research that bright children normally came from families where parents having a higher level of education, were mostly engaged in professions requiring general knowledge, and had more income than the parent of dull students. In Goswami's (1978) study also the scholastic achievement correlated highly with socio-economic status. *Soman's (1977)* study revealed that the dominant personality factor identified for the over-achievers was individual adjustment factor. Dhami (1974) concluded that there was higher relationship between scholastic achievement and emotional stability in the case of 9th class boys than in the coming public examinations. George (1966) mentioned that the public of 10th class with high intelligence were identified as better adjusted and higher achievers. Goswami (1978) found that scholastic achievement is highly correlated with the concept of adjustment.

Another study on classroom climate conducted in Rajasthan with a sample of 1294 by *Verma (1977)* concludes as; the rural school classes showed slight superiority over the urban school classes as far as acceptance, trustfulness, adaptability and emotional relationship dimensions of the classroom climate were concerned; the academic achievement of the urban and rural schools were at par but there was significant difference in the intellectual standards of the rural and the urban pupils; the mean difference of the classroom climate for adaptability and emotional relationship were significant in favour of the classrooms of the private schools; the classes of the privately managed schools have a more learning-conducive climate; the socio-emotional climate of the classroom not only predicted and influenced the pupil's academic achievement but also affected his classroom behavioral development; the classroom climate was positively correlated with the studiousness factor of the sociometric test; the classroom climate was negatively correlated with the behavioral development of the pupils, classroom behavior was positively correlated with their academic achievement. All the components of the studiousness factor and the composite studiousness factor were positively correlated and the mischievousness factor and its components were negatively correlated with the pupil's academic achievement.

In *Salunke's (1979)* study it was observed that educational facilities and emotional happiness in the home contributed positively difference between the high and the low achieving females in health, social, emotional and educational areas of adjustment.

Khanna (1980) observed that the academic achievement of the children of educated parents, illiterate parents, and educated mothers was significantly correlated with the socio-economic status of the family. Menson (1972) also noticed that higher occupational and educational level of father, educational level of mother; family income and parental attention were related to high achievement.

Reddy (1981) studied the interrelationship between organizational climate, socio-economic status, students' perception of rewarding behavior and the academic achievement of random stratified sample of 1607 pupils from 103 schools of Telangana area in A.P. and concluded that academic achievement level of schools having the organizationl climate profile of (*i*) controlled, (*ii*) controlled –cum-paternal-cum-closed, (*iii*) controlled-cum-autonomous, and (*iv*) controlled-cum-open to be 305.34, 303.47,325.73 and 364.54 respectively out of a total of 600 marks.

Subramanyam's (1981) study highlighted the importance of conditions at school vis-à-vis of the data showed that personal characteristics of the children contributed to a large extent to a large extent to their reading achievement and between the two factors, namely, school condition and home better achievement. In another study made by Srinivasa Rao and Subramanyam (1982) it was revealed that among the school factors, accommodation, educational level and experience of teachers, availability of instructional material, books and reading room facilities influenced the reading attainment of children positively.

Science achievement has a significant role to play in predicting scientific aptitude *(Gupta, 1985)*. For scientific aptitude, both achievement and information in the scientific fields may be prerequisites for mastery over the basic scientific skills which in turn, would lead to the unfolding of other mental abilities.

Patnaik (1986) tries to measure the achievement in general science of class V pupils. She found that the pupils of U.P. schools were much superior to those of M.E. schools. And at the same time she also found that the pupils of municipality schools were superior to those in the schools under D.I. of schools at 95 per cent confidence level.

Second international Science Study had a significant comparative study about biology achievement in thirteen countries. The first Year Biology Test with 30 item was administered to 2,582 students in 118 schools of 13 countries. The Advanced Science Biology Test was given to 674 second year biology students in 43 secondary schools. This reflected a response rate of over 80 per cent of the school contacted. The 'mean per cent correct' of biology students who had two or more years of biology education are compared with the scores of students of 13 other countries along with the U.S. The results of this study were : Students in the U.S. who had studied biology for two years ranked 13th among 13 countries in achievement in biology. Singapore had the highest mean achievement score in biology. Students of U.S. with 2 years of biology scored about 10 per cent higher than students who had one year of biology.

Sundararajan (1989) found that the higher secondary boys studying in urban schools did not show greater achievement in biology than the boys studying in rural schools.

The higher secondary school girls studying in urban school showed greater achievement in biology than the girls studying in rural schools (Sundarajan, 1989). This was agreement with the findings of Das (1985), and there were significant differences in respect of understanding and application of objectives of sciences (Williams, 1987).

Foreign Studies Related on Normal Students

Among the 9 studies one study was conducted by Shah and *Kapadia (1971)* in Mathematics among the students of VIII standard in a rural area. The study has shown favourable results to PLM.

The investigator reviewed 4 studies in Biology which are presented below. *Kasthuri (1978)* has taken up her project comparative study of the outcomes of teaching of some selected units in Biological science by conventional method and method of programmed learning. The study reveals that PLM was partially effective. But on the whole, PLM was found to be more suitable than the other method.

The investigator had reviewed 2 studies on Education. The first study, the investigator had chosen was conducted by *Shah (1980)*. The investigator developed a system of 4 components for the course of Educational Evaluation at the B.Ed level. The study was conducted for 2 consecutive years and the strategy was found effective for 3 components (viz) programmed learning. Similarly Bhusan & Goswamy (1978) conducted the investigation on 50 class VIII students having 3 groups of students at 3 levels of intelligence with a view to comparing linear programme and a structural communication strategy. A 2×3×3 factorial design was employed. It was concluded that the structural communication strategy proved steadily superior for the higher categories in the Bloom's hierarchy.

All the fifteen studies reviewed on the effectiveness of programmed learning material in teaching were in different area. Apart from the above 15 studies on PLM made by the investigator she had reviewed another 14 studies on the effect of CAI in teaching.

Of the five studies located by the investigator on the effect of two Computer Assisted Instruction programs for an introductory Physics laboratory of High School students were compared by Moore (1980) Both sets of Computer Assisted Instruction materials contained the same material in virtually identical displays. But one set required that the student participate in the presentation by giving constructed responses of a sort that only a Computer Based Instruction could process. The other set allowed the student to advance upon giving the simpler kinds of responses typical of a programmed test. The results showed that the students using the program forced them to demonstrate understanding performed significantly better than the other group when they were required to make decision in the laboratory.

In an another study conducted by *Pandey (1980)* to find the use of programmed Instruction on Teaching Mathematics at primary Level, the group following programmed text differed favourably and significantly from the other group.

In another one study conducted by *Vazghes (1983)* conducted a study on a Physics course. It was reported that the Computer Assisted Instruction made significant difference and also resulted in higher preference level than the conventional method.

In an another study *Metha J.M. (1983)* studied the construction of different type of programmes on the unit of 'INTEREST' in Mathematics of std IX and study the relative efficiency of those. The main objective was to study the relative efficiency of three types of programmes on the unit 'INTEREST' in mathematics. The sample consisted of 104 students which were divided into 4 equivalent groups. The 3 groups were taught through the three different types of programmes while the 4th group was taught through conventional method. It was better than the one taught through normal (Conventional methods).

The finding of the, study of *Wainw right (1985)* seemed different from the earlier studies in Physics. He found that the use of micro effective learning on the selected topics in Physics', when the investigation was made on the effectiveness of a Computer Assisted Instruction package in supplementing teaching of selected concepts in secondary school Physics. The experimental group received drill, review and reinforcement by using the micro computer for lessons three days a week for a three week period.

It was reported by *Ayoubi (1986)* that Computer Assisted Instruction helped medium ability students to achieve significantly higher, when an experimental study was carried out on the effectiveness of computer assisted instruction on achievement in Physics among high school students. Data were collected from 125 students in a selected urban school. Seventy seven were in the experimental and 48 were in the control group. Pre post test design was used in the study.

In another study conducted by *Bindhu K.C. (1986)* on the effectiveness of teaching zoology for XI std students through PLM, the. Study reported that the performance in the post test was invariably better than the pretest. Totally PLM was found more effective than lecture method. In a similar study Stepics Jeyson (1986) conducted to find the effectiveness of teaching Biology (Biological Science. The study concluded that PLM offers a vast ground for future investigation to work on as it was the latest innovation in the field of education.

In a study conducted by *Desai R.M. (1988) on* a study of effectiveness of programmed learning strategy in teaching physics in the eleventh grade. Main objective was to prepare PLM for XI std. students. The study employed the experimental design. The method of cluster sampling was used for the selection of 200 pupils from Science classes of XI std. A pretest was administered in a small sample to ascertain the pupils' previous knowledge. The tools employed were i) a questionnaire for pupils to ascertain the pupils' previous knowledge in science prepared by the researcher and ii) Ahuja's Group Test of Intelligence. Major findings were: i) pupils took natural interest in reading and learning though programmed material. The PLM approach proved better than the lecture methods in the study of physics.

Similarly, Thangam P. (1991) conducted a study on the effectiveness of teaching physics for students of XI std. through PLM. The study concluded that the experimental treatment (PLM) was more effective that lecture method.

Similarly Dharmar, K, (1992) conducted a study on the effectiveness of teaching Biological Science for B.Ed students through PLM. He concluded that science through PLM using computer was found to be more effective than teaching through conventional methods namely lecturing in colleges of Education.

A similar study was conducted by *Sharma (1996)* on a comparative study of outcomes of teaching Algebra by Conventional Classroom method and method of P.I. He employed a deluged post test to compare the relative effectiveness under the methods. The mean score of Experimental group taught through PLM was found to be more than that of the Control group taught through Conventional (Lecture) method.

The study was conducted by *Terrell (1996)* to determine the effect of changes in resolution and number of colors of performance of a visual search task within a computer-based multimedia environment. Students were randomly assigned to a multimedia task using one of nine possible combinations of resolution and colour depth. Student performance, as measured by speed and accuracy of task completion was analysed for any effect of either resolution or colour. No significant difference was found for either colour or resolution on accuracy or speed.

Many evaluations *Kozma et al., 2004; Light et al., 2010; Linden et al., 2003;* 2010 in developing countries rely on correlation designs to test whether variables are associated with each other and utilize a qualitative or case study approach. Such an approach provides a detailed look into why and how may be used within educational settings to boost learning outcomes, but not whether their usage leads to desired outcomes over time. Moreover, there exists an ongoing discussion on how to define and measure impact in this field, creating a substantial barrier to conducting rigorous research and developing comparable evaluation designs. Challenges also exist at the program implementation level.

Suzanne Stokes (2009) suggests that using visuals in teaching results in a greater degree of learning. The basic premise of this body of research is the concept of visual literacy, defined as the ability to interpret images as well as to generate images for communicating ideas and concepts. This paper provides an introduction to visual literacy and includes a review of studies that investigate the effects of instruction that incorporates varying degrees of visual components including no visual support, still visual aids, and animated visual sequences. The purpose of this literature review is to stimulate interest in using visual enhancements in teaching and to promote the development of learners' visual skills in combination with their development of verbal, reading, and mathematical skills.

Analogy

Out of total 78 studies identified, the investigator found 52 studies conducted in India and 26 studies conducted in abroad. Majority of the studies belonged to survey studies and few of them are experimental studies.

Most of the studies followed random sampling technique in the collection of data and the size of the selected samples range from 50 to 2582 samples. In majority of the studies data was collected from the school students and in few of the studies data was collected from the normal student and child labour students. In majority of the studies the questionnaire, opionnaire rating scale developed by the investigator was utilized as a tool. Since all the reviewed studies were related to achievement in science of Vth Std normal and child labour students. In majority of the studies of the data was collected only from the school students and majority of the standardized tool and very few of them of no standardized tool were utilized mean, standard deviation and 't' test were the statistical technique followed in the majority of the studies.

The findings of the various studies reported that the achievement tests in science among normal students are significantly relationship. Similar result were obtained from the studies conducted by *Reddy (1981) Patnaik (1986).*

The findings of the various studies reported that the achievement tests in science among Child labour students are significantly relationship. Similar result were obtained from the studies conducted by *Weiner (1991) Tripathy (1991).*

Conclusion

The so far conducted concerned mainly on the achievement science subject among Normal and Child labour students. It is felt only a few studies were done on Normal and Child lanour students. So the investigator wishes to know whether variables like gender, type of school, literate and illiterate have achievement in science among child labour and Normal students. The following chapter deals with the methodology of the present study.

Chapter 8
Methodology of the Study

Overview

The Methodology followed in the present study is described in this Chapter. The present study is a Survey Method which aimed to measures the Achievement in Science among the Students of Child labour Schools and Normal Schools. The Design of the study construction of the Tool, Validity and Reliability, Size of the Sample, Selection of the Sample, Administering the Tool among the Students, Scoring Methods, Statistical Techniques utilized etc., have been reported in detailed manner in this present Chapter and ends with the Limitations of the study.

Design of the Study

Research design is a plan, a structure and a strategy of investigation conceived to obtain answers to various issues in research. The object of research design is to test the research hypotheses. The research design, therefore, is built in the principle of maximization of the results of the study, minimization of variance. A research design however, is not a highly specific plan to be followed without direction. Rather, it is series of guideposts to keep right direction. Thus, research design is the process of planning a research, choosing methods and procedures that can be expected to yield meaningful and most interpretable results.

Table 8.1 : Schematic Representation of the Research Design

S.No.	Type	Sources
1.	Nature of the research	Survey Method
2.	Tools Developed	Achievement in Science among the Students of Child Labour School and Normal School (ASSCN)
3.	Variables	Vth Standard Students in Child Labour School and Normal School
4.	Demographic Variables	1. Gender 2. Types of School 3. Parents Education
5.	Sampling Technique	Stratified Random Sampling Technique.
6.	Size of the Sample	Students-100 Child Labour-50 Normal School-50
7.	Statistical Techniques used	Mean, Standard Deviation and 't' test

The present study belongs to Survey Method. The Demographic Variables used are Gender, Type of School and Parents Education. The Tools use in the Study is Achievement in Science among the Student of Child Labour and Normal School at Namakkal District, along with a Personal Data Sheet to know the background of the Students; Random Sampling technique was followed in this study. Data was collected from 100 Students in different locations of Namakkal District. The Statistical Techniques used Mean, Standard Deviation and 't' test.

Objective of the Study

1. To find out the level of Achievement in science among the Vth std Normal Students and Child Labour Students.

2. To find out the level of significant difference on the achievement in science among the Vth std normal students and child labour students.
3. To find out the level of significant difference on the achievement in science among male between normal students and child labour students in Vth std.
4. To find out the level of significant difference on the achievement in science among female between normal students and child labour students in Vth std.
5. To find out the level of significant difference on the achievement in science among Illiterate parents of normal students and child labour students in Vth std.
6. To find out the level of significant difference on the achievement in science among Literate parents of normal students and child labour students in Vth std.

Hypotheses of the Study

1. There is no significant difference on the achievement in science among the Vth std normal students and child labour students.
2. There is no significant difference on the achievement in science among normal and child labour male students in Vth std.
3. There is no significant difference on the achievement in science among normal and child labour female students in Vth std.
4. There is no significant difference on the achievement in science among Illiterate parents of normal students and child labour students in Vth std.
5. There is no significant difference on the achievement in science among literate parents of normal students and child labour students in Vth std.

Blueprint

Table 8.2 : Blueprint for Achievement Test

Objectives	Knowledge			UnderStanding			Application			Skill			Total
Forms of questions/ Content Unit	E	S.A	O	E	S.A	O	E	S.A	O	E	S.A	O	
Physics	-	-	7	-	-	4	-	-	4	-	-	2	17
Chemistry	-	-	4	-	-	3	-	-	5	-	-	3	15
Biology	-	-	5	-	-	4	-	-	6	-	-	3	18
Sub total			16			11			15			8	50
Total (in %)		**32**			**22**			**30**			**16**		**100**

Note : **E** – Essay Type

S.A. – Short Answer
O – Objective Type

Tools Used for the Study

To access the Student Achievement in Science among Child Labour Students and Normal Students in Namakkal District, the Achievement Test was utilized.

Personal Data Sheet

To know the background of the Students, The investigator used personal data sheets along with the Developed Questionnaires. It asked for details of Gender, type of School, Literate and Illiterate. The students were asked to fill in all the particulars given in the personal data sheets.

Size of the Sample

There are so many Child Labour Schools and Normal Schools in Namakkal District among that the investigator select the Five Child Labour Schools and Two Normal Schools. The School as follows:

1. Child Labour Schools at Kumarapalayam – 5
2. Normal Schools at Rasipuram - 2

From the above areas the investigator has taken from this study.

Table 8.3 : List of Child Labour Schools and Normal Schools samples

S.No.	Category	Students
1.	Child Labour Schools	50
2.	Normal Schools	50
	Total	**100**

The present study is done by Survey Method. The Stratified Random Sampling Technique is followed. The size of the sampling was 100 Students only.

Administering the Cool

The achievement test was administered separately among the 100 Students, 50 Child Labour Schools Students and

50 Normal Schools Students of the following in Namakkal district.

Scoring Procedure

The completed response sheets were scored properly by using the key. The questionnaire consisted of objective type questions and each questions carried one mark with the help of the key all the response sheets were valued and marks were recorded for analysis.

Delimitation of the Study

Broadly speaking, any study is impossible without delimitation. Research studies is general will have delimitation due to many factors. This study too has some delimitations. It is the responsibility to the researches to see that the study is contacted with maximum care in ordered to be reliable.

However, the following delimitations were unavoidable in the present study:

- The study has been limited to Tamil Nadu only.
- The study has been restricted to the normal students and child labour only.
- The Study has been restricted to the Vth Std students only.
- This study adopted survey method using questionnaires to collect data from respondents.
- In this study examination marks were considered as achievement.
- 0A purposive stratified random sample was used to choose the subject to be included in the study.
- This study is focused mainly on the variables Illiterate, Literate, Male, Female, Father and Mother.

The ensuring chapter deals with the Data Analysis of the study.

Conclusion

The design of the study various stages involved the experimentation and the data collection procedures were explained in this chapter in detail. The analysis and interpretation of data related to the hypotheses framed have been presented in the next chapter.

Chapter 9

Analysis and Interpretation

Introduction

Any research work could be meaningful when the data were analyzed and interpreted properly. Therefore the researcher has given much important to this part. The data collected from the sample analyzed and interpreted in the following heads.

(*a*) Descriptive analysis

(*b*) Differential analysis

Descriptive Analysis

It includes comparison of measures of central tendency such as the mean and the measures of variability such as standard deviation. The calculated values are used to describe the properties of the different sub-samples. In Namakkal district 100 students are taken as samples. The variables are studies in the present study are Gender, Type of School, literate and Illiterate. After the data was collected, it was classified as the above mentioned variables.

Differential Analysis

It contains the determinations of the statistical significance of the difference between references to selected variables. It contains 't' test. A 't' test is a numerical procedure that takes into account the difference between the means of the sample present in the scores. Thus the 't' test is a technique to find out whether the difference the mean performance is significant or not.

Level of Significance

Experimenters and research workers choose several arbitrary standards for their convenience. These arbitrary standards are called level of significance. Most commonly used level of significance is 0.01 and 0.05 level. For the present investigation, the researcher has used 0.05 levels as significance to analyze the existence of various hypotheses.

Differential Analysis

From the above table 9.1 the calculated overall means value, Normal students have more achievement in science between Vth standards than the child labour students.

Table 9.1 : Significant difference on the Achievement in Science between Vth Std Normal Students and Child Labour

S. No.	Variables	N	Percentage
1.	Normal Students	50	69.9%
2.	Child Labour Students	50	57.3%

Table 9.2 : Significant difference on the Achievement in Science between Vth Std Normal Students and Child Labour Students

S.No.	Variables	N	Mean	Standard deviation	't' Value	Significant Level of 0.05
1.	Normal Students	50	69.9	18.02	3.7724	1. 98*
2.	Child Labour Students	50	57.3	15.323		

*Significant **No Significant

From the above table 9.2. It shows calculated 't' value is grater then the tabulated 't' value at 0.05 level of significance. So there is Significant difference on the Achievement in Science between Vth Std Normal Students and Child Labour Students. Hence formed hypothesis is rejected.

Table 9.3 : Significant difference on the Achievement in Science between Vth Std Male Normal students and Male Child Labour Students.

S.No.	Variables	N	Mean	Standard deviation	't' Value	Significant Level of 0.05
1.	Normal Male Students	24	67.16	19.50	0.8856	2.01**
2.	Child Labour Male Students	29	63.1	12.257		

*Significant **No Significant

From the above table 9.3. It shows calculated 't' value is less than the tabulated 't' value at 0.05 level of significance . So there is no significant difference on the Achievement in Science between Vth Std Normal Male Students and Child Labour Male Students. Hence formed hypothesis is accepted.

Tablea 9.4 : Significant difference on the Achievement in Science between Vth Std Normal Female Students and Child Labour Female Students.

S.No.	Variables	N	Mean	Standard deviation	't' Value	Significant Level of 0.05
1.	Normal Female students	26	71.7	15.205	5.204	2.02*
2.	Child Labour Female students	21	55.9	10.58		

*Significant **No Significant

From the above table 9.4. It shows calculated 't' value is less than the tabulated 't' value at 0.05 level of significance. So there is Significant difference on the Achievement in Science between Vth Std Normal Female Students and Child Labour Female Students. Hence formed hypothesis is rejected.

Table 9.5 : Significant difference on the Achievement in Science between Vth Std Normal Students Father Illiterate and Child Labour Students Father Illiterate.

S.No.	Variables	N	Mean	Standard deviation	't' Value	Significant Level of 0.05
1.	Normal Student Father Illiterate	19	73.4	15.42	3.83	2.02*
2.	Child Labour Father Illiterate	23	58.11	13.896		

*Significant **No Significant

From the above table 9.5. It shows calculated 't' value is grater then the tabulated 't' value at 0.05 level of significance . So there is significant difference on the Achievement in Science between Vth Std Normal Students Father Illiterate and Child Labour Students Father Illiterate. Hence formed hypothesis is rejected.

From the above table 9.6. It shows calculated 't' value is less than the tabulated 't' value at 0.05 level of significance. So there is Significant difference on the Achievement in Science between Vth Std Normal Students Mother Illiterate and Child Labour Students Mother Illiterate. Hence formed hypothesis is rejected.

Table 9.6 : Significant difference on the Achievement in Science between Vth Std Normal Students Mother Illiterate and Child Labour Students Mother Illiterate.

S.No.	Variables	N	Mean	Standard deviation	't' Value	Significant Level of 0.05
1.	Normal Student Mother Illiterate	23	69.8	18.37	2.658	2.01**
2.	Child Labour Mother Illiterate	30	57.84	12.934		

*Significant **No Significant

Table 9.7 : The Achievement in Science between Vth Std School level Father Qualification Normal Students and School level Father Qualification Child Labour Students.

S.No.	Variables	N	Mean	Standard deviation	't' Value	Significant Level of 0.05
1.	Normal Student Father Qualification School Level	31	66.46	16.09	1.746	2.01**
2.	Child Labour Student Father Qualification School Level	27	59.648	17.91		

*Significant **No Significant

From the above table 9.7. It shows calculated 't' value is less than the tabulated 't' value at 0.05 level of significance. So there is no Significant difference on the Achievement in

Science between Vth Std Normal Students Father Qualification School Level and Child Labour Students Father Qualification School Level. Hence formed hypothesis is Accepted.

Table 9.8 : Significant difference on the Achievement in Science between Vth Std School level Mother Qualification Normal Students and School level Mother Qualification Child Labour Students.

S.No.	Variables	N	Mean	Standard deviation	't' Value	Significant Level of 0.05
1.	Normal Student Mother Qualification School Level	27	69.20	17.24	1.4793	2.02**
2.	Child Labour Student Mother Qualification School Level	20	61	19.868		

*Significant **No Significant

From the above table 9.8. It shows calculated 't' value is less than the tabulated 't' value at 0.05 level of significance. So there is no Significant difference on the Achievement in Science between Vth Std Normal Students Mother Qualification School Level and Child Labour Students Mother Qualification School Level. Hence formed hypothesis is Accepted.

Conclusion

Thus the analysis of the data generated by the administration of the tool on the sample of 100 Vth Std School Students in Namakkal District has yielded many interesting results. Which are Summarized in the succeeding chapter-V.

Chapter 10

Findings, Conclusions and Recommendations

Introduction

In this chapter an attempt had been made to consolidate all the findings of the present study, the investigator also made some recommendation, which include the relevant area for this research and lastly the conclusion the findings are based on the result collected from the opinioned.

The Study in Restrospect

The aim of the present investigation was to find out the "Achievement in science among the students of Child labour School and Normal School in Namakkal District".

Methodology in Brief

For the present study, Normative survey method was adopted. The sample of the present study comprises 100 students of Namakkal District were selected in which 50 students are Normal students and 50 students are Child labour students. The tool used for the collection of data is based on Science Achievement.

Statement of the Study

The problem under the study is entitled as "Achievement in science among the students of Child labour School and Normal School in Namakkal District".

Objectives of the Study

The Major Objective of the study was to find out the level of Achievement in Science. The Specific objectives is to find out the Significance difference towards Achievement in science among the students of Child labour School and Normal School are as follows.

Major Objective

The first and foremost objective is to find out the level of Achievement in Science of Vth Std studying.

Specific Objectives

The specific objective is to find out the significant difference towards Achievement in science among the students of Child labour School and Normal School based on the following variables

1. Gender (Male/Female)
2. Type of School (Normal School/Child labour School)
3. Parent Education

Major Findings of the Study

From the present study the investigator gave the following findings:

The level of achievement (score) in science of Vth Std Normal students and child labour students is 69.95 per cent and 57.3 per cent respectively.

There is no Significant difference on the Achievement in Science between Vth Std Normal Male Students and Child Labour Male Students.

There is Significant difference on the Achievement in Science between Vth Std Normal Female Students and Child Labour Female Students.

There is Significant difference on the Achievement in Science between Vth Std Normal Students of Illiterate parents and Child Labour Students of Illiterate parents.

There is no Significant difference on the Achievement in Science between Vth Std Normal Students parents Qualification School Level and Child Labour Students parents Qualification School Level.

Discussion

From the above Findings normal students and normal Female students are significantly differed with child labour students and child labour female students in their Achievement test in science. Because normal students and normal female students are studding in regular classes but child labour students and child labour Female students are not have proper teaching-learning and no parent motivation.

According to the variables, literate parents, normal and normal male students are similar level of achievement with child labour student and child labour male student in Science.

Discussion Related to the Review

From the review of related literature there is no kind of researches in the area of child labour and normal student's achievement in Science. So this research in is investigated as well as one and all findings of this research derived are newly. So these findings are not matched and related with the reviews.

Educational Implication

To achieve the democratic principle of providing equal educational opportunities irrespective of disableness, the government should strengthen the facilities on teaching aids specially meant for child labour. More skilled specialized teachers are to be trained in this area so that education of the child labour may me enhanced. Parents of the child labour students may be called for frequent counseling and motivation training on encouraging child labour students on their education. The parents must be given some financial grant to buy some special devices so as to continue their studies when they are at home. Voluntary organizations are to be identified and linkages are to be made for getting not only financial but also academic assistance, of the child mean that the depend always on the government and parents.

Areas of Research for the Future

Research is a chain activity. There purpose of any research in education is to find solutions for problems related to teachers, students, learning etc... But one problem always leaves many related research questions that can be investigated by other researchers, some of the areas for research in the future may be as follows, the present study can be repeated with wide sample.

- A similar study can be conducted on the professional college students.
- There is need for a change in parental attitude about rights of the child such as health care, nutrition, basic education and recreation for children. Appropriate values should be inculcated with respect to rights of children and responsibilities of parents at community level. Need based strategies should be evolved at micro level to prevent the child labour problem.
- Parents committees should be formed at primary school level. Each school should be given a catchments area and the teacher working in them should be made responsible for the enrollment and

regular attendance of all the children below the age of 14 years. By adopting both carrot and stick policies, teachers should be made responsible to avoid school dropouts minimize absenteeism and to make the school lovable for children.

- School dropouts are becoming child workers under the pretext of learning skills in mechanical field. But, the real solution lies in strengthening compulsory education, neighborhood function education and in providing vocational skills.
- The rehabilitation programmers of the child workers should take into consideration the earning potential and the acquisition of skills in the work process. As a complimentary measure, non formal schooling at convenient hours to working children should be planned with sufficient incentives and entertainment.
- Inspiring efforts should be made through mass media by politicians, academicians, social workers and elite of the society to bring awareness in the community about the various issues involved in the education of working children.
- There should be a campaign in increase awareness about child labour. Use of mass media can be made for creating awareness with respect to the need of eliminating child labour.
- Regular inspection and supervision of various industries and factories need to be made to control the employment of children. For regulating the employment of children in agriculture and its allied activities, Panchayati raj institutions and Village Education Committee may be delegated judicial powers to ensure that the children are not employed and the attend the regular schools.
- There is a need to strengthen employment generation, minimum wage and such other programmes

to provide employment to men and women in the family so that their children need not go work.

- There is a need to improve school education to move from non-consistent local initiatives which end up offering free meals and poor educational services, to a sustainable government policy for the rehabilitation of working children, with transparent and measurable indicators.
- In order to support families who do invest in their children's education, social benefits should be linked to school a attendance of their children. Innovative programmes which may pay families a small stipend to make up for the lost wages of children can improve future prospects of today's child labour.
- Existing statistics on child labour are problematic. The effect is that situations of children engaged in hazardous work do not get the degree of attention they deserve. Therefore comprehensive data collection regarding working children is must then only effective policy measures and action plans can be formulated.
- NGOs can be given incentive to work for the cause of eliminating child labour because they are in a better position to have easy access to the relevant information and their message will have more credibility among the local people. The will be more likely to generate a change in the attitude of the majority population via increasing their participation. Co-operation of government and voluntary organization is needed to eradicate child labour completely.

Conclusion of the Study

The study found that the child labour students are not equally competent with normal students. Teaching strategies and teaching aids are to be strengthened at the school for the Child labour for achieving equal educational opportunities. Moreover, the child labour students may be brought to the normal school and study under integrated system. Hence it is concluded that integrated Education is the system which analysis the experience that are provided to child labour and Normal students. Through that system, the child labours are more benefited than the normal students in getting higher experiences.

teaching aids are to be strengthened at the school for the Child labour for achieving equal educational opportunities. Moreover, the child labour students may be brought to the normal school and study under integrated system. Hence it is concluded that Integrated Education is the system which analysis the experimenter that can be promoted to child labour and normal students. Through that system the child labours are more benefited than the normal students in gaining higher experiences.

PART—III

Awareness on Traffic Rules Among Student Teachers

Chapter 11

Introduction

Education in the largest sense is any act or experience that has a formative effect on the mind, character or physical ability of an individual. In its technical sense, education is the process by which society deliberately transmits its accumulated knowledge, skills and values from one generation to another.

The word education is derived from *educare* (Latin) "bring up", which is related to *educere* "bring out", "bring forth what is within", "bring out potential" and *ducere*, "to lead".

Teachers in educational institutions direct the education of students and might draw on many subjects, including reading, writing mathematics, science and history. This process is sometimes called schooling when referring to the education of teaching only a certain subject, usually as professors at institutions of higher learning. There is also education in fields for those who want specific vocational skills, such as those required to be a pilot. In addition there is an array of education possible at the informal level, such as in museums and libraries, with the Internet and in life experience. Many non-traditional education options are now available and continue to evolve.

Systems of Formal Education

Education is the process by which people learn:

- *Instruction* refers to the facilitating of learning, usually by a teacher.
- *Teaching* refers to the actions of a real live instructor to impart learning to the student.
- *Learning* refers to learning with a view toward preparing learners with specific knowledge, skills, or abilities that can be applied immediately upon completion.

Traffic

Traffic in English is taken from the Arabic word *taraffaqa*, which means to walk along slowly together.

Traffic on roads may consist of pedestrians ridden or herded *animals*, *vehicles*, *streetcars* and other *conveyances*, either singly or together, while using the public way for purposes of travel. *Traffic laws* are the *laws* which govern traffic and regulate vehicles, while *rules of the road* are both the laws and the *informal rules* that may have developed over time to facilitate the orderly and timely flow of traffic.

Organized traffic generally has well-established priorities, lanes, *right-of-way*, and traffic control at *intersections*.

Traffic is formally organized in many jurisdictions, with marked *lanes*, *junctions*, *intersections*, *interchanges*, *traffic signals*, or *signs*. Traffic is often classified by type: heavy motor vehicle (*e.g.*, *car*, *truck*); other vehicle (*e.g.*, *moped*, *bicycle*); and *pedestrian*. Different classes may share *speed limits* and easement, or may be segregated. Some jurisdictions may have very detailed and complex rules of the road while others rely more on drivers' common sense and willingness to cooperate.

Organization typically produces a better combination of travel safety and efficiency. Events which disrupt the flow and may cause traffic to degenerate into a disorganized mess include: *road construction*, *collisions* and *debris in the roadway*. On particularly busy freeways, a minor disruption may persist in a phenomenon known as *traffic waves*. A complete breakdown of organization may result in *traffic jams* and *gridlock*. Simulations of organized traffic frequently involve *queuing theory*, *stochastic processes* and equations of *mathematical physics* applied to *traffic flow*.

Rules of the Road

Rules of the road are the general practices and procedures that *road* users are required to follow. These rules usually apply to all road users, though they are of special importance to *motorists* and *cyclists*. These rules govern interactions between vehicles and with *pedestrians*. The basic traffic rules are defined by an international treaty under the authority of the *United Nations*, the 1968 *Vienna Convention on Road Traffic*. Not all countries are signatory to the convention and, even among signatories, local variations in practice may be found. There are also unwritten local rules of the road, which are generally understood by local drivers.

As a general rule, drivers are expected to avoid a collision with another vehicle and pedestrians, regardless of whether or not the applicable rules of the road allow them to be where they happen to be. In addition to the rules applicable by default, *traffic signs* and *traffic lights* must be obeyed, and instructions may be given by a police officer, either routinely (on a busy crossing instead of traffic lights) or as *road traffic control* around a construction zone, accident, or other road disruption. These rules should be distinguished from the mechanical procedures required to operate one's vehicle.

Traffic Rules in India

The transport department of each and every city around the world has been entrusted with the responsibility of providing a smooth public transportation system on roads, controlling pollution under permissible limits, keeping a record of registration of vehicles, insurance of vehicles, issuing permits and collection of taxes. These departments function by devising policies, implementing them and then monitor and regulate the functioning of the transport in the city.

Traffic rules of the roads are both the laws and the informal rules that may have been developed over time to facilitate the orderly and timely flow of traffic. With the replacement of ancient horse driven carts with cars and trucks, the speed of the traffic increased paving way for the need of smooth roads and yet smoother traffic. So, to curb the need of the smoother traffic, some rules were devised to assure that the traffic runs smooth. Almost all of the roadways traffic rules are built with devices meant to control traffic.

The basic idea to devise rules is to make the traffic more organized. These establish a direct contact with the driver and help making the ride easy and controlled by delivering information which complements the laws, guiding directions, speed limits and parking zones. All these efforts collectively assure that traffic is orderly and safe. An organized traffic has well established priorities, lanes flowing in particular directions. The benefit is that it reduces the travel time. Some rules and regulations have been formulated for an easy driving. The drivers are not allowed to drive without a few documents. These documents should be produced on demand.

Road Traffic Signs-Signals

Basic Rules of the Road

The rules enlisted under this category are to be meant for all the people sharing the roads. The idea behind formulating such rules is that the roads are meant not only for the drivers (including motorists/cyclists/motorcyclists), but are shared by the pedestrians and animals by the road side. The rules belonging to these categories are mandatory to be followed while using the roads. You can observe all the above-stated rules only if you are patient, considerate and careful.

Traffic Signals

A traffic light, traffic signal or a stop light is a signaling device positioned at a road intersection to indicate when it is safe to wade through. The traffic signal passes on its information using a universal color code.

Road Signals

Signs form a vital and integral part of the trafficking system for the safety of the road users. As per Indian Roads Congress Road Signs are for indications on the road the roads signs are categorized into 3 types:

- Mandatory Signs or Regulatory Signs
- Cautionary Signs or Warning or Precautionary
- Informatory Signs

Hand Signals

Hand Signals or Manual Regulation Signs are the gestures used to regulate traffic on the road using the hand movements. Traffic policemen use these actions to regulate traffic particularly at intersections while the drivers use these signals to notify the other users on the road about his intentions. Based on the person these can be categorized as:

- Hand Signals by Policeman
- Hand Signals by Drivers

Road Markings and Pavement Markings

Road markings or pavement markings were introduced in 1920s. Initially, they were used to indicate the road's centerline. But, as they traffic increased, so did the roads and the lanes and later with the multi lane roads they were used to define lanes. With the times, they too have evolved a lot adorned with the information to aid motorists in passing safely.

Traffic Authorities in India

The transport Department is one of the largest revenue earning departments. dealing with various transport related matters like driving licenses, registration of motor vehicles, grant and renewal of permits and other regulatory and enforcement services. The transport department works under the provision of the section 213 of the MV Act, 1988. The transport department is primarily established for enforcement of the provisions of the motor vehicle act, 1988.

Working Authorities

Transport Department works with two of the concerned authorities, under Section 68 of the Motor Vehicles Act, 1988. These are discussed below:

State Transport Authority

The main functions of the State Transport Authority are:

- To co-ordinate and regulate the activities and policies of the Regional Transport Authorities.
- Entering into bilateral agreements with other States.
- To decide the quota for counter signature permits.
- Grant of All India and State wide permits.

Regional Transport Authority

To exercise and discharge the powers and functions conferred on them under the provisions of Motor Vehicles Act, which mainly relate to control of transport by way of grant of permits.

Services Provided by R.T.O.

Regional Transport Office provides the following services:

1. Related to Driving License

- Issuing learner license.
- Renewal of learner license.
- Issuing driving license.
- Renewal of driving license (issued in same and other office).
- Endorsement in driving license.
- Noting change of address in learner and driving license.

- Issuing International driving permit.
- Conductor license

2. Related to Registration of Vehicles

- Temporary registration of vehicles.
- Permanent registration of vehicles.
- Transfer of ownership.
- Entry of hypothecation/hire-purchase/lease agreement.
- Termination of hypothecation/hire-purchase/lease agreement.
- Change of address.
- Issue of no objection certificate.
- Issue of clearance certificate

3. Collection of Tax

- Payment of tax

Enforcement

The services granted by these authorities are regulated, monitored and enforced by two of the Enforcement Agencies:

- Enforcement wing of the transport department.
- Traffic police

Road Race-A Menace

Literally, "Road Rage" is a term used to refer to the violent incidents caused by stress while driving on high traffic zones on roadways. It is usually associated with "Aggressive Driving". But, in lay man's language, "Road Rage" can be defined as an incident in which an angry or impatient motorist or passenger intentionally injures or kills another motorist, passenger, or pedestrian, or attempts or threatens to injure or kill another motorist, passenger, or pedestrian. "Road Rage" often occurs with exchange of swear words and furious shouts at the fellow commuter.

It has been found that most of the drivers have a feeling of "Road Rage" because it is a cultural norm. Angst and frustration while driving on Indian roads comes naturally which translates into "Road Rage". People learn this behavior from childhood when being driven by parents and adults. In day to day life, more of the incidents can be experienced during peak traveling hours, during fair weather, under moderately congested conditions in urban areas. "Alcohol" has many a times been found to be associated with many of the incidents.

There are many conditions associated with "Road Rage"; including: traffic congestion, driving habits, weather conditions, noise levels, time constraints. Some time it can be an instructive response of careless driving by another driver. With reference to the historical records, in 1997, the U.S therapists have worked to claim "Road Rage" a medical disorder. Although, a few insist that defining "Road Rage" as a medical disorder will allow criminals to plead and provide them an excuse to shrug off.

It is usually emphasized that "Road Rage" and "Aggressive Driving" are not synonymous. "Road Rage" is uncontrolled anger that results in violence or threatened violence on the road; it is Criminal Behavior. These are serious crimes that just happen to occur within the roadways environment. "Aggressive Driving" does not rise to the level of criminal behavior. "Aggressive Driving" includes tailgating, abrupt lane changes, and speeding, alone or in combination. These potentially dangerous behaviors are traffic offenses, but are not criminal behavior. Infect, "Road Rage" can be distinguished from any other traffic incident by its "Willful and Criminal" nature.

In general, "Road Raging" involves menace provoking activities including:

1. Speeding and Aggressive Acceleration.
2. Tailgating.

3. Cutting others off.
4. Weaving in and out of traffic.
5. Forming a "convoy" to block access to a traffic lane.
6. Honking the vehicle's horn or flashing lights excessively.
7. Rude gestures.
8. Verbal abuse.
9. Deliberately hitting another person, vehicle or object with one's own vehicle.
10. Hitting a person or vehicle with a weapon other than a vehicle.
11. Threatening to use a deadly weapon.
12. Revengeful feeling.

"Road Rage" is considered as a menace because it can lead to physical injuries and in some cases it can lead to death also.

First Aid in Road Accidents

Many deaths and impact of injuries can be prevented with First Aid if causalities are treated immediately. First aid is the initial care given to an injured person. Mostly, this timely care prior to the arrival of the medical help means the difference between life and death. It must start immediately when the injury or illness occurs and continue until medical help arrives or the casualty recovers. The basic aims of first aid are:

1. To save life.
2. To protect the casualty from getting more harm.
3. To reduce pain and Priorities of Casualty Treatment.

Traffic Rules and Regulations

Sections: Every driver should possess adequate knowledge and understanding of the following provisions of Motor Vehicle Act 1988:

Section (122) Leaving vehicle in dangerous position: No person shall park his vehicle in public place in such a way that it causes danger, obstruction or inconvenience to other road users.

Section (123) Riding on running board: Carriage of persons on running board and on the top or on the bonnet of motor vehicle is strictly prohibited.

Section (125) Obstruction to the driver: No person driving a motor vehicle shall allow any person to stand or sit or anything to be placed in such a manner as to hamper the driver in his control of the vehicle.

Section (126) Stationary vehicle: While keeping the vehicle stationery in public place its Mechanism should be stopped, brakes must be applied or such measures should be taken as to ensure that vehicle cannot accidentally be put in motion.

Section (128) Pillion Rider: No driver of two-wheeled motor cycle shall carry more than one person, on pillion seat.

Section (130) Production of Documents: (A) the driver of motor vehicle in any public place shall on demand produce his driving license and certificate of registration of the vehicle for examination. (B) Beside these documents driver of transport vehicle shall produce Road Permit Fitness Certificate, Authorization if any Certification of Taxation on demand.

Section (134) Duty of Driver in case of Accident: If you are involved in an accident then you should:

- Stop
- Give your own and vehicle owners name and address to any person who gives his name and address
- Give possible medical aid to injured person.
- Report the matter to the nearest Police Station as soon as possible or within 24 hours.

Section 185) Driving by drunken person or by a person under the influence of drugs: Whoever, while driving, or attempting to drive, a motor vehicle shall be punishable for the first offence with imprisonment for a term which may extend to six month, or with fine which may extend to Rs. 2000 or with both.

Section 186) Driving when mentally or physically unfit to drive: Whoever drives a motor vehicle in any public place when he is to his knowledge suffering from any disease or disability, calculated to cause his driving of the vehicle to be a source of danger to the public, shall be punishable for the first offence with fine which may extend to Rs. 200.

Section (207) Power to detain the vehicle: The Motor Vehicle Inspector may detain the vehicle used:

- Without certificate of registration.
- Without permit.
- Without driving license

Overtaking: Driver must take following precautions before overtaking

- Overtaking is prohibited at blind turns, corners, hill top, when indicated not to overtake by traffic signal or road markings.
- Overtaking only from right hand side. (expect when vehicle ahead is turning right)
- Make your intentions clear before overtaking & do not overtake unless driver ahead permits you to do so.
- While overtaking, distance of vehicle coming opposite direction, its speed and road gradient plays an important role.
- Before starting to overtake look in your rear view mirror & confirm that nobody else is overtaking you.
- If in doubt do not overtake.

- When being overtaken driver shall not increase speed or do anything to other vehicle passing it.
- Come back to your own lane as soon as the vehicle which you have overtaken is seen in the mirror.

Caution at Road Junction and Give Way

The driver of a motor vehicle shall slow down when approaching a road intersection, a road junction, pedestrian crossing or a road corner, and shall not enter, until he has become aware that the he may do so without endangering the safety of persons thereon and shall give way to all traffic approaching on the right hand side of the road. On mountains road or steep roads vehicles traveling downhill shall give precedence to vehicle going up hill.

Fire Service Vehicles and Ambulance to be Given Free Passage

Every driver shall on the approach of fire service vehicle or of an ambulance allow it free passage by drawing his vehicle to the left side of the road.

Pedestrian Crossing

The pedestrian have right of way at any pedestrian crossings (Zebra crossing). When a solid yellow or while line is painted on road at pedestrian crossing no driver shall drive a motor vehicle so that part thereof beyond that line.

Towing

- No vehicle other than mechanically disabled vehicle shall be towed by any vehicle.
- There shall be license holder driver in the vehicle being towed or its steering wheels shall be elevated from the road.
- On the rear of vehicle being towed letters "ON TOW" shall be displayed.

- Distance between two vehicles shall not be more than 5 mts.
- Speed of the vehicle towing another vehicle shall not be more than 42 km/Hrs.

Distance from Vehicle in Front

The driver of vehicle moving behind another shall keep sufficient distance from the vehicle in front (one vehicle length distance for every 15 km/hr). More the speed more is the distance between two vehicles.

Carrying Persons in Tractor and Goods Vehicles

A driver when driving a tractor shall not carry or allow to person on tractor. Goods vehicles driver shall not carry passengers on Hire or Reward.

Projection of Load

No Person shall drive any motor vehicle with is loaded in manner likely to cause danger to any person in such manner that the load projects laterally beyond the side of body or to the front or the rear or in height beyond permissible limits.

Driving Reverse Gear

No driver shall drive in reverse gear without first satisfying himself that it will not cause danger to others.

Use of Horns and Silence Zones

A driver of a vehicle shall not:

- Sound the horn needlessly or continuously or more than necessary to ensure safety.
- Sound the horn is silence zones.
- Drive a vehicle creating undue noise when in motion.
- Drive a vehicle with a muffler causing alarming sound.
- Sound the multi tuned horn or shrill horns.

Organized Traffic

Priority (right of way)

Vehicles often come into conflict with other vehicles and pedestrians because their intended courses of travel intersect, and thus interfere with each other's routes. The general principle that establishes who has the right to go first is called "right of way", or "priority". It establishes who has the right to use the conflicting part of the road and who has to wait until the other does so.

Signs, signals, markings and other features are often used to make priority explicit. Some signs, such as the *stop sign*, are nearly universal. When there are no signs or markings, different rules are observed depending on the location. These default priority rules differ between countries, and may even vary within countries. Trends toward uniformity are exemplified at an international level by the *Vienna Convention on Road Signs and Signals*, which prescribes standardized traffic control devices (signs, signals, and markings) for establishing the right of way where necessary.

Crosswalks (or pedestrian crossings) are common in populated areas, and may indicate that pedestrians have priority over vehicular traffic. In most modern cities, the *traffic signal* is used to establish the right of way on the busy roads. Its primary purpose is to give each road a duration of time in which its traffic may use the intersection in an organized way. The intervals of time assigned for each road may be adjusted to take into account factors such as difference in volume of traffic, the needs of pedestrians, or other traffic signals. Pedestrian crossings may be located near other traffic control devices; if they are not also regulated in some way, vehicles must give priority to them when in use. Traffic on a public road usually has priority over other traffic such as traffic emerging from private access; rail crossings and *drawbridges* are typical exceptions.

Uncontrolled Traffic

Uncontrolled traffic occurs in the absence of *lane markings* and *traffic control signals*. On *roads* without marked lanes, drivers tend to keep to the appropriate side if the road is wide enough. Drivers frequently overtake others. Obstructions are common.

Intersections have no signals or signage, and a particular road at a busy intersection may be dominant—that is, its traffic flows-until a break in traffic, at which time the dominance shifts to the other road where vehicles are queued. At the intersection of two perpendicular roads, a traffic jam may result if four vehicles face each other side-on.

Turning

Drivers will often want to cease to travel a straight line and turn onto another road or onto private property. The vehicle's directional signals (blinkers) are often used as a way to announce one's intention to turn, thus alerting other drivers. The actual usage of blinkers varies greatly amongst countries, although its purpose should be the same in all countries: to indicate a driver's intention to depart from the current (and natural) flow of traffic well before the departure is executed (typically 3 seconds as a guideline).

This will usually mean that turning traffic will have to stop in order to wait for a breach to turn, and this might cause inconvenience for drivers that follow them but do not want to turn. This is why dedicated lanes and protected traffic signals for turning are sometimes provided. On busier intersections where a protected lane would be ineffective or cannot be built, turning may be entirely prohibited, and drivers will be required to "drive around the block" in order to accomplish the turn. Many cities employ this tactic quite often; in *San Francisco*, due to its common practice, making three right turns is known colloquially as a "San Francisco left turn". Likewise, as many intersections in *Taipei City* are too busy to allow direct left turns, signs often direct drivers to drive around the block to turn.

Turning rules are by no means universal. In New Zealand, for example, left turning traffic must give way to opposing "right turning" traffic, *i.e.*, traffic turning into a driver's path (unless there are multiple lanes to turn into).

On roads with multiple lanes, turning traffic is generally expected to move to the lane closest to the direction they wish to turn. For example, traffic intending to turn right will usually move to the rightmost lane before the intersection. Likewise, left-turning two rightmost lanes will be of authority; for example, it is common for drivers to observe (and trust) the turn signals used by other drivers in order to make turns from other lanes. For example if several vehicles on the right lane are all turning right, a vehicle may come from the next-to-right lane and turn right as well, doing so in parallel with the other right-turning vehicles.

Speed Limits

The higher the speed of a vehicle, the more difficult collision avoidance becomes and the greater the damage if a collision does occur. Therefore, many countries of the world *limit the maximum speed allowed* on their roads. Vehicles are not supposed to be driven at speeds which are higher than the posted maximum.

To enforce speed limits, two approaches are generally employed. In the *United States*, it is common for the police to patrol the streets and use special equipment (typically a *radar* unit) to measure the speed of vehicles, and pull over any vehicle found to be in violation of the speed limit. In *Brazil* and some European countries, there are computerized speed-measuring devices spread throughout the city, which will automatically detect speeding drivers and take a photograph of the license plate (or number plate), which is later used for applying and mailing the ticket. Many jurisdictions in the U.S. use this technology as well. A mechanism that was developed in *Germany* is the *Grüne Welle,* or *green wave,* which is an indicator that shows the optimal speed to travel for the synchronized green lights along that corridor. Driving faster or slower than the speed set by the behavior of the lights causes the driver to frequently encounter red lights. This discourages drivers from speeding or impeding the flow of traffic. See related *traffic wave*.

Overtaking

Overtaking (or passing) refers to a maneuver by which one or more vehicles traveling in the same direction are passed by another vehicle. On two-lane roads, when there is a split line or a dashed line on the side of the overtaker, drivers may overtake when it is safe. On multi-lane roads in most jurisdictions, overtaking is permitted in the "slower" lanes, though many require a special circumstance.

When a street is wide enough to accommodate several vehicles traveling side-by-side, it is usual for traffic to organize itself into *lanes*, that is, *parallel* corridors of traffic. Some roads have one lane for each direction of travel and others have multiple lanes for each direction. Most countries apply pavement markings to clearly indicate the limits of each lane and the direction of travel that it must be used for. In other countries lanes have no markings at all and drivers follow them mostly by *intuition* rather than visual stimulus.

On roads that have multiple lanes going in the same direction, drivers may usually shift amongst lanes as they please, but they must do so in a way that does not cause inconvenience to other drivers. Driving cultures vary greatly on the issue of "lane ownership": in some countries, drivers traveling in a lane will be very protective of their right to travel in it while in others drivers will routinely expect other drivers to shift back and forth.

Designation and Overtaking

The usual designation for lanes on *divided highways* is the fastest lane is the one closest to the center of the road, and the slowest to the edge of the road. Drivers are usually expected to keep in the slowest lane unless *overtaking*, though with more traffic congestion all lanes are often used.

When Driving on the left:

- The lane designated for faster traffic is on the right.
- The lane designated for slower traffic is on the left.
- Most *freeway* exits are on the left.
- Overtaking is permitted to the right, and sometimes to the left.

When driving on the right:

The lane designated for faster traffic is on the left.

- The lane designated for slower traffic is on the right.
- Most *freeway* exits are on the right.
- Overtaking is permitted to the left, and sometimes to the right.

Needs of the Study

Due to increase in population the use of vehicle is increased. So the road accident and many of them are died. We want to know about the traffic rules. So we want to learn about this from childhood onwards. Hence the investigator made an attempt to study the awareness on traffic rules among Student Teachers.

Statement of the Study

The study taken by the investigator stated as *"Awareness on Traffic rules among Student Teachers at Namakkal District"*.

Definition of the Terms

Awareness

The foremost objectives are to help students acquire an awareness and sensitivity to the total environment and its allied problems.

Traffic Rules

Traffic is formally organized in many jurisdictions, with marked lanes, junctions, intersections, interchanges, traffic signals, or signs. Traffic is often classified by type: heavy motor vehicle (*e.g.*, car, truck); other vehicle (*e.g.*, moped, bicycle); and pedestrian. Different classes may share speed limits and easement, or may be segregated. Some jurisdictions may have very detailed and complex rules of the road while others rely more on drivers' common sense and willingness to cooperate.

Education

Education is a lifelong process which helps on individual through experience. Learning or training to seek his proper adjustment and attain maximum possible harmonious development of his potentialities for the welfare of his self and service to the society.

B.Ed Students

B.Ed trainees are one who is capable of developing a desire to learn the techniques principles and methods of teaching and capable of modifying their behavior pattern in order to bring about desired behavior changes in pupil under the change in future.

Objectives of the Stujdy

1. To find out the level of awareness on the Traffic rules among Student Teachers.
2. To find the level of significant difference on the awareness of Traffic rules between Male and Female Student Teachers.
3. To find the level of significant difference on the awareness of Traffic rules between Under Graduate with B. Ed and Post Graduate with B. Ed Student Teachers.

4. To find the level of significant difference on the awareness of Traffic rules between science and Arts Subjects Student Teachers.
5. To find the level of significant difference on the awareness of Traffic rules between rural and urban area Student Teachers.
6. To find the level of significant difference on the awareness of Traffic rules between Under Graduate with B. Ed and Post Graduate with B. Ed Male Student Teachers.
7. To find the level of significant difference on the awareness of Traffic rules between Under Graduate with B. Ed and Post Graduate with B. Ed Female Student Teachers.
8. To find the level of significant difference on the awareness of Traffic rules between Science and Arts Subjects Male Student Teachers.
9. To find the level of significant difference on the awareness of Traffic rules between Science and Arts Subjects Female Student Teachers.
10. To find the level of significant difference on the awareness of Traffic rules between rural and urban area Male Student Teachers.
11. To find the level of significant difference on the awareness of Traffic rules between rural and urban area Female Student Teachers.

Hypotheses of the Study

1. There is no significant difference on the awareness of Traffic rules between Male and Female Student Teachers.
2. There is no significant difference on the awareness of Traffic rules between Under Graduate with B. Ed and Post Graduate with B. Ed Student Teachers.

3. There is no significant difference on the awareness of Traffic rules between science and Arts Subjects Student Teachers.
4. There is no significant difference on the awareness of Traffic rules between rural and urban area Student Teachers.
5. There is no significant difference on the awareness of Traffic rules between Under Graduate with B. Ed and Post Graduate with B. Ed Male Student Teachers.
6. There is no significant difference on the awareness of Traffic rules between Under Graduate with B. Ed and Post Graduate with B. Ed Female Student Teachers.
7. There is no significant difference on the awareness of Traffic rules between Science and Arts Subjects Male Student Teachers.
8. There is no significant difference on the awareness of Traffic rules between Science and Arts Subjects Female Student Teachers.
9. There is no significant difference on the awareness of Traffic rules between rural and urban area Male Student Teachers.
10. There is no significant difference on the awareness of Traffic rules between rural and urban area Female Student Teachers.

Scope of the Study

The topic is an investigation of awareness on Traffic rules among B.Ed Student Teachers. Since this is the survey study. The investigator attempt to know the awareness on Traffic rules among B. Ed Students. This study will be of great help for the educationists particularly for the teachers since the concept of education has been changing from time to time. The awareness may differ from person to person one can learn and do anything with involvement only when he had a better awareness towards it. If we compel anybody to do any work in which one does not have good awareness, then it may be the root cause for many problems. It may give a lot mental fatigue to a person. Thus he can't do it effectively. In this context the investigator attempts to study the influence and awareness of Traffic rules among B. Ed Students in various categories.

Delimitations of the Study

- The present investigation is confined to the B. Ed Students Studying in Namakkal District of Tamil Nadu.
- The study is confined only to a sample of 306 student teachers from private college of Education located in rural and urban area.

Organisation of the Study

The report of the thesis will be presented according to the following sequences.

The first chapter gives introduction, definitions of terms, Statement of problem, objectives and delimitations of the study.

Second chapter deals with the review of related literature which are done in India and abroad related to this study.

Third chapter gives a detailed account of research procedures and methodology used in this study.

Fourth chapter deals with the tabulation of analysis and the interpretations of the data in detail.

Fifth chapter describe the findings, conclusions and certain recommendations about the study.

This is followed by the bibliography and appendices which consist of the tools used for the study and the related matters.

Conclusion

In this chapter, the investigator described the statement of the problem taken for the research study, objectives of the study, delimitations of the study and the need for the study.

In the following chapter, a review of related literature and studies conducted in relevant areas will follow.

Chapter 12 Review of Related Literature

Introduction

As essential aspect of a research of research project is the review of the related literature such a review represents the third set of the scientific method outlined be Dewey and other educational philosophers and the serious student of research will find an exhaustive Survey of what has already been done on the problem an indispensable step in its solution.

Practically all human knowledge can be found in books and libraries. Unlike other animals that must start a new with each generation a man builds upon the accumulated and recorded knowledge of the past. A survey related literature was found necessary to have an idea of what has been done in similar area to scrutinize. the methodology used in coordinated study with others to find gaps to avoid duplication and to direct the work along useful lines.

Review of literature is arranged with a view to look into the findings of few researches which were conducted earlier and which are related to the problem of this current study. The analysis of the previous research findings helps the researcher to known how the hypotheses are constructed types of data, tools for research etc...

Need for Review of Related Literature

For any worthwhile study in any field of knowledge, the research worker needs an adequate familiarity with the library and its many resources practically all human knowledge can be found in books and in libraries. A very effective search for specialized knowledge will be possible only with the help of the related literature. This will help in understanding various aspects of the problem. A review of literature would develop the insight of the researcher. The importance of the review is quite obvious in delimiting the research problems and in defining it better. A complete and elaborate survey of literature will largely enable the investigator to overcome the problems in all quarters of his study. It imparts some sort of confidence in the investigator and consequently the investigator would get a clear picture of the area, his investigation is affiliated to.

Purposes of Review of Related Literature

The survey of related research literature is not without purpose. The following are some of the purposes of such a survey.

- Complete survey of related literature gives to the researcher's necessary insight into the problem. It enables him to put forth vigorously the rationale for the study.
- It becomes an important part of the introduction of the thesis.
- It helps to orient the readers with types with types of research that has been conducted in the field previously.
- It widens the horizon of the researcher.
- It suggests appropriate methods to tackle the problem under study.
- It helps avoiding unnecessary duplication of research of the same nature.

- It provides basis for formulating valuable hypothesis.
- It helps to locate data that can be used in comparative interpretation of results.

Studied Conducted in India

Dr. Archana Kual, Dr. U.S. Sinha, Dr. Y.K. Pathak, Dr. Aparajith Singh, Dr. A.K. Kapoor, Dr. Susheel Sharma & Dr. Sanju Singh (2005) conducted a study on "Fatal Road Traffic Accidents, study of distribution, nature and type of Injury". During one year study period medico legal autopsies were conducted on 950 cases of fatal road traffic accidents at the mortuary of SRN Hospital, MLN Medical College, and Allahabad. M/F Ratio 3:1. 33.68 per cent of cases were in the age group of 25-44 years. Pedestrians were most vulnerable accounting for 35.79 per cent of total fatalities followed by motorized wtwo wheelers 30.52 per cent. Heavy Vehicles were found to be mostly involved 58.52 per cent of cases and most accidents 83.05 per cent occurred on highways. Majority of cases sustained multiple injuries. Primary impact injuries were recorded in 455 cases and pedestrians 36.26 per cent were mostly affected followed by pedal cyclists 20 per cent. 505 cases sustained secondary impact injuries and pedestrians and motor cyclists were primarily involved. Of 697 secondary injuries, 29.99 per cent were sustained by motorcyclists followed by pedestrians 22.67 per cent. Mostly lower extremities 27.39 per cent and pelvis 25.99 per cent received the primary impacts; the head and neck 55.62 per cent the secondary impacts, while secondary injuries were mostly located in the lower extremities 28.38 per cent. Largest number of injuries was recorded in lower extremities 804 number, followed by head & neck 748 numbers. Vehicle occupants mostly sustained thoracic injuries. In majority of cases, of cases, the site of initial impact of the responsible vehicle was frontal (45.14%) followed by rear (25.83%) and side (7.01%). In 179 cases (22.02%) site of responsible vehicle were not known.

Arvind Kumar Mavoori (2005) conducted a study on "An activity plan for Indian Road Safety". Road safety is a major issue affecting the road sector. Road accidents remain a serious impediment to sustainable human development in many of the developing member countries (DMCs) of the Asian Development Bank (ADB). Road accidents continue to be an important social and economic problem in developing countries like India. Growth in the number of motor vehicles, poor enforcement of traffic safety regulations, poor quality of roads and vehicles, and inadequate public health infrastructures are some of the road safety problems facing in India.

The object of this Thesis is to present a status report on the nature of the government policy towards the Activity plans implemented till now and which has to be implemented later for the reduction of road fatalities and for the safe roads, and also giving the guidelines for financing of remedial measures, institutional framework, physical characteristics of the road, traffic control and calming measures, road safety education and enforcement issues.

The aim of the activity plans is to analyze the present situation of road safety in India and to indicate main problems in individual sector of the Activity implemented by comparing and taking the examples of some the ASEAN Region who are successes in implementing in the individual sectors. The effect of the programme to real safety situation is estimated, and further plans could be corrected if it is necessary. Implementation of the goals for the coming years to reduce the number of accidents at maximum extent and give people, the safe and the steady flow of traffic in India. The vision of a tremendous change next 5 to 10 years is based on a big potential for improvement and a joint effort of all involved groups on all levels of traffic safety, centrally coordinated by the National Road Safety Authorities.

The Action Plan is deliberately divided into 14 key Sectors of activity in broadly the same way as the individual country road safety action plans. The sectors involve many different disciplines and a very wide range of multi sector activities but all are based on applying scientific, methodical approaches to the problem.

At the end of the thesis gives the recommendations and conclusion for the safe Roads in India.

H.M. Awami, S. Puri, & V. Bhatia (2006) conducted a study on "Road Safety Awareness and practices Among School Children of Chandigarh". It has been estimated that 1 million deaths & 15 million RSA (Road Side Accidents) occur on roads worldwide every year. Globally, RSA is 10th & in SEAR, 7th leading cause of death in all age groups. According to WHO estimates, RSA is the 9th leading cause of death as per on the basis of DALY. However, this is likely to reach at no. 3 by 2020. It was estimated that over 75 per cent of RSA occur in the so called developing countries, even though these countries account for only 32 per cent of total motor vehicle fleet, which involves 65 per cent of pedestrians and 35 per cent of school children. Child pedestrian injury, an important cause of morbidity and mortality remains one of the leading causes of death in developed and developing countries. Each year in US approximately 850 children under the age of 15 years are killed & another 30,000 are injured in pedestrian raised by 300 per cent in Asian and African countries in contrast to 30-40% in developed countries. There is limited literature available regarding accident related behaviour in developing countries. The chances of RSA can be averted to a large extent, if school children who are going to be adults of tomorrow are made aware of road safety measures. Hence present study was focused on school children to study knowledge of various risk factors pertaining to road side accidents and their practices.

Forty percent of students lacked correct knowledge of traffic safety rules. In particular, knowledge of correct speed limit was lacking in 67.3 per cent of the respondents. Girls were more aware of traffic rules to be followed at traffic lights (63%) and while crossing zebra lines (41.2%), whereas boys were more versed with rules for pedestrians (49.8%). Around 60 per cent of school children had correct knowledge of risk factors. The awareness was almost same in both government & private Schools as well as in males & female students. Results of this study were similar to that done in other countries. In a study done in Bangladesh, 62 per cent of road traffic accidents were accounted by pedestrian casualties. 62 per cent of students agreed that risk factors that expose one to accidents are driving without helmet, driving at night without headlights (59.5%) and not wearing seatbelts (59.1%).

Gururaj (2008) conducted a study on "Road traffic deaths, injuries and disabilities in India: Current scenario". In 2005, road traffic injuries resulted in the death of an estimated 110,000 persons, 2.5 million hospitalizations, 8-9 million minor injuries and economic losses to the tune of three per cent of the gross domestic product (GDP) in India. If the present trend continues, India will witness the deaths of 150000 persons and hospitalizations annually by 2015. Nearly 10 per cent-30 per cent of hospital registrations are due to road traffic injuries and a majority of victims of road traffic injuries are men in the age group of 15-44 years and belong to the poorer sections of society. Also, vast majority of those killed and injured are pedestrians, motorcyclists and pillions riders, and bicyclists.

A clearly defined road safety policy, a central coordinating agency, allocation of adequate resources, strict implementation systems are urgently required. Greater participation from and coordinated approach is essential. Health professionals can contribute in numerous ways and should take a lead role in reducing the burden of road traffic injuries in India.

Studied Conducted in Abroad

A. Ghaffar, A. A. Hyder, R. H. Morrow & D. Bishai (2002) conducted a study on "Interventions for Control of Road Traffic Injuries: review of effectiveness Literature". In 1998, road traffic injuries were estimated to be the 9th leading cause of loss of healthy life globally and are projected to become the 3rd leading cause by 2020, the majority of this burden can be located in the developing world where most of the projected Increase will occur. Yet health systems are least prepared to meet this challenge in these countries. At the same time, there are effective Interventions for road traffic Injuries being implemented in the developed world, an extensive review of the literature reveals more than 16 different interventions in four categories that have been implemented. Renewed testing of these and new interventions will take both time and funds-resources that are scarce in developing countries, As a result, it is imperative to study the effectiveness of those Interventions already tested and attempt to evaluate their potential implementation In developing countries. The method was used Literature review to Identify effective interventions end the magnitude of the effects. The findings were Four broad classes of interventions can be identified from the literature; health education/awareness, legislation, product design and environmental modifications.

The issues for the developing countries are affordable, infrastructure and socio cultural in implementation of these strategies. The road traffic injuries are also underreported and hence under represented at the priority setting stage, Road safety should be high on the agenda as it can save a lot of lives and disability. Public health professionals should assess and advocate road safety in developing countries (JPMA 52:69, 2002).

Gururaj (2004) conducted a study on "Alcohol and Road Traffic Injuries in South Asia: Challenges for Prevention". Among the one million people killed on the roads during 2000, nearly 75 per cent died in developing countries of the world about half of them in Asia. A selective examination of RTIs in the region indicates that they constitute the second of third leading cause of death in the 5-44 years age group. The increase in direct and indirect health risk associated with alcohol usage has been well-documented in recent years. Alcohol is a major risk factor for RTIs as it impairs judgment and increases the possibility of involvement in other high risk behaviours (*e.g.*, speeding, violating traffic rules, etc.,). Precise information on the involvement of alcohol in RTIs and deaths is clearly not available from South Asian countries. With the recognition that road safety needs to focus on reducing drinking and driving, many high-income countries have formulated and implemented a number of coordinated, integrated and sustainable progammes based on scientific research. Considering the gravity of the situation, ongoing efforts to reduce the problem and lessons learnt from high-income countries, it is important to change strategies and mechanisms to reduce drink driving in south Asia.

Fahad Al-Rukaibi, Mohammed A. Ali, and Ahmad H. Aljassar (2006) conducted a study on "Investigating the Driving Behavior and Traffic Safety Attitudes of University Students in Kuwait". Road safety has become one of the most important issues in Kuwait along with traffic congestion. On an average, one person is lost every day to road accidents in Kuwait, this is in addition to scores of major and minor injuries. Kuwait Government has implemented new and stiffer traffic rules and regulations in November 2001. Along with these new rules, the Ministry of Interior has installed several cameras at mid-block and intersection locations. Most of the dead and seriously injured drivers in road accidents in Kuwait belong to the group of young Kuwaitis. It is becoming more and more evident that enforcement and engineering alone may not be able to help alleviate the dangerous situation of traffic accidents the country is in today. Education is probably the only effective action to complement the engineering and enforcement measures.

This paper presents the results of a study undertaken to investigate the driving behavior and traffic safety attitudes of young university student drivers. It also examines the road traffic accidents statistics in Kuwait. Findings of the study indicate that even though students report of their awareness of traffic rules and that they usually follow them, they seem to be ignorant of the disastrous consequences of higher travel speeds. Educational measures should be effectively used to improve the degrading traffic safety situation in Kuwait. Education and training before issuing the license and graduate licensing policies should also be investigated for implementation in Kuwait.

The findings of the study, strongly point towards introducing a structured traffic safety course in schools and colleges, to increase awareness among the young students about the traffic laws and the consequences of traffic accidents. It is also recommended based on the findings of the study that an increase in the enforcement personnel and number of hidden cameras is also required. The positive role that the media plays in public education and awareness has been highlighted in the literature. The electronic and print media should also effectively be utilized. Graduate licensing practices prevalent in other countries could also be introduced in Kuwait.

Jose Ricardo Marar & Marco Lemgruber & Joaquim Jose Guilherme Aragao (2008) conducted a study on "Legal issues surrounding public-private partnerships (PPP) in Transport projects". In Brazil, the improvement of the efficiency of public transport systems requires the use of Public-Private Partnerships for promoting competitiveness and delivering modern and high quality public services. Experiences from European countries have shown advantages and disadvantages of using PPP in transport projects. Lack of financing in transport infrastructure could deliver opportunities for testing this mechanism in developing countries. The main aim of this study is to understand the crucial role that legal analysis plays in developing new financing transport projects. The paper concludes with a discussion of legal issues in international experiences in the field of infrastructure concession.

Conclusion

In this chapter theoretical introduction and review of related literature have been considered. The review of related studies has been helpful to the investigator to formulate design of the study, identification of variables, tool and hypotheses

Chapter 13

Methodology

Introduction

The main objective of the study was to find out the awareness on Traffic Rules among student teachers. The need for the study, objectives and the scope of the study were split out in chapter I. An extensive review of related literature covering the awareness on Traffic rules among student teachers and some other related fields were presented in chapter II. This chapter deals with the design and procedure adopted for the present study.

In the simplest way research design is a plan structure and strategy of investigation in order to obtain answer to the research question. "Design is the blue print of the procedures that reaching valid conclusions about relationships between independent and dependent variables" says *Best (1978)*. Hence to the right towards the goal, it is necessary to have a design for the research being carried out at the very beginning. But it is also true that "selection of a particular design", as *Best (1978)* suggests, "is based on the purpose of the experiment, the types of variables to be manipulated and the conditions or limiting factors under which it may be conducted". So it is apparent that the designs differ, as the problems differ. The ultimate aim of such a science is to provide knowledge that will permit the educator to achieve his goals by the most effective methods. Scientific problems can be resolved only on the basis of data, and the major responsibility of the scientist is to set up a research design capable of providing the data necessary to the solution of the problem".

Observed by *George J. Mowly (1964)* the selection of methods for research work depends upon the nature of the problem selected. Mainly methodology consists of tools, techniques and procedures. The success of investigation depends on the priority of the method and the tools and techniques the researcher uses. Research methodology is a way to solve the research problem systematically. It is necessary for the researcher to know not only the research methods and techniques but also the methodology.

The methodology varies from problem to problem. The researcher has to specify very clearly what decisions were selected and why he did select them and how they can be evaluated by others. The purpose of study may vary from researcher to researcher. But in any form of research the investigator has to follow certain methods. George J. Mowly has classified research methods into three basic types, namely

1. Historic or documentary method.
2. Experimental method.
3. Normative survey method.

1. The Historic or Documentary Method: Historical research is the application of the scientific method of inquiry to historical problems. Historical research is one of the most difficult types of investigation to conduct adequately. In historical method the source of data is by direct observation and through indirect observation through documents. It gives the accurate record of past events, interpretations, relationships and evaluation of present day problem and procedures.

2. Experimental Method: Experimentation is the most scientifically sophisticated research method. It is defined as observation under controlled conditions. It studies observable changes that take place in order to establish a cause and deliberate and controlled modification of the conditions determining an event and in the observation and interpretation of the changes that occur in the event itself.

3. Survey Method: The word "survey" has been derived from the words "sur" or "ser" and "vecir" or "veidor" which means "over" and "see" respectively that is the term normally implies the determination of normal or typical conditions.

The normative survey method of educational research is very common. It is the method of investigation which attempts to describe and interpret what exists at present in the form of conditions. Practices, processes, trends, effects, attitudes, beliefs, awareness etc, it is concerned with the phenomena that are typical of the normal conditions.

Characteristics of Survey Method

- It gathers data from a relatively large number of samples.
- It involves defined problem and define objectives.
- It provides information useful to the solution of local problem.
- It is not concerned with the characteristics of individuals.
- It does not seek to develop an organized body of scientific principles.

In the present study the investigator intended to measure the Awareness on Traffic rules among student teachers. So this study aims at measuring the activity of leaning. Here normative survey method is the best method for conduction research study.

Design of the Study

Research design is a plan, a structure and a strategy of investigation conceived to obtain awareness to issues in research. The object of research design is to test the research hypothesis. The research design therefore is built in the principle of maximization of the results of study and minimization of variance. A research design however, is not a highly specific plan to be followed without direction. Rather, it is a series of guideposts to keep right direction. Thus research design is the process of planning a research, choosing methods and procedures that can be expected to yield meaning and most interpretable results.

Table 13.1 : Schematic Representation of the Research Design

S.No.	Type	Source
1.	Nature of the Research	Normative Survey Method
2.	Tools Developed	Type of Tool Awareness on Traffic Rules among student teachers at Namakkal District.
3.	Variables	1. Gender 2. Locality 3. Educational qualification 4. Subject
5.	Sampling Technique	Random Sampling Technique
6.	Size of the Sample	Students = 306 (Boys = 128, Girls = 178)
7.	Statistical Techniques used	Mean, Standard Deviation, and 't' test

The present study belong to Normative survey Research. The variables used are Gender, Locality, Educational qualification, Subject among B.Ed., student teachers. It is developed by the investigator to access the awareness on the Traffic Rules among B.Ed., student teachers at Namakkal district separately, along with a personal data sheet to know the back ground of the students. In this study Random Sampling Techniques was followed data were collected from 306 students of 5 college of Education at Namakkal district.

The statistical techniques Mean, Standard Deviation and 't' test were used.

Objectives of the Study

The objectives of the study are:

12. To find out the level of awareness on the Traffic rules among Student Teachers.
13. To find the level of significant difference on the awareness of Traffic rules between Male and Female Student Teachers.
14. To find the level of significant difference on the awareness of Traffic rules between Under Graduate with B. Ed and Post Graduate with B. Ed Student Teachers.
15. To find the level of significant difference on the awareness of Traffic rules between science and Arts Subjects Student Teachers.
16. To find the level of significant difference on the awareness of Traffic rules between rural and urban area Student Teachers.
17. To find the level of significant difference on the awareness of Traffic rules between Under Graduate with B. Ed and Post Graduate with B. Ed Male Student Teachers.
18. To find the level of significant difference on the awareness of Traffic rules between Under Graduate with B. Ed and Post Graduate with B. Ed Female Student Teachers.
19. To find the level of significant difference on the awareness of Traffic rules between Science and Arts Subjects Male Student Teachers.
20. To find the level of significant difference on the awareness of Traffic rules between Science and Arts Subjects Female Student Teachers.

21. To find the level of significant difference on the awareness of Traffic rules between rural and urban area Male Student Teachers.
22. To find the level of significant difference on the awareness of Traffic rules between rural and urban area Female Student Teachers.

Hypotheses of the Study

11. There is no significant difference on the awareness of Traffic rules between Male and Female Student Teachers.
12. There is no significant difference on the awareness of Traffic rules between Under Graduate with B. Ed and Post Graduate with B. Ed Student Teachers.
13. There is no significant difference on the awareness of Traffic rules between science and Arts Subjects Student Teachers.
14. There is no significant difference on the awareness of Traffic rules between rural and urban area Student Teachers.
15. There is no significant difference on the awareness of Traffic rules between Under Graduate with B. Ed and Post Graduate with B. Ed. male Student Teachers.
16. There is no significant difference on the awareness of Traffic rules between Under Graduate with B. Ed and Post Graduate with B. Ed Female Student Teachers.
17. There is no significant difference on the awareness of Traffic rules between Science and Arts Subjects Male Student Teachers.
18. There is no significant difference on the awareness of Traffic rules between Science and Arts Subjects Female Student Teachers.

19. There is no significant difference on the awareness of Traffic rules between rural and urban area Male Student Teachers.
20. There is no significant difference on the awareness of Traffic rules between rural and urban area Female Student Teachers.

Method of the Study

In order to realize the aforesaid objectives, the normative survey method is employed. Normative survey method studies, describes and interprets what exists at present. They are concerned with existing conditions or relations, preventing practices, beliefs, awareness and attitude, etc. Such investigations are termed in research literature as descriptive survey or normative survey.

Sample of the Study

A sample is small proportion of a population selected for observation and analysis. "A good sample of a population with great accuracy" (Corwell.1960). By considering here the research which proposes to ascertain what is the normal or typical condition or practice at the present time" (Sukhia, et.al1969). It is the only means through which opinions, attitudes and suggestions for improvement and such other data can be obtained. Survey studies help in contributing to other type of investigations and cover a large number of traits and characteristics of the groups.

A sample of 306 student teacher of B. Ed level was selected from the following five different B. Ed institutions in Namakkal District of Tamilnadu.

1. Rasi College of Education - Rasipuram
2. S.R.B College of Education - Muthukalipatti
3. Vidya Mandhir College of Education - Gurusamy-palayam

4. Kongu Nadu College of Education - Velagoundampatti
5. C.M.S College of Education - Ernapuram

The investigator collected the response of all B.Ed. Students of each Institution.

Table 13.2 : The sample are shown according to the following variables

S.No.	Category of the variable		No. of Samples	Total
1.	Gender	Male	128	306
		Female	178	
2.	Locality	Rural	212	306
		Urban	94	
3.	Educational qualification	UG	238	306
		PG	68	
4.	Subject	Arts	176	306
		Science	130	

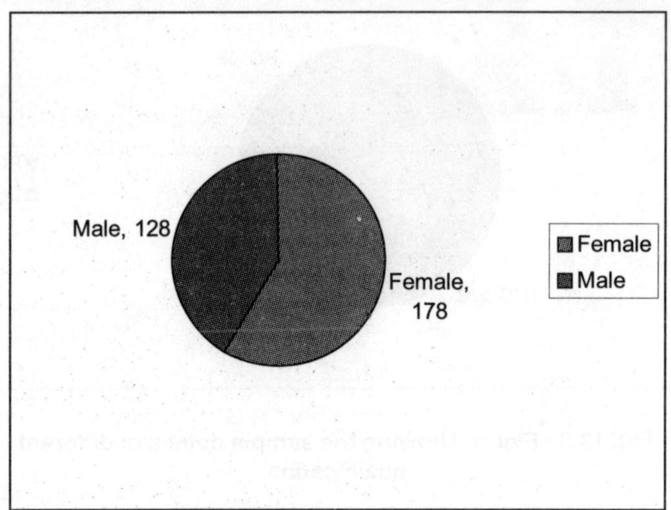

Fig. 13.1 : Figure showing the sample details of gender

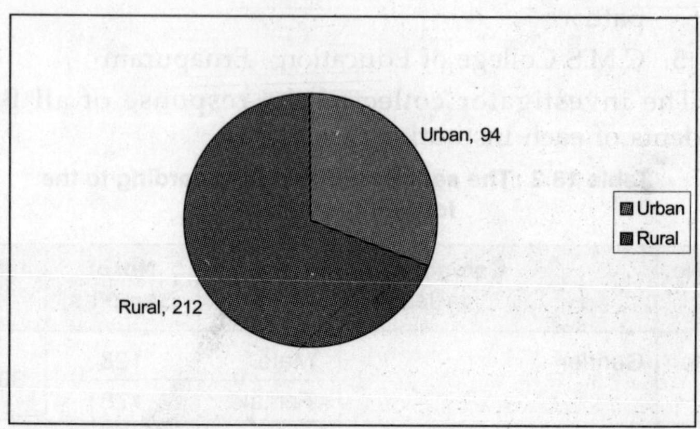

Fig. 13.2 : Figure showing the sample details of different Locality

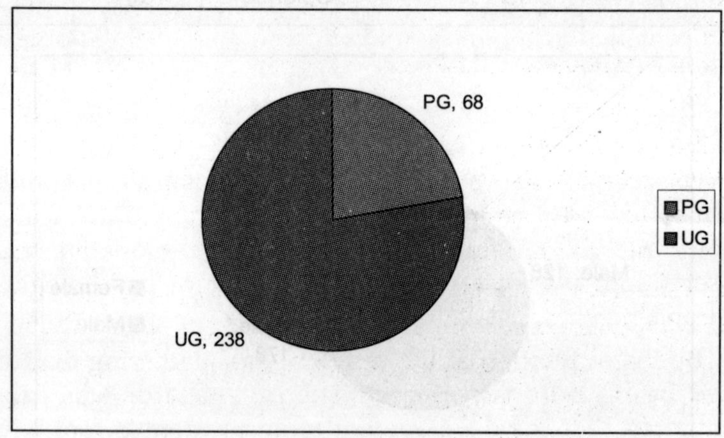

Fig. 13.3 : Figure showing the sample details of different qualification

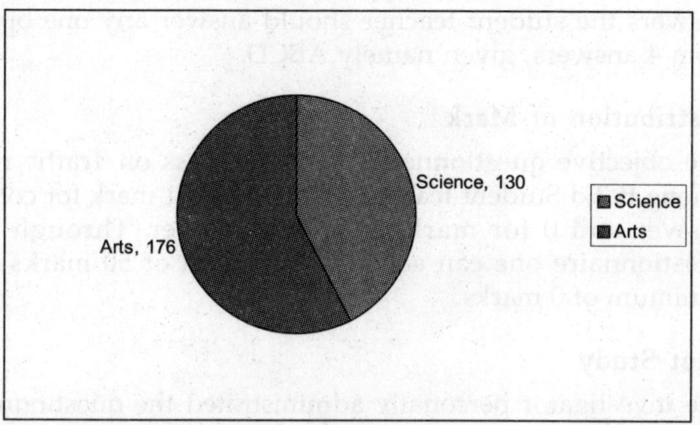

Fig. 13.4 : Figure showing the sample details of different subject

Tools Used

The instruments employed for collecting data are called tools. "Tools employ distinctive ways of describing and qualifying the data". Best 1992. The tools of research are instruments that provide for the collection of data upon which hypothesis may be tested.

There is large number of tools and techniques available for data collection in research from these tools, the researcher selects the most appropriate forms of information that could be most useful. The important tools of educational research should include schedules, questionnaire, opinionative, and observation, checklist, rating scale, interview, psychological test and pentagrams.

By the evaluation of the different data gathering devices used in educational research, the investigator was fully convinced that the development of an awareness tool with objective type will help in collecting data.

Construction of Tool

The investigator framed questionnaire on "Awareness on Traffic rules among B. Ed Student teachers". It constitutes of

50 marks with objective type. In order to bring out correct answers the student teacher should answer any one option from 4 answers, given namely ABCD.

Distribution of Mark

The objective questionnaire of "Awareness on Traffic rules among B. Ed Student teachers" will award 1 mark for correct answer and 0 for marking wrong answer. Through this questionnaire one can achieve maximum of 50 marks and minimum of 0 marks.

Pilot Study

The investigator personally administrated the questionnaire to the subjects and explained to them the purpose of the study and how the subjects should answer for the items in the questionnaires of five sections. The subjects were allowed to answer the item avoiding the influence of mutual consolation. They were asked to underline ambiguous words or sentences that would help the investigator delete these ambiguous or confusing ones while preparing the final questionnaire. No item limit was fixed. The subjects were encouraged to answer all items without omission.

Collection of Data

The investigator obtained adequate number of copies of the awareness tool scale for the actual collection of data. Selected College of Education was visited and their principal and lecturer were contacted for getting permission and co-operation for the collection of data. The awareness scale was then distributed among the student teachers. Adequate instructions were given for marking the responses. Strict uniform procedures were adopted in the administration of the awareness tool to student teachers of different Colleges. The following steps were invariably followed while administrating the awareness scale.

- Distribution of the individual awareness tool to each student.

- Giving directions of how to mark the responses in the awareness tool.
- Clearing the doubts of the students and giving additional instructions wherever necessary.
- Giving sufficient time to mark the responses.
- Strictly enquiring the marking of independent responses.
- Collecting all distributed awareness tool

Personal Data Sheet

The personal data sheet serves to collect personal information. Trainees were asked to write their name, sex, and name of the Institution, educational qualification and subject, that they studied in higher secondary course.

Reliability and Validity

Reliability applies to a measure when similar results are obtained over time and across situations. It should be noted that reliability is a necessary condition for validity, but a reliable instrument may not be valid. A reliable but invalid instrument will yield consistently may not be valid. A reliable but invalid instrument will yield consistently inaccurate results.

The investigator used the objective type questionnaire method, the 't' values found in the questionnaire such as 0.80. Then the tool was accepted as the valid tool for administering in this study.

Statistical Techniques Used

(a) Mean: Mean is used to measure the entire data by one value. It is obtained by adding to gather all the items and by dividing the total by the number of items.

$$\bar{X} = A + \left[\frac{\Sigma fd}{N} \times C\right]$$

Where,

c = Class interval

Σdf = Total of the products of each class frequency with the steps deviation of the respective class

N = Total frequency

$\bar{X}$ = Arithmetic mean

(b) Standard Deviation: The standard deviation concept was introduced by Karl Pearson in 1823. It is used to measure dispersion standard deviation is also known as root of the mean of the square deviation from arithmetic mean.

$$\text{S.D.} = \sqrt{\frac{\Sigma fd^2}{N} - \left(\frac{\Sigma fd}{N}\right)^2} \times c$$

Where,

N = No. of samples

c = class interval

$d = \frac{X - A}{C}$

x = Midpoint of the class interval

A = Assumed mean

Σfd = Total of the products of each class frequency with the steps deviation of the respective class

Σfd^2 = Total of the products of each class frequency with the square deviation of the respective class.

(c) Techniques used for testing hypotheses: Student 't' test is used to find out the significance of the means of different groups of students. For example boys and girls. The hypotheses formulated are tested using relevant statistics (*i.e.*) 't' test.

The test of significance of the difference between the two means is known as 't' test. 't' is calculated by using the below formula,

$$t = \frac{M_1 - M_2}{\sqrt{\frac{\sigma_1^2}{N_1} + \frac{\sigma_2^2}{N_2}}}$$

Where,

M_1 and M_2 are the means of the two variables

N_1 is number of cases in first sample

N_2 is number of cases in second sample

σ_1^2 is standard deviation of first sample

σ_2^2 is standard deviation of second sample

Conclusion

This chapter deals with methodology of the present investigation as enumerated. Thus it gives brief details about selection of sample, pilot study, administration of tool in the study, data collection and statistical technique use in this study. Hawing described the detailed methodology of the study in the chapter analysis and interpretation of the data for the present study is next chapter.

Chapter 14

Data Analysis

Introduction

The analysis of data represents the application of the inductive and deductive logic to the research process. It is a very important step in the total procedure of research. Analysis of (variable or data) means studying the tabular material.

It involves breaking down existing complex factor into simple parts and putting the parts together in new arrangements for the purpose of interpretation. Interpretation of calls for a critical examination of the results of one's analysis in the light of all the limitations of this data gathering.

Analysis of data means studying the tabulated material in order to determine the inherent falls or meaning. Data accepted by the investigator got their meanings, when they are chanalized into the process of statistical analysis. It will give the investigator an insight into the problem. It simplifies the masses of number and facts and presents them in an understandable manner. Therefore analysis must lead to interpretation of data.

The purpose of present investigation is to study the awareness of Traffic Rules among student teachers. The data for the study was collected from the students by means for a questionnaire. The analysis of data was attempted as per the objectives of the study. In the present study, the data are analyzed using mainly the following statistical techniques.

1. Percentage
2. Arithmetic Mean
3. Standard Deviation
4. 't' Value

Testing of Hypothesis

After formulating the hypothesis, it is necessary to

- Deduce its consequence;
- Selected or develop tools that will determine whether these consequences actually occur; and
- Use the tools there by collecting facts that will confirm the hypothesis.

"A hypothesis is never proved; it is merely sustained (or) rejected".

Table 14.1 : The Level of Awareness on the Traffic Rules Among Student Teachers

Category	Samples (N)	Mean	S.D
Traffic Rules awareness	306	71.3	10.65

The above table 14.1 shows Mean Standard deviation of the student teacher. The total number of sample is 306 from B.Ed students at Namakkal District. An almost homogeneous group of 306 (128 Male and 178 Female) was selected for this study.

From the above table 14.2 it shows the calculated 't' value is greater than the tabulated 't' value at 0.05 level of significance. So there is significant difference on the awareness of Traffic Rules between Male and Female student teachers

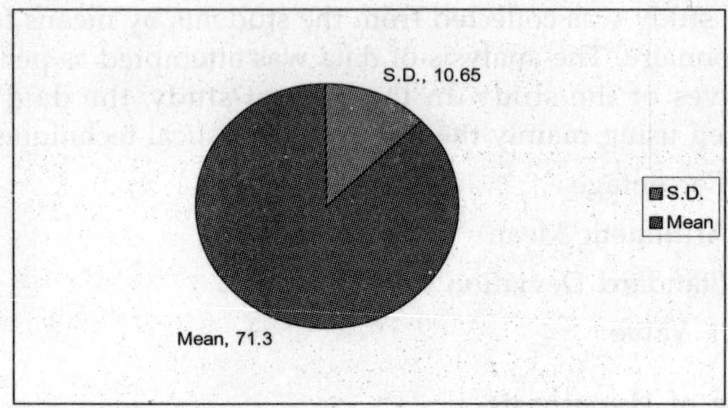

Fig. 14.1 : The Mean and S.D. values of awareness on the Traffic Rules among Student Teachers.

Table 14.2 : Significant difference the Awareness of Traffic Rules between Male and Female Student Teachers

Variable	N	Mean	SD	't' value	Level of Significance (0.05)
Male	128	74.48	9.28	4.50	1.97
Female	178	69.26	10.91		

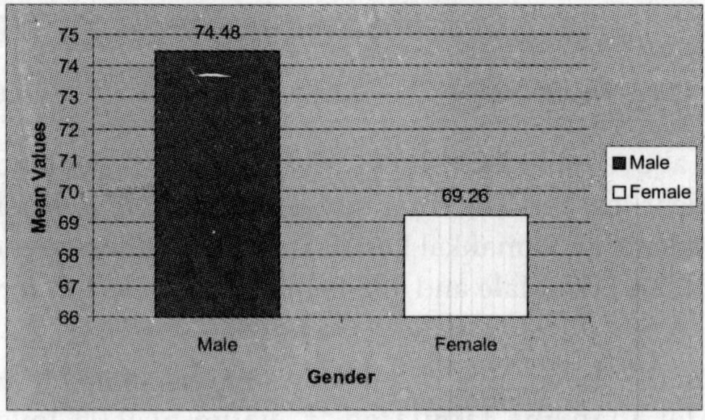

Fig. 14.2 : The Mean value of between Male and Female student teachers

Table 14.3 : Significant difference the awareness of Traffic Rules between Under Graduate with B.Ed and Post Graduate with B.Ed student teachers

Variable	N	Mean	SD	't' value	Level of Significance (0.05)
UG	238	71.59	11.02	1.01	1.97
PG	68	70.21	9.64		

From the above table 14.3 it shows the calculated 't' value is less than the tabulated 't' value at 0.05 level of significance. So there is no significant difference on the awareness of Traffic Rules between Under Graduate with B. Ed and Post Graduate with B. Ed studying student teachers.

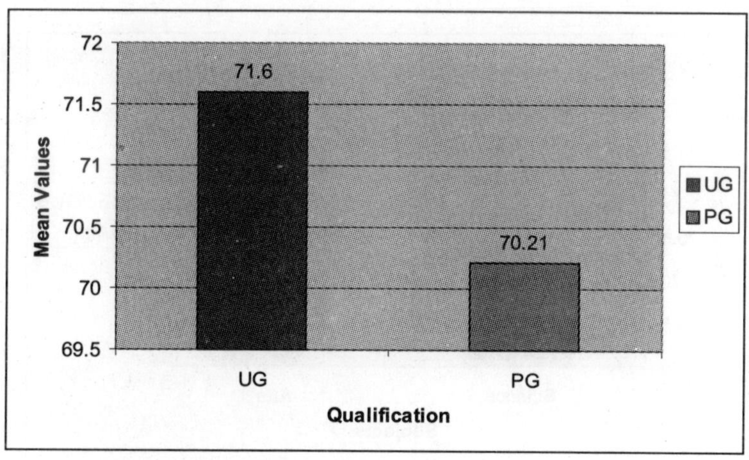

Fig. 14.3 : The Mean values of Under Graduate with B.Ed and Post Graduate with B.Ed Student Teachers

Table 14.4 : Significant Difference the Awareness of Traffic Rules between Science and Arts subject Student Teachers

Variable	N	Mean	SD	't' value	Level of Significance (0.05)
Science Students	178	72.15	10.69	1.59	1.97
Arts Students	130	70.19	10.61		

From the above table 14.3 it shows the calculated 't' value is less than the tabulated 't' value at 0.05 level of significance. So there is no significance difference on the awareness of Traffic Rules between Science and Arts subjects student teachers.

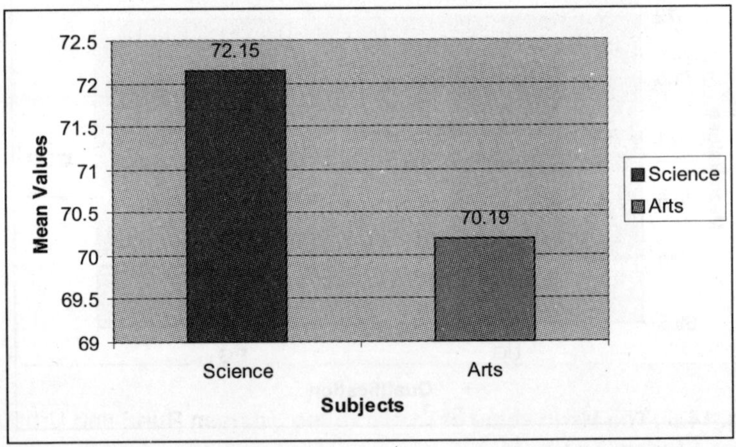

Fig. 14.4: The Mean Value of Traffic Rules between Science and Arts subject Student Teachers.

Table 14.5 : Significant Difference on the Awareness of Traffic Rules between Rural and Urban Area Student Teachers

Variable	N	Mean	SD	't' value	Level of Significance (0.05)
Rural Students	212	71.58	10.33	0.95	1.97
Urban Students	94	70.29	11.18		

From the above table 14.5 it shows the calculated 't' value is less than the tabulated 't' value at 0.05 level of significance. So there is no significance difference on the awareness of Traffic Rules between Rural and Urban student teachers.

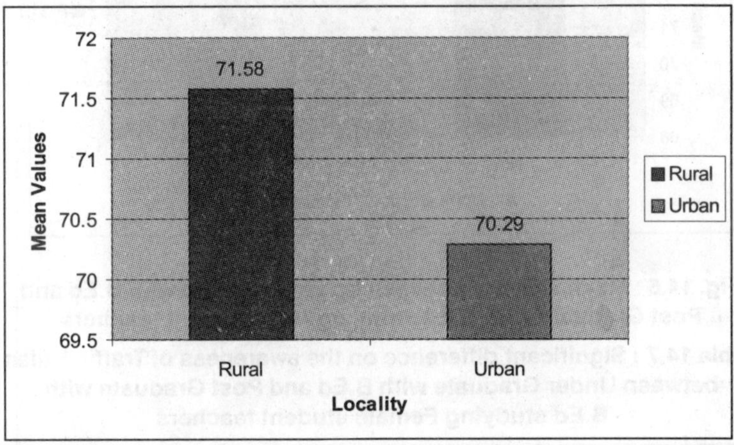

Fig. 14.5 : The Mean value of Traffic Rules between Rural and Urban Area Student Teachers.

From the table 14.6 it shows the calculated 't' value is greater than the tabulated 't' value at 0.05 level of significance. So there is significance difference on the awareness of Traffic Rules between Under Graduate with B.Ed and Post Graduate with B.Ed studying Male student teachers.

Table 14.6 : Significant difference the awareness of Traffic Rules between Under Graduate with B.Ed and Post Graduate with B.Ed studying Male student teachers

Variable	N	Mean	SD	't' value	Level of Significance (0.05)
Male UG	99	74.89	9.93	2.18	1.98
Male PG	29	70.67	8.95		

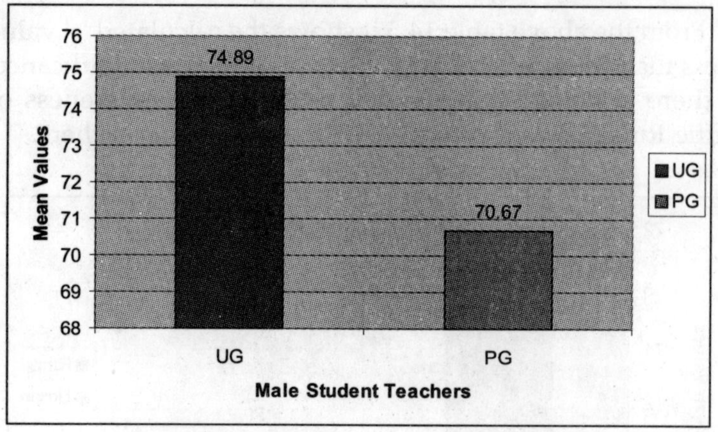

Fig. 14.6 : Mean value of between Under Graduate with B.Ed and Post Graduate with B.Ed studying Male student teachers

Table 14.7 : Significant difference on the awareness of Traffic Rules between Under Graduate with B.Ed and Post Graduate with B.Ed studying Female student teachers

Variable	N	Mean	SD	't' value	Level of Significance (0.05)
Female UG	139	69.1	11.14	0.41	1.97
Female PG	39	69.86	10.05		

From the table 14.7 it shows the calculated 't' value is less than the tabulated 't' value at 0.05 level of significance. So there is no significance difference on the awareness of Traffic Rules between Under Graduate with B.Ed and Post Graduate with B.Ed studying Female student teachers.

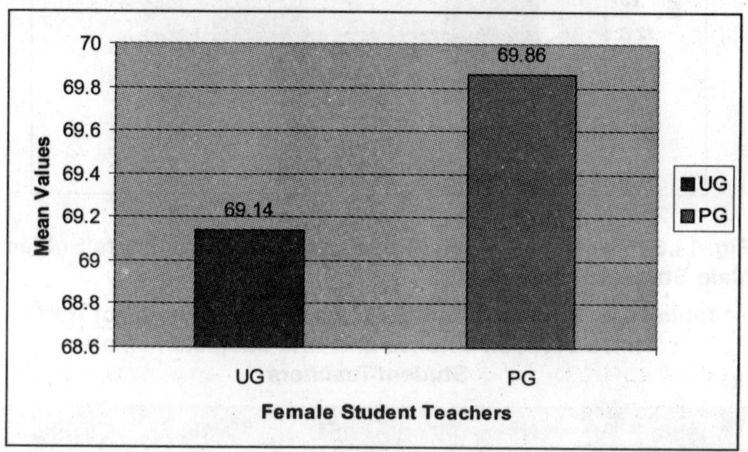

Fig. 14.7 : Mean Values of between Under Graduate with B.Ed and Post Graduate with B.Ed Studying Female Student Teachers.

Table 14.8 : Significant Difference on the Awareness of Traffic Rules between Science and Arts subjects Male Student Teachers

Variable Male Student Teachers	N	Mean	SD	't' value	Level of Significance (0.05)
Science Subject	75	75.1	10	1.31	1.98
Arts Subject	53	72.86	9.14		

From the above table 14.8 it shows the calculated 't' value is less than the tabulated 't' value at 0.05 level of significance. So there is no significance difference on the awareness of Traffic Rules between Science and Arts subjects Male student teachers.

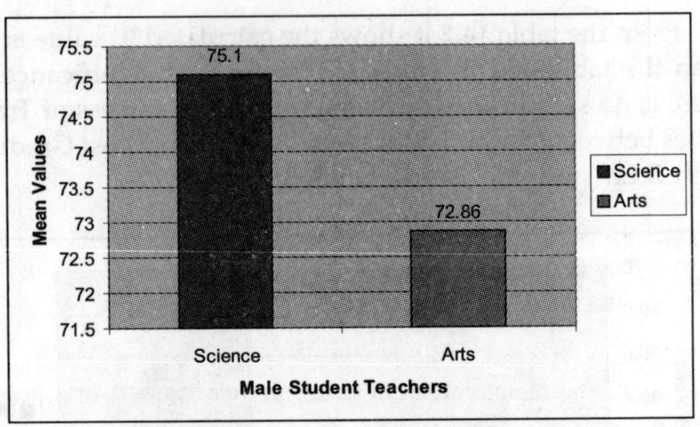

Fig. 14.8 : The Mean Values of between Science and Arts Subjects Male Student Teachers

Table 14.9 : Significant difference on the Awareness of Traffic Rules between Science and Arts subjects Female Student Teachers

Variable Female Student Teachers	N	Mean	SD	't' value	Level of Significance (0.05)
Science Subjects	101	69.96	10	1.04	1.97
Arts Subjects	77	68.23	11.24		

From the above table 14.9 it shows the calculated 't' value is less than the tabulated 't' value at 0.05 level of significance. So there is no significance difference on the awareness of Traffic Rules between Science and Arts subjects Female student teachers.

From the table 14.10 it shows the calculated 't' value is less than the tabulated 't' value at 0.05 level of significance. So there is no significance difference on the awareness of Traffic Rules between Rural and Urban Male student teachers.

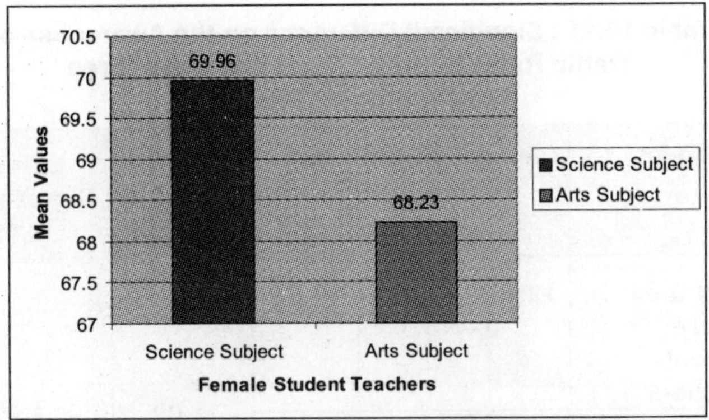

Fig. 14.9 : The Mean values of between Science and Arts subjects Female student teachers.

Table 14.10 : Significant Difference on the Awareness of Traffic Rules between Rural and Urban Area Male Student Teachers

Variable	N	Mean	SD	't' value	Level of Significance (0.05)
Rural area Male Students	87	74.6	9.3	0.68	1.98
Urban area Male Students	41	73.3	10.5		

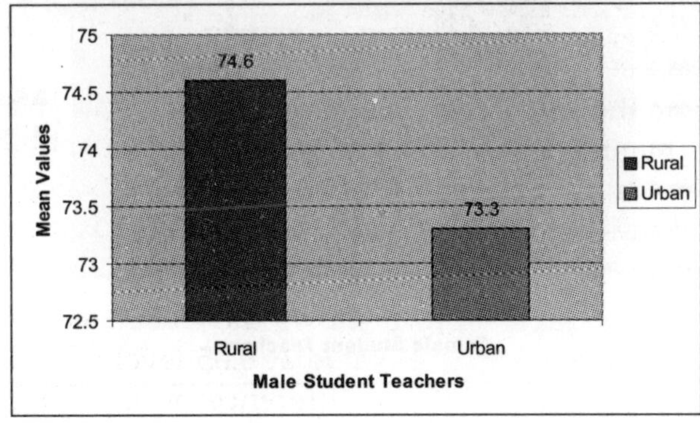

Fig. 14.10 : The Mean value of Traffic Rules between Rural and Urban Area Male Student Teachers

Table 14.11 : Significant Difference on the Awareness of Traffic Rules between Rural and Urban area Female Student Teachers

Variable	N	Mean	SD	't' value	Level of Significance (0.05)
Rural area Female Student Teachers	125	69.8	10.68	1.02	1.97
Urban area Female Student Teachers	53	67.95	11.3		

From the above table 14.11 it shows the calculated 't' value is less than the tabulated 't' value at 0.05 level of significance. So there is no significant difference on the awareness of Traffic Rules between Rural and Urban area Female student teachers.

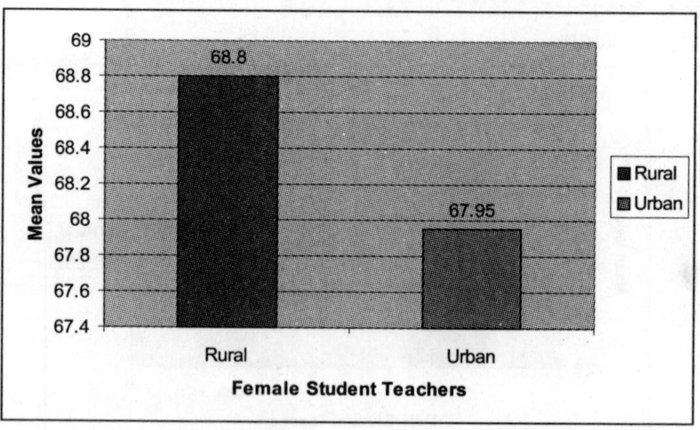

Fig. 14.11 : The Mean value of between Rural and Urban Area Female Student Teachers

Conclusion

Data analysis is ultimately necessary for any research. The obtained data was subjected to necessary statistical computations. The results thus analyzed in terms of the corresponding table value are interpreted accordingly. The findings were calculated without any researcher's bias, which serve as a recommendation for further study.

Chapter 15

Findings and Conclusions

Introduction

In this chapter an attempt had been made to consolidate all the findings of the present study, the investigator also made some recommendation, which include the relevant area for this research and lastly the conclusion. The findings are based on the result collected from the awareness tool.

The Study in Retrospect

The aim of the present investigation was to find out the Awareness on Traffic Rules.

Methodology in Brief

For the present study normative survey method and cluster sampling technique was adopted. For the sample of the study, 306 B.Ed Student teachers in Namakkal District were conducted the awareness tool was administrated. The tool used for the collection of data is awareness.

Statement of the Study

The problem under the study is entitled as *"Awareness on Traffic rules among Student Teachers at Namakkal District"*.

Major Findings of the Study

21. There is significant difference on the awareness of Traffic rules between Male and Female Student Teachers.

22. There is no significant difference on the awareness of Traffic rules between Under Graduate with B. Ed and Post Graduate with B. Ed Student Teachers.

23. There is no significant difference on the awareness of Traffic rules between science and Arts Subjects Student Teachers.

24. There is no significant difference on the awareness of Traffic rules between rural and urban area Student Teachers.

25. There is significant difference on the awareness of Traffic rules between Under Graduate with B. Ed and Post Graduate with B. Ed Male Student Teachers

26. There is no significant difference on the awareness of Traffic rules between Under Graduate with B. Ed and Post Graduate with B. Ed Female Student Teachers.

27. There is no significant difference on the awareness of Traffic rules between Science and Arts Subjects Male Student Teachers.

28. There is no significant difference on the awareness of Traffic rules between Science and Arts Subjects Female Student Teachers.

29. There is no significant difference on the awareness of Traffic rules between rural and urban area Male Student Teachers.

30. There is no significant difference on the awareness of Traffic rules between rural and urban area Female Student Teachers.

Discussion Conclusion of the Study

(*a*) On noticing the results with regard to the student teachers between male and female. There is significant different on the awareness of traffic rules. Because the Male student teachers having more awareness about Traffic rules. Generally male pupils use the 2 wheelers and four wheelers than the Female pupils.

(*b*) On noticing the results with regard to the student teachers between under graduate and post graduate with B.Ed studying. There is no significant difference on the awareness of Traffic Rules. Because the undergraduate and post graduate student teachers having similar awareness about Traffic Rules. Because the under Graduate and post graduate student teachers having similar awareness about Traffic Rules. Now days all the graduate pupils use the two wheelers. So those know very well about the Traffic Rules. Although under graduate student teachers have more awareness to post graduate Student Teachers.

(*c*) On noticing the results with regard to the student teachers between Science and Art subjects. There is no significant different on the awareness of Traffic Rules between Science and Art subjects student Teachers. Because the Science and Art subjects Student Teachers having similar awareness about Traffic Rules. Generally both Science and Art Subjects pupils use two and four wheelers. Although Science Student Teachers have more awareness to Art Student Teachers.

(*d*) On noticing the results with regard to the student teachers between Rural and Urban area. There is no significant different on the awareness of Traffic Rules between Rural and Urban area Student Teachers. Because the Rural and Urban area Student Teachers having similar awareness about Traffic Rules. Generally both Rural and Urban area students having vehicle. Those are gone to town for their personal works. Although Rural area Student Teachers have more awareness to Urban area Student Teachers.

(*e*) On noticing the results with regard to the male student's teachers between undergraduate ad post graduate with B.Ed studying. There is significant difference on the awareness of traffic Rules between under graduate with B.Ed and Post Graduate with B.Ed studying male Student Teachers. Because the male UG Student Teachers having more awareness about Traffic Rules compare when to the male PG Student Teachers. Generally UG Male Student having more awareness than the PG male students. Because UG students are mostly enjoyed their self like went to cinema, beach, and hotels with friends. So they have more awareness about Traffic Rules.

(*f*) On noticing the results with regard to the Student Teachers between under graduate and post graduate with B.Ed studying. There is no significant different n the awareness of Traffic Rules on the awareness of Traffic Rules between under graduate with B.Ed and post graduate with B.Ed studying Female Student Teachers. Because the undergraduate with B.Ed and post graduate with B.Ed studying Female student teachers having similar awareness about Traffic Rules. Now a day's Female students also use vehicles. So both the UG and PG Female students know very well about the traffic Rules. Although PG Female Student Teachers have more awareness to UG Female Student Teachers.

Areas of Research for the Future

Research is a chain activity. There purpose of any research in education is to find solutions for problems related to teachers, students, learning etc... But investigation on one problem always leaves many related research questions that can be investigated by other researchers; some of the areas for research in the future may be as follows:

- The present study can be repeated with wide sample.
- A similar study can be conducted on the professional college students.
- A study can be conducted to find out the demographic and motivational variables associated with Traffic Rules activities.
- A similar study can be conducted on the Higher Secondary School Students.
- The present study could be undertaken at various States in India.

- A study can be conducted on the primary, Secondary and Higher Secondary school Teachers.
- The gender difference in Traffic Rules awareness can be studied.
- Development of CA, package on the awareness of Traffic Rules.
- A study on the modern techniques to develop the awareness of Traffic Rules among the D.T.Ed training students.
- A comparative study on the awareness of Traffic Rules among the students of different categories like secondary and higher Secondary Students.
- A critical study on evolving strategies promoting the awareness of Traffic Rules among the Arts and Science Students.

Educational Implications of the Study

- More measures are to the taken at rural and urban Schools to create Traffic Rules awareness.
- More programmes related to Traffic Rules awareness are to be conducted to the students.
- The students may be trained to give some activities like quiz debate discussion, seminar, workshop etc., on Traffic Rules awareness.
- The teacher may be trained to teach their lesson linked with traffic Rules.
- Government should introduce and enrich awareness on Traffic Rules programmes.
- The government has to modify the syllabus according to the needs and mental level of students.

Conclusion

The present study made on awareness of Traffic Rules among student teachers. The findings of the present study reveal that the B.Ed., student teachers having more awareness among Gender, Qualification, Subjects, and Locality with respect to the questionnaire.

PART—IV Awareness on Yoga Education

Chapter 16

Introduction

Education

Education is a process and it is a continuous, complex, dynamic and lifelong process. The importance of Education has been realized by everyone and every nation. The root meaning of Education is given as bringing up or leading out or making manifest the inherent potentialities in a pupil. Broadly speaking, education refers to any act or experience that has a formative effect on the personality of an individual. The role of Education is to make growth and development in the individual's life. It includes that all the influence which acts upon an individual during his passage from cradle to grave. In other words Education is life and life is Education. It is not giving of facts and detain alone, but it is a man making process.

Education is the process by which people acquire knowledge, skills, habits, values or attitude. It is the chief means of acquiring and teaching the essential knowledge and skills. Education is very closely linked with solving social problems such as improvement in the state of health, population control, and the eradication of poverty, thus constituting a major to a country is socio-economic development, and as such it represents one of the most important in international co-operation.

Knowledge in basic skills, academics, technical, discipline, citizenship Our society says only academic basics are important and that is based on collecting knowledge without understanding its value. the processing of knowledge, using inspiration, visionary ambitions, creativity, risk, ability to bounce back from failure, motivation There is a huge disconnected gap and this is a problem for high school students in particular answer is, all elements in the opening paragraph and more, relate to education and all should be considered.In short, Education is a dynamic in the life of every individual, influencing his physical, mental, social, emotional and ethical development.

Education is an important social activity planned and shared by the parents and the society. Education is a process of learning to live the life of a community Education has been defined by different people in different ways. The meaning of education has been changing according to people, places and times. Some took education to mean the process, others the result, still others the methodology. Since the concept has changed the definitions have also changed. Yet, there are certain definitions, which are all time popular and also acceptable.

A compare pensive definition of education must take into consideration a few factors. They are: (*i*) The individual who is to be educated; and (*ii*) The society in which education is to take place. Education can be best described as "the nature of personal growth". When Education is considered as the conservation transmission and renewal of entire culture, then it becomes an instrumental by which a community maintains itself.

Education is a process of human empowerment for the achievement of better and higher quality of life. It tells man how to think and how to make decisions. Training of a human mind is incomplete without Education. Only through the attainment of Education, Man is enabled to receive information from the external world, to acquaint him with past history and receive all necessary information regarding the present. Without Education, man is as though in a closed room and with education he finds himself in a room with all its windows open towards outside world.

Developing multimedia Course ware in teaching exercise Physiology for physical Education major – May 2006.

Definitions of Education

- *"Aristotle"* - has defined education as "creation of a sound mind in a sound body".
- *"Pestalozzi"*- defined education as a "natural harmonious and progressive development of men's innate power's.
- *"Mahatma Gandhi"*- wrote, "by Education, I mean an all round drawing out of the best in child and man body, mind and spirit".
- *"Vivekananda"*- "Education means the manifestation of divine Perfection already existing in man".
- *"John Dewey"* - Education is the development of all those capacities in the individual which will enable him to control his environment and fulfill his possibilities.

Yoga

Yoga is one of the gifts of our rich heritage. Dr. Radhakrishnan said, "Yoga is a way of life". It is a system that makes us cultured human beings. The value of yoga is not doubt immeasurable, and now-a-days yogic training is being more and more recognized especially as India's unique contribution to physical Education activities, yoga is a scientific and systematic discophile for a successful organization of all the energies and faculties of internal human being with a view to attaining the highest caustic communion with the cosmic reality of god. Yoga is an ancient practice combining meditation with training the body which originated in India five thousand year ago *(vikneskar & kuvalayananda, 1971).*

Yoga the science of man based on our ancient wisdom and culture has laid down technology consisting of various psycho physiological processes for dealing with the body – mind complex. It tries to harmonious and physical Benefits of yogasanans: (*a*) The endow cranial system is controlled and regulated and correct quantities of different hormones are secreted from all glands in the body; (*b*) Through regular practice, in paired organs can be rejuvenated and carry out their normal functioning; (*c*) systems like circulatory, respiratory, nervous, excretory, glandular, muscles, and bones are coordinated to help one another.

Yogic practices helped to deal with delinquency and criminal behavior and improved academic performance. Yoga was helpful to deal with headache, meditation intake and symptoms of stress perception. Yoga helped to solve the confusion between self-ideal disparity and ideal self. Yoga helped to decrease anxiety level in the gymnastic group. It helped to improve the mental health and emotional maturity of adolescent girls hatha yoga improved and fastened a psychophysical balance. The modern yoga students understand the importance of this ancient tradition, it is effective in reducing stress using breathing exercises and mindful meditation, reducing stress using breathing exercises and mindful meditation, reducing anxiety level and improving mental health, improving mental health and self-concept and reducing stress using breathing exercises and mindful meditation reducing anxiety level and improving mental health, improving mental health and self-concept, and reducing anxiety and improving adjustment. Yoga and meditation enhance self-esteem, self-disclosure, improves emotional intelligence and enhances social adjustment of jail inmates, and helped to decrease depression. So, yogic practices help to improve physical health, reduce anxiety, depression, and stress, and improve mental health, self-concept and emotional maturity of individuals. Yoga is the richest and noblest legacy the ancient Indians have gifted to the world.

It is a timeless programmatic science; it is an experimental science; it is an age old science; it is a culture—cum-science; it is the grandest of all sciences; it is the science of the integral man; it is the science of sciences. It is the mother of all sciences. Yoga is the culture of tomorrow.

Yoga is a method of education in the society. It is an art of successful living. It is a way of healthy living at all levels. It is a tool for positive change. It is the remedy for all worldly miseries. It is the science of creativity and personality development. It is a voyage of discovering truth or knowing the reality. It is a utilitarian commodity. Yoga is a total experience of human life. Thus, yoga is as old as civilization. Yoga is as old as mankind. Yoga is creation. Yoga is intimate and ultimate.

Yoga in India has a long history. Its earliest beginnings are lost in the obscuring of ancient Indian history. Yoga is a universal way of life, which in above all castes. Creeds, regions, languages and nations. It is an education that completely provides human beings good health for better living. Yoga is a health providing activity having its influence in all aspects of health, namely physical, mental and spiritual.

Developed in India, yoga is a psychophysical discipline with roots going back about 5,000 years. Today, most yoga practices in the west focuses on the physical postures called "Asanas", breathing exercise called "Pranayama", and meditation. However, there's more to it than that, and the deeper your go the richer and more diverse the tradition becomes. The word "yoga" means union linguistically; it is related to the old English "yoke". Traditionally, the goal of yoga is union with the Absolute, known as Brahman, or with Atman, the true self. These days the focus is often on the more down to – earth benefits of yoga, including improved physical fitness, mental clarity, greater self-understanding, stress control and general well being. Spirituality, however it is a strong underlying, theme to most practices. The beauty of yoga is in its versatility, allowing practitioners to focus on the physical, psychological or spiritual, or a combination of all three. For thousands of years yoga was a secret technique with little or no written material and was practiced by memorization and demonstration from the Guru to the Discipline. Yoga was a special feature of the Dravidian civilization. They mainly really upon the evidence brought forward by the of the Indus civilization. Certain relics like that of mother Goddess, and certain phallic symbols suggest a type of tundra yoga. Certainly yoga must have been much older than the archeological record, which is the only reliable source we have at present.

Yoga is said to be an integral subjective science. Its division into spiritual, mental and physical cannot be separated from each other. The word yoga is derived from the Sanskrit root "yujir" meaning to 'yoke' or 'union' or 'to join'. Yoga is equanimity and control of the senses and the mind. Yoga is a spiritual technique, a way, a path, a method that has something to offer to everyone, religions and the non- religious, men and women irrespective of age and faith. Yoga is a way to a healthier, happier and harmonious life.

Yoga has a complete message of humanity it has a message for the human body. It has a message for the human mind and it has also a message for the human soul. Will intelligent and capable youths come forth to carry this: message to every individual not only in India, but also in every other part of the world".

Efficiency and performance quotient. Yoga is one of the greatest disciplines in the world and can be practiced at each stage with positive results. It aims at controlling one's physical, mental and spiritual climate. The circulation of blood, the degree of tension in the muscles and in the nerves is all subjected to progressive control *(Devi, 1994).*

The main aim of yoga is integrating the body mind and thoughts, so as to work for good ends. In our modern life style the human body is easily affected by many diseases, mostly due to our food habits, daily routines, and also because of air and water pollution, etc. through systematic and regular yoga practices our body may be made healthier and its resistance power to fight against the diseases could be enhanced mind gets sharpened, and the concentration and memory power may be developed. Thus, power of mind could be Realized for thinking the right good thoughts. Then the good and healthy thoughts can develop in the right direction. yoga paves the way for an individual to do any action peacefully and perfectly. The main objectives of the yogic practices are making a man from diseases, ignorance, egoism, miseries, the affiliation of old age, fear of survival and so forth. In recent times yoga has become integral part of physical education and sports. Athletes and sportsman are mentally prepared and physically warmed up by yogic techniques to improve their efficiency in their performance in the play ground.

People who start yoga usually find that after a few weeks they feel more robust and energetic, lighter and springier. The postures directly affect the muscles, joints and skin but also the whole organism glands, never, internal organs, bones, circulation and respiration.

Yogic techniques, which aim at physical and mental self – culture, have convincing scientific bears and produce consistent physiological changes. It has been reported that yoga's are capable of achieving remarkable, feats of endurance and controlling their autonomic functions, there is evidence that the practice of yoga improves cardiac-respiratory

Meaning of Yoga

The word yoga is derived from the Sanskrit root *yuj* meaning to mind, Join, attach and *yoke,* to direct and concentrate one's attention in to use and apply. It also means union or communion. It is the true union of our will with the will of God. It thus means the yoking of all the power of body, mind and soul to God, it means the disciplining of the intellect, the mind the emotions, the will, which that yoga presupposes, it means a poise of the soul which enables one to look at life in all it is aspects evenly.

The word yoga is derived from the *Sanskrit* root 'YUJIR' meaning to *'yoke'* (or) *'union'* (or) *'to join'* a combination of body, mind and thought. In due course of time the body is opting to deteriorate and succumb to diseases. Mind is life, it can be used for good purpose or for bad purposes. It remains warring and gets no peace. By proper and regular yogic practices, the body becomes healthier and increases its resistance power to diseases yoga sharpens the intellect and increases the power of concentration and purifies the soul. Thus the body, mind and the soul gets unified and works for the betterment of a harmonious life.

The *Bhagavath Gita* also gives other explanations of the term yoga and lays stress up on karma yoga. It is said work alone is your privilage, never the fruits there of Never let the fruits of action be your motive and never case to work. Work in the name of the Lord, abandoning selfish desires. Be not affected by success or failure, this equipoise is called yoga.

Yoga is not for him who gorges too much, not for him who starves himself. It is not for him who sleeps too much, not for him who stays awake. By moderation in eating and in resting, by regulation in working and by regulation in working and by concordance in sleeping and awaking, yoga destroys all pain and sorrow. Yogi stages are practices and followed in life, virtues like mortality, morally sound conduct and good character is developed in man. Be sides there is all round progress in human life, physically intellectually and spiritually and man attains physical fitness and mental equanimity.

Definitions of Yoga

- *Swami Sivananda*—"Yoga is universal in its application leading to an all round development of body, mind and soul."
- *Sri Aurobindo*—"Yoga is amethodical effort towards self perfection by the development of the potentialities of the individuals."

- *Bhagavad Gita*—"Yoga is a power of creation."
- *Krishnamoorthy*—"Yoga is awareness".
- *Patanjali*—"Yoga is a process of gaining control over the mind", "Clarity of thought is yoga."
- *Amarakosa*—"Yoga is training in the techniques of Harmony and also a preparation for the total integration of human personality."
- *Vyasa Bhashya*—"Yoga implies integration of the personality of man as a whole."
- *Swami Nithyananda*—"Yoga is the ultimate practice for body, mind and being."

Nature of Yoga

Yoga is one of the six system of Hindu philosophy. Unlike so many other philosophies of the world, it is a philosophy that is wholly practical.

Yoga philosophy holds not only the answers to all problems, but also offers a scientific way to transcend his problems and suffering. The philosophy of yoga is caring, sharing and empowering. Yoga philosophy provides knowledge, strength, solace and peace. The purpose of yoga is to overcome ignorance and gain awareness of self. Western traditions of health and healing have tended to separate body and mind. But yoga tradition has a very strong link between the two.

Yoga helps man to have power to cure his disease as well as to control his premature death. Where all the methods of modern medical treatment fail, the yogic treatment succeeds. Hatha yoga has the capacity to replace medical hospitals. Science is partially unified knowledge; yoga is completely unified knowledge.

Yoga has been designed in such a way that it can complete the process of evolution of the personality in every possible direction. That is why yoga has so many paths- Hatha yoga, Karma yoga, Bhakthi yoga, Raja yoga, Jnana yoga, Kundalini yoga and so on. Yoga helps to reach the highest state of Ananda. Ananda means moral, divine and intellectual perfection. Yoga way of life is an experience which cannot be understood intellectually and will only become living knowledge through practice and experience. It leads to super-consciousness.

Yoga thus has transformed this earth the play ground of animal-men into a play ground of godly men. It enhances the practice of any religion. It is a way of life for the followers of all religions. Yoga has become into its own. Thus, yoga enhances spirituality.

The Aim of Yoga

According to the Yoga Sutras of Patanjali, the ultimate aim of Yoga is to reach "Kaivalya" (emancipation or ultimate freedom). This is the experience of one's innermost being or "soul" (the purusa). Then one becomes free of chains of cause and effect (Karma) which tie us to continual reincarnation. In Kaivalya one is said to exist in peace and tranquility, having attained absolute knowledge of the difference between the spiritual which is timeless, unchanging and free of sorrows, and the material which is not.

This is considered desirable as life is analyzed as ultimately full of sorrows and pain even pleasure and joy leave pain and loss when they have gone as nothing in the material world is permanent.

Yoga is therefore a spiritual quest. However, along the path of path of yoga, the aspirant also gains health, happiness, tranquility and knowledge which are indicators of progress and an encouragement to continue their practice. Buddhism and other Eastern spiritual traditions use many techniques derived from yoga.

Concept of Yoga

Yoga is one of the world's oldest branches of spiritual inquiry and one of the long-standing, most intense experiments on the human spirit.

The word *"yoga"* comes from the *Sanskrit* root *"yuj"* which means to *"yoke"* or *"To join together"*. It is a technique to join the body, mind and spirit and to create a feeling of union. Yoga can also be defined as "Mindfulness", or process of directing the attention towards whatever it is we are doing at the moment.

Yoga is a method o training designed to lead to integration or union. It includes physical exercise, but its ultimate goal is the yoking of individual soul to universal spirit. Although yoga today is often taught and practiced as a pursuit for health and fitness in order to accommodate a changing world, the spiritual roots still nourish today's authentic yoga.

Aim of yoga is the attainment of the physical, mental and spiritual health. Yoga is one of the orthodox systems of Indian philosophy, was systematized by Patanjali in his yoga sutra. He advocated the eight-fold path of yoga, popularly Known as "Ashtanga yoga" for all-round development of human personality. They are Yama (restraint), Niyama (Observance of austerity), Asana (Physical Posture), Pranayama (Brething Exercise), Pratyahara (Restraining the Sense Organ), Dharana (contemplation), Dhyana (Meditation) and Samadhi.

Importance of Yoga

The body becomes strong and healthy, excersive fat disappears, the face glows, the eyes are bright and the whole personality radiates, a special charm. The whole body is purified and the mind improves in ability to concentrate of the importance are:

- The blood in the different blood vessels is purified through different yoga sanas.
- Yogasanas helps the mind to experience tranquility. This is progressive intellectual development because of the calm mind.

Stages of Yoga

The proper function of the body depends on the several limbs. The absence or the sicknesses of any one limb affect the health of the whole body. The same principle applies to the study of yoga and its branches. Any inadequauacy in the study and the perfection of any the eight steps of yoga will not lead to self-realization.

Need for the Study

Education is the only way to boost yoga awareness. In the long run, Behavior can be modified through the process of Yoga Education. Yoga education would have to aim t producing a health, creating a constituency of yoga-oriented people that is knowledgeable regarding the physical and problem, aware of how to solve these problems and motivated enough to work towards their solution. Such a challenge has to be taken up by educational institutions, and among these, universities and colleges will have to show the leadership.

It is vital to effectively educate man regarding his relationship to the total environment, the relationship which is based on than on superior-subordinate relationship. Hence major goals of yoga education should be to help individuals acquire.

1. The basic responsibility of the society and government to work for solving yoga problems.
2. Development of yoga ethics which will motive people to participate in the decision-making process and to demand protection of the yoga so as to advance human welfare and dignity.

Yoga education should aim to provide factual information to students which will lead to the understanding of the intricate system of health balance and man's place in it. Namakkal education district is situated in the coast of Tamilnadu. It is an educational area. This induced the investigator to make an attempt to study the awareness on yoga among the higher secondary students at Namakkal educational district.

This is an age of science; every human being on the earth is the product of science and technology. Science has made man luxurious by providing comforts of physical life. Due to the materialistic attitude is leading the modern man to the life bondage, miseries, gain, money, reputation and selfishness. Today, we have overstrained ourselves and it may result in body or mind breakdown. In such a condition a person needs timely guidance for diversion of his mind towards creative channel to save himself from disaster of entering the dark world of miseries, frustrations etc. Hence, the need of yoga appears. It can certainly be proved as a big blessing to provide mental, physical and spiritual health and complete well-being. Yoga provides individual with refreshing positive thinking, self-confidence, analytical approach, smooth and calm mental stage with emotional stability and strong will power. Effects of yoga exercises is no doubt vary wide and it influences every activity of an individual.

Statement of the Problem

Yoga awareness is of keeping the importance of keeping the health clean and mind relaxation. So the study focuses on the topic entitled "A study higher secondary school students at Namakkal Educational District".

Background of the Study

In view of increasing importance of the yoga, students who are the citizens of the nation and will be employed in various walks of life cannot afford to keep themselves from this potential medium. The government has therefore, decided to provide the yoga education by importing profound knowledge and skills developing positive attitude and interest in the yoga.

Today our educational system is knowledge and examination oriented that test only the rote memory of the students. The effective domain such as attitudes is neglected in our teaching. Thus the children should also be encouraged to developed positive attitude towards yoga. Hence the main outcome of the introduction of yoga is the inculcation of proper attitude towards it. Therefore, the present investigation has been undertaken with a view to find out how far the attitude of yoga education developed among higher secondary students.

Operational Definitions of the Terms

Awareness

Paraphrasing Webster's congenital dictionary. Awareness implies vigilance in observing something or experience and alertness in drawing inference from what one observes. Awareness in a personal development sense is a consciousness impact that you are being and the impact that you are having on others. Higher your awareness by imaging a small creature on your shoulder who watches over what you think and what he observes in your ear.

Yoga

Yoga is one of the greatest disciplines in the world and can be practiced at each stage with positive results. It aims at controlling one's physical, mental and spiritual climate. The circulation of blood, the degree of tension in the muscles and in the nerves is all subjected to progressive control *(Devi, 1994).*

Yoga Awareness

It is a state of being conscious about yoga. It may be defined as to help the individual to gain variety of information and experiences to acquire basic knowledge and understanding of yoga and problems associated with it.

Higher Secondary Students

After the completion of the high school level of education, students enter the secondary level. (*i.e.*) in standard XI in higher secondary school. New they attain the adolescence stage as teenagers.

Namakkal District

Since Namakkal is a growing busionalized and educational town it is apt for the study.

Objectives of the Study

The following objectives were formulated for the present study.

To find out the yoga awareness of higher secondary school students in Namakkal Educational District.

To find out the significance difference in the yoga awareness of Boys and girls (gender)

Locality of the student (Rural & Urban)

Types of the school (Government & Metric)

Parent's occupation (Government & Private)

Subjects. (Arts & science)

Hypothesis of the Study

- There is no significant difference between boys and girls towards awareness on yoga.
- There is no significant difference between rural boys and girls towards awareness on yoga.
- There is no significant difference between urban boys and girls towards awareness on yoga.
- There is no significant difference between Government school boys and girls towards awareness on yoga.
- There is no significant difference between Matriculation school boys and girls towards awareness on yoga.
- There is no significant difference between Government occupation of male and female parents towards awareness on yoga.

- There is no significant difference between private occupation of male and female parents towards awareness on yoga.
- There is no significant difference between arts group boys and girls towards awareness on yoga.
- There is no significant difference between science group boys and girls towards awareness on yoga.

Scope of the Study

The topic is an investigation of the awareness of yoga among higher secondary students at Namakkal District .this is the survey study. The investigation attempt to know the awareness on yoga among higher secondary school students at Namakkal District.

This study will be of great help for the education particularly for the teacher since teacher since the concept of education has been changing from time to time.

The awareness may different student to student. One can learn and do anything with involvement only when he had a better awareness towards it. In this content investigator attempts to study the awareness on yoga in higher secondary student in various categories

Delimitation of the Study

1. The study has been limited to NamakkaL District only.
2. The study has been restricted to the higher secondary school students only.
3. This study has been restricted to the 11th standard students only.
4. This study adopted survey method using questio-nnaires to collect data from respondents.
5. A purposive stratified random sample was used to choose the subject to be included in the study.

6. This study is focused mainly on the Variables, Gender, Locality, Various subjects, Types of schools, Parents occupations.

The ensuring chapter deals with the data analysis of the study

Organization of the Thesis

The report of the thesis will be presented according to be following sequences.

The first chapter gives introduction, definition of terms, statement of problem, Hypothesis objectives and Delimitation of the study.

Second chapter deals with the review of related literature which are done in India and abroad related to this problem.

Third chapter gives a detailed account of research procedures and methodology used in this problem.

Fourth chapter deals with the tabulation of analysis and the interpretations of the data in detail.

Fifth chapter describes the findings, conclusion and certain recommendations about the problem.

This is followed by the Bibliography and appendices which consist of the told used for the problem and the related matters.

Conclusion

In this chapter the investigator described the statement of the problem taken for the research study, objectives of the study delimitations of the sturdily and need for the study.

In the following chapter, a review of related literature and studies conducted in relevant areas will following.

Chapter 17

Review of Related Literature

Introduction

A good thesis is one that how to replicate or extend the previous work with improvements to reduce bias, eliminate flaws consider pertinent variables, settle unsolved issues to check contradictory or uncertain finding". The aim of this chapter is to record briefly a survey of literature related to the problems under study. It is necessary to enter on any research project. This will help in understanding the various aspects of the problem.

The purpose of this chapter is to record briefly the findings of research studies carried out on various topics that are related to the problem under study. An essential of research project is the review of the related literature In the words of Good, the key to the vast store house of published literature may open doors to sources of significant problems and explanatory hypotheses, and provide helpful orientation for definition of the problem, back ground for selection of procedure, and comparative data for interpretation of results. In order to be truly creative and original, one must read extensively and critically as stimulus thinking.

The research worker must be acquainted with up-to-date information about what has been thought and done in the specific area from which he intends to take up a problem of research. A review of related literature gives the scholar an understanding of the previous work that has been done in the area, it enables him to know the means of getting to the frontier in the field of his problems, methods and limitations and it enables him to locate comparative data useful in the interpretation of results.

Review of related literature is an essential step in educational research, in reflective thinking, the second step is the survey of all ready available data that should also be considered as a necessary step which would enable the researcher to base his rational argument for the justification of the study.

Review of Related Literature

A review of related literature is a direction to find out the reality and the beneficial nature and the reliability of a work undertaken, keeping in mind the material that are available in connection with the topic. A review will give the investigator a vivid idea of what he should do and how he should go about his investigation. Clarke, D.H. and Clarke, H.H. (1970) gave the importance of review of related literature as that of before completing a plan for a research understanding, the investigator needs to conduct a literature search in the area of the proposed investigations.

The review of related literature is an instrument in the selection of the topic formulation of hypothesis and defective reasoning leading to the problem. It helps to get a clear idea and supports the findings with regard to the problem under study (Tirumalai Swamy1995).The research scholar had come across several books, periodicals, journals, internet and unpublished thesis while searching for relevant facts and findings that are related to this present study. Such of these facts are given below for a better understanding and to justify his study.

The phrase Review of literature consists of two words Review and Literature of a particular are of any discipline which includes theoretical practical and its research studies. The literature in any field forms the foundation upon which all future work will be build. If we fail to build foundations of knowledge provided by the review of literature one work is likely to be shadow and that has already done better by someone else.

A search for knowledge cannot yield something meaningful if this relation with the existing knowledge has not been examined. A research study is never conducted in a vacuum. Hence an attempt was made, as far as possible, to find out what has already been done. A review of literature gives both thematic as well as methodological direction. In a rare case a study may justify accomplishment of a new knowledge without paying attention to what has been done carrier. In an age where we already find vast store of knowledge, it is necessary to examine what has been done before we boast of a new achievement (Barotia and Sharma, 1999). Hence, a brief review of the studies related to the present problem is described in this chapter.

Purpose of Review Literature

The following are the some of the purposes of the review of literature:

1. It provides ideas, theories, explanations or hypothesis valuable in formulation the problem.
2. To avoid the risk of duplicating some of the studies already undertaken.
3. To suggest methods or research methodology appropriate to the problem.
4. It widens the horizon of the researcher.
5. It suggests valuable basis for hypothesis.
6. It helps delimit the problem.

7. It helps the investigator not to allow the mistake (or) pit fall which occurred in the previous findings.
8. To locate comparative data useful in the interpretation of results.
9. It contributes to the investigator for the general scholarship.
10. It helps to locate data that can be used in comparative interpretation of results

Indian Studies on Yoga

Bhole et al., (1970) – found the yogic exercises significantly improving the vital capacity. It was reported that significant increase in hemoglobin contents of the blood and the lymphycytes after yogic treatment (significance level 5% noted).

Udupa (1971) and others selected twelve subjects and gave Hatha yoga practices for a period of three months and they found that lower level of pulse rate was maintained for three months. It was concluded that physical stress of fast running had increased the pulse rate the difference was not statistically significant.

Pollock (1971) and others conducted a study on effects of waling on body composition and cardiovascular function of middle aged men. In this study sixteen sedentary men were trained four days per week for twenty weeks. The vigor of walking was progressively increased in accordance with the tolerance of each individual by the last week, the men averaged 4.7 miles per hour sub stained improvement occurred in maximum oxygen consumption sub-maximal heart rate and resting diastolic blood pressure and reductions of body weight and present of fat, showing that vigorous waling can be effective as an adult training activity.

Gopal (1973) and others studied the effect of yogasanas and pranayamas on blood pressure, pulse rate and some respiratory function. Two groups of male volunteers 20-33 years in age and having the same average height and weight were studied. The experimental group consisted of 14 subjects in yogasanas and pranayamas for a period of six weeks. The control group consisted of 14 normal untrained subjects, who carried out non-yogic exercise *i.e.,* long walk and playing light games. Pre-test and posttest were conducted to both the groups before and after training. The results of both the groups were compared. The trained persons and greater vital capacity, more tidal volume and less respiratory rate than the untrained group. The prescribed standard exercise increased the respiratory rate in both the groups but the increase was less in the trained group who instead exhibited a corresponding increase in total volume.

Gopal (1973) – found a men heart rate about 71 beats per minute for a group which had been trained in yoga for six months for a group which regularly engaged in long walks and light games. Afterwards both groups did 20 jumps and sit-ups. The yoga groups mean heart rate increased to 100 and 7 less than of the light exercises group. A group with at least 6 weeks of certain Hatha yoga practice followed strenuous exercises with 1 minute sitting and then 3 minutes of either sitting, mild exercises or savasana Relaxation. Just after the exercises the heart rate Averaged over 180 and after one minute of sitting it dropped to 130. after 3 more minutes of sitting, it dropped to 17 more beats per minute, a lesser drop than that following 3 minutes of savasan relaxation. This suggests that savasana relaxation facilitates pulse deceleration following exercises.

Gharote (1973) – conducted a study on the effect of yogic training on physical fitness. He employed flies man basic fitness test. 17 males and 12 females were his subjects and they were given three weeks training in selected yogic exercises. He found significant increases of 7.74 in fitness index in males and 11.75 in females.

Gharote and Ganguly (1973) – observed that nine weeks practice in yogic culture was helpful to improve general physical fitness level of 49 cadet police who were already conditioned to physical activities. But the control group was engaged only in school schedule. The physical fitness of the subjects was judged through: (*a*) Fleishman–basic fitness tess; (*b*) cureton's flexibility test; (*c*) skin-fold; and (*d*) Harvard-step test. The improvement was most significant in flexibility.

Dhanaraj (1974) studied the effect of yoga on selected physiological parameters. The results indicated increases in basal metabolic rate. Tidal volume in basal state. Thyroxine, hemoglobin, vital capacity, chest expansion breath holding time and flexibility after yoga training. He observed decreased in basal heart rate and basal respiratory rate when yogic training was discontinued for six weeks following six weeks treatment, a significant decline in flexibility and breath holding time were noticed.

Nayar (1975) and others investigated the effect of yogic exercise on human physical efficiency. The studies were conducted on 53 cadets of National Defense Academy (NDA) representing there groups, doing routine NDA training, NDA training plus athletics and NDA training plus yogic exercises. Each cadet was assessed both under basal state and during a fixed exercise on bicycle ergometer. The parameters of assessment included ventilation minute volume, the rate of respiration, oxygen consumption, pulse rate, blood pressure, mechanical efficiency and maximum oxygen take capacity. Four additional assessments were made under resting condition, via vital capacity (VC) maximum breathing capacity (MBC) forced expiratory volume (FEV 10 sec) and breath-holding time. All the three groups showed a significant decreased in pulse rate during exercise. The yogic group in addition recorded a highly significant increase in breath-holding time (from 54 to 106 sec) and VC (from 1.98 to 2.89 L/M2 body surface area). It is also recorded a significant increase in FEV 1.0 sec (from 1.69 to 1.94 liters per M2 body surface area). The remaining two groups (doing routine NDA training and NDA training plus athletics) recorded only significant increase in VC. Ventilation minute volume, rate of respiration, blood pressure, mechanical efficiency, maximum oxygen uptake capacity and MBC remained unaltered in all the three groups.

Ghorate, Ganguly and Moorthy (1976) reported in the study of430 school boys in the age group of 6 to 20 years of yogic training for 3 weeks showed on improvement of 36.8 per cent in comparison of 20 per cent improvement on minimum muscular fitness.

Gharote (1977) says, health and physical fitness can be maintained only by carefully selected physical activities, which are called exercise. It could be evaluated only in terms of the effects that are obtained in promoting particular factors of physical fitness.

Astrand and Rodhal (1977) brought out the difference between heart rate and pulse rate. Thus heart rate is the number of ventricular beats per minute as compared from records of the electrocardiogram or blood pressure curves. The heart rate can easily be determined by osculation with a stethoscope or by palpitation over the heart, both during rest and exercise. Pulse rate is the frequencies of pressure waves propagated along the peripheral arteries, in normal healthy individuals. But this is not necessary so in patients with arrhythmias in such cases the output of blood by some beats may be too small to give rise to a detectable pulse wave.

Omen (1981) – investigated the comparative effects of isometrics, yogic physical culture and combination training on body composition and physical fitness status of high school boys. ANACOVA revealed that all the three experimental groups showed significant improvement in physical fitness status and significant reduction in percentage of fat (body composition). And when all the groups influenced significantly than that of the other two groups in developing physical fitness status and reducing percentage of body fat.

Karwande (1981) made a study on the comparative effect of yogic and physical exercises on anxiety level and mental fatique of children. This study was carried with sixty male students from VII and VIII standard. The average age of the subjects was 12 years. The test of anxiety level and mental fatigue were taken as criteria measures for the purpose of the study. The test was taken before and after the experimental period of six weeks. He concluded that anxiety level can be reduced either by training in selected Asanas was superiority to the training in physical exercise for both variables though the difference was not statistically significant.

Thankamma Ommen (1981) compared the isometrics yogic physical culture and combination training on body composition and physical fitness status of high school boys. Result of this study has shown that all the three exercise groups showed a significant increase in toe-touching scores. The inter group differences show that yogic physical culture group is more helpful in developing flexibility than the isomeric and combination groups, and in dynamic flexibility. Comparatively yogic exercises were the best in developing dynamic flexibility.

Ganguly (1981) found that daily one hour training in yigic physical culture for three weeks as per N.F.C progaramme was found to improved cardio-vascular endurance significantly as measured by 20 Harvard step test.

Uppal (1982) in his study, investigate endurance training employing show continou8s running method, which significantly reduces resting systolic and diastolic pressure of forty boys at secondary school. Slow continuous running method significantly lowers systolic blood pressure after exercises of the secondary school level boys, no significant change found out in resting and exercise blood pressures in the case of control groups as it was obviously a reflection of inactivity.

Moorthy (1982) conducted a study on minimum muscular fitness of school children of age group from 6 to 12 yrs and compared the influence of selected yogic exercises and physical exercises on them. In that study, 1000 children (571 boys and

429 girls) from 2nd standard to 11th standard attended at three schools in pune 90 boys and 90 girls who had failed were randomly.

Moorthy (1982) – surveyed the minimum muscular fitness of school children of age group six to eleven years and also compared the influences of selected yogic and physical exercises on them.

Thousand children from second standard to seventh standard at three schools in Pune were selected at random as subjects. Based on their low fitness level, ninety children were selected for experimental purpose. The children were randomly allotted to yogic exercises group, physical exercises group and control group of thirty each. They were undergone their respective treatment for six weeks. Finally he concluded from the results of the study that both the experimental groups significantly improved the minimum muscular fitness after six weeks training when compared to control group. Further, he concluded that yogic exercise group improved significantly the minimum muscular fitness when compared to physical exercise group.

The effect of pranayama a controlled breathing practice, on exercise tests was studied in athletes in two phases, sub-maximal and maximal exercise tests. At the end of phase 1 (one year) both the groups (control and experimental) achieved significantly higher work rate and reduction in oxygen consumption per unit work. There was a significant reduction in blood lactate and an increase P/L ratio in the experimental group, at rest. At the end of phase II (two years), the oxygen consumption per unit work was found to be significantly reduced and the work rate significantly increased in the experimental group. Blood lactate decreased significantly at rest in the experimental group only. Pyruvate and pyruvate-lactate ratio increased significantly in both the group after exercise and at rest in the experimental group. The results in both phases showed that the subjects who practiced pranayama could achieve higher work rates with reduced oxygen consumption per unit work and without increase in blood lactate levels. The blood lactate levels were significantly low at rest (Raju, 1994)

Hoare (1984) conducted a study and concluded that yoga release energy and helps us to channel it creatively: it breaks physical and mental tension and habits which conditions our response to life and it helps us to live freely with spontaneity and awareness. Yoga is a perfectly balanced physical and mental exercise and towards all efforts that one made toward achieving its knowledge.

Victory Ronrcy (1985) conducted a study of comparative study of the pulse rate and systolic Blood pressure of college sprinters and long distance runners. For the 30 long distance runners were taken as subjects. The long distance runners have a decreased pulse rate than the sprinters. In the systolic blood pressure, there is significance but not much difference between sprinters group and long distance runners.

Makwana (1988) conducted a study to find out the effect of short-term yoga practice on ventilatory function tests. For this purpose they used 35 healthy normal male subjects, their age ranging from 20-50 years. The experimental group of 25 subjects underwent 10 weeks of yogic practices 90 minutes daily in the morning. Yoga training limited the exercise *i.e.* surya namaskar, sharirsanchalam, eleven asanas, pranayama and prayer. A control group of 15 subjects were not performing yoga or any other physical exercise. All the subjects were tested as ventilatory function in the beginning before starting yoga training and practices and again after a period of 10 weeks of yogic practices.

Mall (1989) – found Sava Sana, a yoga relaxation method to be of great utility in reducing the heart rate, systolic and diastolic pressure of all the four recovery techniques. Nine weeks training in yogic physical culture was helpful to improve general physical fitness level of forty-nine cadet police who were already conditioned to physical activities as against the control group of forty-nine engaged only in school schedule as judged through (*a*) Fleischer man.

Backialakshmi (1990) – evaluated the influence of selected asana and aerobic exercises on selected motor fitness and physiological variables. Ninety boys from Kendra Vidalia, Karaikudi, were divided into three homogeneous groups as control, asana and aerobic exercises group based on their initial performance. Asana and aerobic exercises groups were given treatment for six weeks duration. Finally she came to a conclusion that both the asana and aerobic exercises had significantly improved motor fitness.

Krishnan (1991) – estimated the effect of selected yogic and Bharathiam exercise on physiological variables. Ninety boys between the age group of 13 to 15 years were selected as subjects for this study. The subjects were divided into three groups of 30 each by lot method. Group A was treated as control and group B and C were given yoga asana and Bharathiyam exercises respectively for a period of six weeks. The results indicated that both yogic and Bharathiyam exercises programmers had significantly improved the physiological variables. Further he concluded that yogic training programmed significantly improved the physiological variables than Bharathiam exercise training programmed.

Kirshnan (1991) conducted a study on the effect of exercise and yogic exercises on physiological variables among school boys. In this study 90 students were selected from thirumayam. Three groups were randomly selected of which one served as control group and other two served as experimental groups. With Bharathiyam and yoga Sana exercises, respectively. They were measured for selected physiological variables like pulse rate, breath holding time, cardiovascular efficiency and vital capacity before training as well as immediately after six weeks of training. The significance of the difference among the means of control group, bharathiyam group and yoga Sana group, pre test and post test were determined by 't'-ratio through analysis of variance, Bharathiyam and yogic group significantly improved the pulse rate, breath holding time, cardiovascular efficiency and vital capacity.

Sahay (1992) and others investigated the changes occurring in various biochemical parameters in normal healthy volunteers subject training in Yogic practices pranayama, vajrasana, bhujangasana, shalabhasana, dhanurasana, makarasana, halasana, naukasana, ardha-matsyendrasana, sirshasana and shavasana for a period of three months. the parameters studied included fasting, blood sugar, serum cholesterol, serum triglycerides, serum lactate dehydrogenase, serum creatine-phosphokinase, serum cholinesterase, blood lactate, blood pyruvate and urinary creatine. The subjects were 53 males aged 28 the mean body weight being 58 kg and 20 female's aged 25 the mean body.

Zant and Kusma (1993) studied the effectiveness of a community based exercise and health education programme to improve cardiovascular fitness and body composition on 25 subjects. Subjects participated in a supervised aerobic training programme for 12 weeks. Resting heart rate, blood pressure, weight, body composition and after training. Date was analyzed using ANOVA. Subjects of the exercise session saw significant ($p<0.05$) reductions in systolic blood pressure, resting, resting and heart rate post exercise hand sum of 6 skinfoldpercentmf 6 skinfoldpercentm of 6 skin fold percent of body fat and fat workload. Subjects significantly increased maximal exercise workload. These results indicate that a community based exercise workload. These results indicate that a community based exercise and health education programme results in beneficial changes in fitness and body composition.

A questionnaire was developed in order to estimate the dietary in takes of garlic per person per month and to record three blood pressure readings on each individual. It was given to 101 adult subjects presenting to the family practice centre of a hospital in the city of Karachi, Pakistan. The various demographic parameters including age, sex, marital status and education were recorded. Those subjects found to be overweight with a known history to hypertension, diabetes mellitus, is chaotic heart disease and smoking and on meditations, which affect blood pressure and were excluded from the study to remove the effect of confounding variables on blood pressure. The data were analyzed, an average garlic use of 134 g per month was found, 67 per cent of the subjects used garlic in cooked food while the rest used it either in the raw form or in pickles, 59 per cent thought that dietary use of garlic is healthy. Subjects with blood pressure on the low side were found to consume more garlic in their diets (waris Qidwai 2000).

Madanmohan, Thombre DP, Balakumar. B, Nambinarayanan TK, Thakur S, Krishnamurthy.N, Chandrabose. A, (1993) – studied the effect of yoga training on reaction time, respiratory endurance and muscle strength. There is evidence that the practice of yoga improves physical and mental performance. The present investigation was undertaken to study the effect of yoga training on visual and auditory reaction times, maximum expiratory pressure, maximum aspiratory pressure, 40 mmHg test, breath holding time after expiration, breath holding time after inspiration, and hand grip strength, twenty seven student volunteers were given yoga training for 2 weeks.

There was a significant ($p<0.001$) decrease in visual RT(from 270.0 ± 6.20 (SE) to 224.81 ± 5.76ms) as well as auditory RT (from 194.18 ± 6.00 to 157.33 ± 4.85 ms). MEP increased from 92.61 ± 9.04 to 126.46 ± 10.75 mmHg; our results show that yoga practice for 12 weeks results in significant reduction in visual and auditory RTS and significant increase in respiratory pressures, breath holding times and HGS.

Raju PS, Madhavi S, Prasad KV, Reddy MV, Reddy ME, Shahay BK, Murthy KJ (1994)—studied the comparison of efforts of yoga and physical exercise in athletes. The effect of pranayama a controlled breathing practice, on exercise test was studied in athletes in two phase; sub-maximal and maximal exercise tests. At the end of phase I (one year) both the groups (control and experimental) achieved significantly higher work rate and reduction in oxygen consumption per unit work. There was a significant reduction in blood lactate and an increase in P/L ratio in the experimental group at rest. At the end of phase II (two years). The oxygen consumption per unit work was found to be significantly reduced and the work rate significantly increased in the experimental group. Blood locate decreased significantly at rest in the experimental group only. Pyruvate and pyruvate llactate ratio increased significantly in both the groups after exercise and at rest in the experimental group. The result in both phases showed that the subjects who practiced pranayama could achieve higher work rates with reduced oxygen consumption per unit work and without increase in blood lactate levels. The blood lactate levels were significantly low at rest.

Dhanaraj (1995) administered a study to investigate the effect of yogic and physical exercises on flexibility and cardio-respiratory endurance of Madurai Kamaraj University players. Hundred and fifty men students were selected at random as subjects. They were randomly divided in three groups of fifty each. Experimental group A underwent selected yogic exercises and group B underwent selected physical activities for 12 weeks and the control group C did not engage in any of these programmes. Analysis of covariance revealed that both yogic and physical training groups had shown significant improvement in the flexibility and cardio-respiratory endurance, and when two experimental groups were compared with each other, the yogic training group was more effective than physical training group.

Radhalakshmi (1997) – conducted a study to assess the effect of selected yogic and physical training on physical fitness of school girls in Kerala. To achieve this purpose 90 girls were selected as subjects from Jawahar Navodaya Vidyala,

Ernakulam, Kerala state. The age range from 12 to 15 years. They were randomly divided into three groups of thirty subjects each as group A (yogic training group), group B (physical training group), and group C (control group). Yoga and physical training were given to group A and group B respectively for 8 weeks whereas group C did not participate in any of these training programme. The concept of ANACOVA revealed that even though yogic and physical training had significantly improved the physical fitness, the yogic training group influenced more significantly than the physical training group in developing physical fitness.

Naveen KV, Nagarathna R, Nagendra HR, Telles S (1997) – studied that the yoga breathing through a particular nostril increases spatial memory scores without lateralized effects. Uninostril breathing facilitates the performance on spatial and verbal cognitive tasks, said to be right and left brain functions, respectively. Since hemispheric memory functions are also known to be lateralized, the present study assessed the effects of uninostril breathing on the performance in verbal and spatial memory tests. School children (N=180 whose ages ranged from 10 to 17 years) were randomly assigned to four groups. Each practiced a specific yoga breathing technique: (*i*) right nostril breathing; (*ii*) left nostril breathing; (*iii*) alternate nostril breathing, (*iv*) breath awareness without manipulation of nostrils. These techniques were practiced for 10 days. Verbal and spatial memory was assessed initially and ofter 10 days. An age-matched control group of 27 were similarly assessed. All 4 trained groups showed a significant increase in spatial test scores at retest, but the control group showed to change. Average increase in spatial memory scores for the trained groups was 84 per cent. It appears yoga breathing increases spatial rather than verbal scores, without a tateralized effect.

Tommijean Thomas, Ph.D, Christopher D.Jori, Ph.D, Benjamin A. Thomas B.A (1998) – assessed the benefits of practicing Iyengor yoga, personality traits, emotional stability, coping and cognitive states among 21 men and 36 women attending an intensive training workshop in celebration of yogacharya Dr. K.K.S. Iyengar's 75th birthday were quantified. It was hypothesized that experienced yoga practitioners would obtain higher scores on the battery of psychological test than normative samples. Statistical Analyses revealed that the coping, stamina and self-control level of the yoga practitioners were significantly elevated and, relative to norms, the mood of the yoga experts was characterized by emotional stability, high energy, exhilaration, and vigorousness with reduced feelings of hostility, tension/anxiety, and apathy. Personal reports indicated that yoga had notable influence on the participants in four areas: (*a*) physical gains; (*b*) mental and emotional functioning; (*c*) personal growth; and (*d*) general life satisfaction. These findings provide support for the proposition that yoga practice is associated with enhanced mental and physical health.Selected for experimental purposes. 30 boys and 30 girls were randomly selected for experimental purposes. 30 boys and 30 girls were randomly allotted for control group. Experimental group I (physical exercises) and Experimental Group (II) (Yogic exercise) were undergoing the treatment for a period of six weeks. He concluded that both experimental groups showed significant improvement after six weeks training when computed to control group. The percentage of improvement was seen much greater in yogic group than in physical exercise group.

Madanmohan, Kaviraja udupa, Ananda Balayogi Bhavanani, Chetan Chinmaya Shatapathy and Ajit sahai (2000) studied the modulation of cardiovascular response to exercise by yoga training. This study reports the effects of yoga training on cardio – vascular response to exercise and the time course of recovery after the exercise. Cardiovascular response to exercise was determined by Harvard test using a platform of 45cm height. The subjects were asked to step up and down the platform at a rate of 30/min for a total duration of 5 min or until fatigue, whichever was earlier. Heart rate (HR) and Blood pressure response to exercise were measured in supine position before exercise and at 1, 2, 3, 4, 5, 7 and 10 minutes after the exercise. Rate-prssure product and double product. Which are indices of work done by the heart were also calculated. Exercise produced a significant increase in HR, systolic pressure, RPP and DOP and a significant decrease in diastolic pressure. After two months of yoga training, exercise induced changes in these parameters were significantly reduced. It is concluded that after yoga training a given level of exercise leads to a milder cardio vascular response, suggesting better exercise tolerance.

Manjunath, Shirley Telles (2001) took twenty girls between 10 and 13 years of age, studying at a residential school they were randomly assigned to 2 groups on group practiced yoga for one hour fifteen minutes per day, 7 days a week, while the other group was given physical training for the same time. Time for planning and for execution and the number of moves required to complete the tower of London task were assessed for both groups at the beginning and end of a month. These three assessment were separately tested in increasingly complex tasks requiring 2 moves, 4 moves and 5 moves. The pre post data were compared using the wilsoxon paired signed Ranks Test. The yoga group showed a significant reduction in planning time for both 2 moves and 4 moves tasks (3.99 and 59.1) execution time in both 4 moves and 5 moves tasks (63.7 and 60.3) and in the number of moves in the 4 moves tasks 120.9 percent). The physical training group showed no change. Hence yoga training for a month reduced the planning and execution time in simple as well as complex tasks (4,5 moves) and facilitated reaching the target with a smaller number of moves in complex tasks (4 moves).

Yogacharya Vishwas Mandlik, (2002) – studied the effect of Jalandhar Bandh on Blood pressure. It is observed that the blood pressure increases during the Kamchatka. It is also warned strictly in all yogic texts to perform all the three Bands have during Kamchatka. The position and the description of the Jalandhar Bandh indicate that there is some relation in between increased blood pressure and Jalandhar Bandh. Jalandhar Bandh created the pressure on the carotidal sinus which in turn reduces the blood pressure.

Hence the Hypothesis is "performing the Jalandhar Bandh in the proper way helps to reduce the Blood pressure".

Gore et al., (2003) effects of yoga and Aerobics Training on cardio respiratory functions in obese people" as an outcome of one month programme of weight reduction using yoga practice and Aerobics, female Residential yoga group (FRYG) of 25-40 age range, showed a significant and consistent reduction in systolic blood pressure (SBP) in all the tasting sessions. Their peak expiratory flow Rate (PEFR) also improved in two of the follow up (RU) testing sessions. FRYG of 41-70 age range reduced their SBP significantly in two of the FU sessions as well as a significant increase in PEFR was recorded. Pulse rate (PR) did not show significant changes. FMRYG (female Non-Residential yoga group) of 25-40 age range with a normal BP and PR initially, showed a significant reduction in DBP in two of the FU testing sessions, while the increase in their PEFR was not significant. FNRYG of Age 41-70 showed a significant improvement in PEFR in post-test and first FU; yet, reduction in 13p was non-significant statistically. Female Aerobic group (FAG) of age range 25-40 showed no significant reduction in BP and PEFR. However, FAG of age range 41-70 age range did not show significant change in BP and PEFR, however, MAG (Male Aerobic group) of the same age range showed significant reduction in SBP only, in one of the FU testing sessions. Their PEFR showed significant reduction, MAG of age range 25-40 showed non-significant reduction in BP and PEFR.

Mishra et al., (2003) cardiac Efficiency of long distance runners and yoga practitioners" cardiac efficiency of 120 male students, in the age range 16 to 17 years from the Aggarsain public school Kurukshetra, Haryana, was tested through Harvard step test. The students were divided in to three equally matched groups viz. Long distance running group (Group A), yoga group (Group B) and control Group (Group C). duration of the experimental period was 6 months which was divided into two sessions of 3 months each. Results of 2×3 factorial ANOVA revealed that yoga practitioners had higher cardiac efficiency those long distance runners.

Govindarajulu (2003) – "Effect of yoga practices on flexibility and cardio Respiratory endurance on high school girls". Sixty (n=60) high school girls (age 12 years) volunteered for a pre-experimental group design, where the practice of selected yoga practice was given as an intervention to the experimental group 'A' (n_1=30) for a period of eight weeks. The control group 'B' (n_2=30) was not allowed to participate in the experimental treatment. The pre-and post tests were conducted on flexibility and cardio-respiratory endurance. The results of ANOVA revealed that there was in improvement in the flexibility and no significant change was evident in the cardio-respiratory endurance. Thus, short-term yoga is useful in improving.

Moorthy (1983) – estimated the detraining effect of yogic and non-yogic exercises on minimum muscular fitness. For this purpose 90 students were selected at random from six to eleven years of age. The data on minimum muscular fitness were collected after discontinuing the training for both yogic and non-yogic exercises group. The minimum muscular fitness was decreased in non-yogic exercise group. The minimum muscular fitness was decreased in non-yogic exercises group whereas yogic exercises group retained for longer duration. Hence the investigator concluded from the results of the study that yogic exercises are more advantageous than non-yogic exercises in improving and maintaining minimum muscular fitness.

Analogy

Out of total 41 studies identified, the investigator found all studies conducted in India. Majority of the studies belonged to survey studies and few of them are experimental studies.

Most of the studies followed random sampling technique in the collection of data and the size of the selected samples range from 60 to 430 samples. In majority of the studies data was collected from the school students. In majority of the studies the questionnaire, opionnaire rating scale developed by the investigator was utilized as a tool. Since all the reviewed studies were related to yoga, yogic exercise, training, practice, yogic culture. Other studies are related to yogasanas, few studies related to body composition and cardiovascular functions, physical functions.

Mean, standard deviation and 't' test where the statistical techniques followed in majority of the study.

Conclusion

The investigator collected the studies related to the yoga awareness based on the studies revealed the investigation designed his research, method, sample size, location and variables of the study. The following chapter deals with methodology of the present investigation.

Chapter

18

Methodology of the Study

Overview

The Methodology followed in the present study is described in this Chapter. The present study is a Normative Survey Research which aimed to measures the Awareness on Yoga among Higher Secondary Students. The Design of the study construction of the Tool, Pilot Study, Validity and Reliability, Size of the Sample, Selection of the Sample, Administering the Tool among the Students, Scoring Methods, Statistical Techniques utilized etc., have been reported in detailed manner in this present Chapter and ends with the Limitations of the study.

Design of the Study

Research design is a plan, a structure and a strategy of investigation conceived to obtain answers to various issues in research. The object of research design is to test the research hypotheses. The research design, therefore, is built in the principle of maximization of the results of the study, minimization of variance. A research design however, is not a highly specific plan to be followed without direction. Rather, it is series of guideposts to keep right direction. Thus, research design is the process of planning a research, choosing methods and procedures that can be expected to yield meaningful and most interpretable results.

Table 18.1 : Schematic Representation of the Research Design

S.No.	Type	Sources
1.	Nature of the research	Normative Survey Research
2.	Tools Developed	Awareness on Yoga among Higher Secondary Students.
3.	Variables	Higher Secondary Students
4.	Demographic Variables	Students
		1. Gender
		2. Types of School
		3. Locality
		4. Parents Occupation
		5. Subject
5.	Sampling Technique	Stratified Random Sampling Technique.
6.	Size of the Sample	Students-150
		Boys-73
		Girls-77
7.	Statistical Techniques used	Mean, Standard Deviation, 't' test

The present study belongs to Normative Survey Research. The Demographic Variables used are Gender, Type of Schools, Locality, Parents Occupation, Subjects. The Tools use in the Study is Awareness on yoga among Higher Secondary Students at Namakkal District, along with a Personal Data Sheet to know the background of the Students; Random Sampling technique was followed in his study. Data was collected from 150 Students in different locations of Namakkal District. The Statistical Techniques used *Mean, S.D* and't' Test.

Objectives of the Study

The following objectives were formulated for the present study.

- To find out the yoga awareness of higher secondary school students in Namakkal Educational District.
- To find out the significance difference in the yoga awareness of:
  - Boys and girls (gender)
  - Locality of the student (Rural & Urban)
  - Types of the school (Government & Metric)
  - Parent's occupation (Government & Private)
  - Subjects. (Arts & science)

Hypothesis of the Study

- There is no significant difference between boys and girls towards awareness on yoga.
- There is no significant difference between rural boys and girls towards awareness on yoga.
- There is no significant difference between urban boys and girls towards awareness on yoga.
- There is no significant difference between Government school boys and girls towards awareness on yoga.
- There is no significant difference between Matriculation school boys and girls towards awareness on yoga.
- There is no significant difference between Government occupation of male and female parents towards awareness on yoga.
- There is no significant difference between private occupation of male and female parents towards awareness on yoga.

- There is no significant difference between arts group boys and girls towards awareness on yoga.

  There is no significant difference between science group boys and girls towards awareness on yoga.

Tools Used for the Study

To access the Factors Influencing the Yoga Education among Higher Secondary Students in Namakkal District with three types of Four Point Rating Scale was developed under the Similar Statements. In the type of tools, with the options such as Strongly Agree, Agree, Disagree and Strongly Disagree were utilized.

Preliminary Draft of the Tool

The investigator being a Higher Secondary Students was going on to write appropriate statements related to the objectives of the study.

Awareness on Yoga among Higher Secondary Students in Namakkal District. The steps on the different issues based on the experience of Teachers and other aspects the investigator refine the written statements in all the three Opionnairres. After the corrections, the Opionnairres had 50 Statements only. Then it was administered as a Pilot Study.

Pilot Study

The above Opionnaires was neatly typed and administered among the 40 Students, their respective our College Staffs and our College B.Ed Students in the time of Pilot Study the two Opinonnaire had 50 statements for students. After completion of the pilot study, gathered valuable suggestions, corrections and deleting of some statements were taken by the investigator and refine the Opionnaires.

Finally the tool was consists of 50 statements, the above the tools were used to a study on finding the Awareness on Yoga Education among Higher Secondary Students.

Table 18.2 : Students Opinnaire-Factors Influencing

S.No.	Students		Total
	Positive Items	Negative Items	
	1, 2, 4, 6, 8, 10, 12, 13, 14, 17, 18, 20, 22, 24, 26, 28, 30, 32, 34, 35, 36, 40, 41, 43, 45, 47, 48, 49, 50.	3, 5, 7, 9, 11, 16, 19, 21, 23, 25, 27, 29, 31, 33, 37, 38, 39,42, 44, 46.	
	30	**20**	**50**

The above table 18.2 shows the student opionnairre to access the influencing factor for the students awareness of special education this tool consists of 4 point scale with 30 positive and 20 negative statements.

Reliability and Validity

Reliability applies to a measure when similar results are obtained over time and across situations. It should be noted that reliability is a necessary condition for algidity, but a reliable instrument may not be valid. A reliable but invalid instrument will yield consistently may not be valid. A reliable but invalid instrument will yield consistently inaccurate results.

The one type of opionnairre was to access the awareness on Yoga Education among Higher Secondary students, Teachers and their students as said about in the pilot study and also discuss with the Senior Lecturers working in the Kasthooribha Gandhi College of Education Numskull for their valid suggestions. A few modifications where down in the wordings and options for a few statements utilized in the Opionnairre

For validating the preliminary draft of the Opionnairres, it was administered the Students, The investigator used the Test and Retest method, the test 't' value found in the Opionnairres such as 0.05, accordingly all the influencing factors. Then the tool was accepted as the valid tool for administering in the study.

Personal Data Sheet

To know the background of the Students, The investigator used personal data sheets along with the Developed Questionnaires. It asked for details of Gender, type of School, Locality, Parents Occupation, Subjected. The students were asked to fill in all the particulars given in the personal data sheets. A specimen copy of the personal data sheet and opionnaire used in this study is given in the Appendix-I Tamil version was used for this study.

Size of the Sample

There are so many School in Namakkal district among that the investigator select the Two School in random sampling method the name of the Schools as follows:

1. N.S.A.U G. Hr. Sec. School at Namakkal
2. Trinity Matriculation Hr. Sec. School at Namakkal

From the above areas the investigator has taken from this study.

Table 18.3 : List of Boys and Girls samples

S.No.	Category	Students
1.	Boys	73
2.	Girls	77
	Total	**150**

The present study is done by Normative Survey Method. The Stratified Random Sampling Technique is followed. The size of the sampling was 150 Students only.

Administering the Tool

The opinnaires were administered separately among the 150 students, 73 Boys Students and 77 girls Students of the following Sampling Schools in Namakkal district. The name of the Sampling Schools in Namakkal District following:

Table 18.4 : Name of the Sampling Schools in Namakkal District from Which the Samples are Collected

S.No.	Name of the School	District
1.	N.S. Arumuga udaiyar Government Hr. Sec. School at Namakkal	Namakkal District
2.	Trinity Matriculation Hr. Sec. School at Namakkal	

The above table 18.4 shows the name and the district of the 2 Schools from which the samples are collected.

Scoring Key

The Opinonnairre consists of 30 Positive Statements and 20 Negative Statements. The Negative questions were scored as 1/2/3/4 and positive questions were scored as 4/3/2/1. They are Strongly Agree, Agree, Disagree and Strongly Disagree. The total maximum scores for the Tools were 150 and the total minimum scores to the same are 50 respectively.

Statistical Measures Used in the Study

After scoring the filled in Opinionnarrie, a Master Table was prepared by plotting the scores. Different Statistical Measures such as Mean, Standard Deviation and 't' test to find out the Significant Relationship between Mean Average Scores were used in the present study for finding out the influence of the problems.

Delimitations of the Study

Broadly speaking, any study is impossible without limitation. Research studies is general will have delimitation due to many factors. This study too has some delimitations. It is the responsibility to the researches to see that the study is contacted with maximum care in ordered to be reliable.

However, the following delimitations were unavoidable in the present study:

1. The study has been limited to Namakkal District only.
2. The study has been restricted to the Higher Secondary Students only.
3. The study has been restricted to the XI th Std Student Only.
4. This study adopted survey method using questionnaires to collect data from respondents.
5. A purposive stratified random sample was used to choose the subject to be included in the study.
6. This study is focused mainly on the Variables, Gender, Locality, Various Subjects, Types of Schools, Parents Occupations.

Conclusion

This chapter deals with methodology of the present investigation as enumerated This it gives brief details about selection of sample, pilot study, administration of tool on the study, data collection and statistical technique use in this study, In the following described the detailed methodology of the study in the chapter analysis and interpretation of the data for the present study is next chapter.

Chapter 19

Analysis and Interpretation

Introduction

Any research work could be meaningful when the data were analyzed and interpreted properly. Therefore the researcher has given much important to this part. The data collected from the sample analyzed and interpreted in the following heads:

(*a*) Descriptive analysis

(*b*) Differential analysis

Descriptive Analysis

It includes comparison of measures of central tendency such as the mean and the measures of variability such as standard deviation. The calculated values are used to describe the properties of the different sub-samples.

One hundred and fifty students from Namakkal District constituted the sample. He variable studied in the present judgment was with reference to some selected variables like gender, locality, types of schools, parents occupation, students subjects.

After the data was collected, it was classified as the above mentioned variables.

Differential Analysis

It contains the determinations of the statistical significance of the difference between references to selected variables. It contains '*t*' test. A '*t*' test is a numerical procedure that takes into accounts the difference between the means of the sample present in the scores. Thus the '*t*' test is a technique to find out whether the difference the mean performance is significant or not.

Level of Significance

Experimenters and research workers choose several arbitrary standards for their convenience. These arbitrary standards are called level of significance. Most commonly used level of significance is 0.01 and 0.05 level. For the present investigation, the researcher has used 0.05 levels as significance to analyze the existence of various hypotheses.

Table 19.1 : Significant Difference between Boys and Girls Towards Awareness on Yoga

S.No.	Variables	N	Mean	Standard deviation	't' Value	Significant Level of 0.05
1.	Boys	77	71.31	5.68	2.13*	1.97
2.	Girls	73	74.03	8.11		

*Significant **No Significant

In order to study the significant of the difference, the '*t*' value is calculated. It is 2.13 at 0.05 level and it is represented in table 19.1 the '*t*' value is higher than the table value. Hence it is concluded that, there is significant difference exists between boys and girls higher secondary school students in their yoga awareness. Thus, the framed hypothesis is rejected.

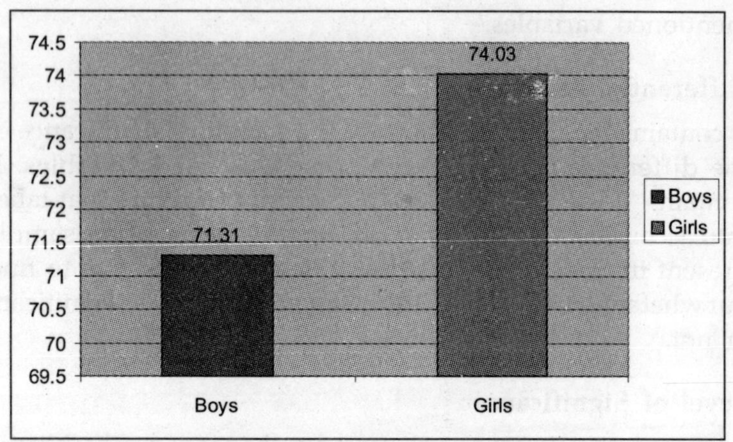

Fig. 19.1 : Significant difference between Boys and Girls towards Awareness on Yoga

Table 19.2 : Significant Difference between Rural Boys and Rural Girls Towards Awareness on Yoga

S.No.	Variables	N	Mean	Standard deviation	't' Value	Significant Level of 0.05
1.	Rural Boys	31	70.41	5.648	2.956*	1.97
2.	Rural Girls	36	74.52	5.738		

*Significant **No Significant

In order to study the significant of the difference, the *'t'* value is calculated. It is 2.956 at 0.05 level and it is represented in table 19.2. The *'t'* value is higher than the table value. Hence it is concluded that, there is significant difference exists between boy's andgirls higher secondary school students in their yoga awareness. Thus, the framed hypothesis is rejected.

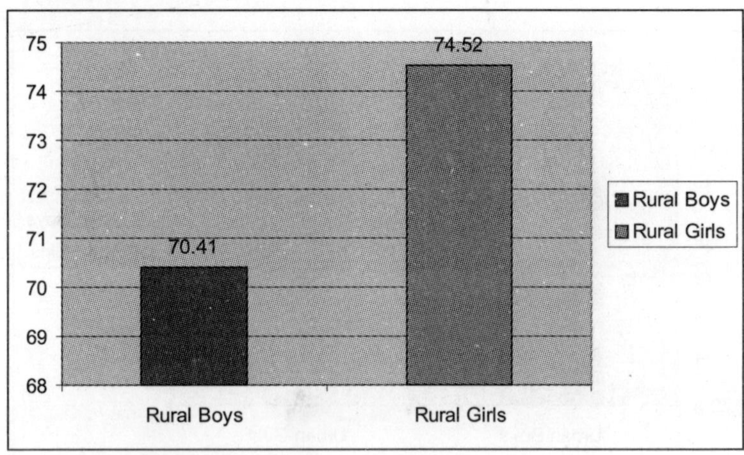

Fig. 19.2 : Significant difference between rural boys and rural girls towards awareness on yoga.

Table 19.3 : Significant Difference between Urban Boys and Urban Girls Towards Awareness on Yoga

S.No.	Variables	N	Mean	Standard deviation	't' Value	Significant Level of 0.05
1.	Urban Boys	46	71.91	4.159	1.518**	1. 97
2.	Urban Girls	37	73.94	7.23		

*Significant **No Significant

In order to study the significant of the difference, the '*t*' value is calculated. It is 1.518 at 0.05 level and it is represented in table 19.3. The '*t*' value is lower than the table value. Hence it is concluded that, there is significant difference exists between boys and girls higher secondary school students in their yoga awareness. Thus, the framed hypothesis is accepted.

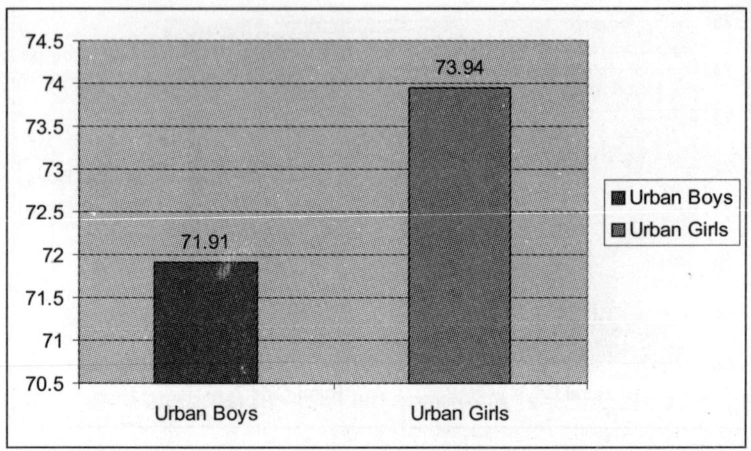

Fig. 19.3 : Significant difference between Urban Boys and Urban Girls towards Awareness on Yoga.

Table 19.4 : Significant difference between Government School Boys and Girls Towards Awareness on Yoga

S.No.	Variables	N	Mean	Standard deviation	't' Value	Significant Level of 0.05
1.	Gov.Boys	34	71.82	5.949	0.158**	1. 97
2.	Gov.Girls	34	72.26	7.68		

*Significant **No Significant

In order to study the significant of the difference, the '*t*' value is calculated. It is 0.158 at 0.05 level and it is represented in table 19.4. The '*t*' value is lower than the table value. Hence it is concluded that, there is significant difference exists between boys and girls higher secondary school students in their yoga awareness. Thus, the framed hypothesis is accepted.

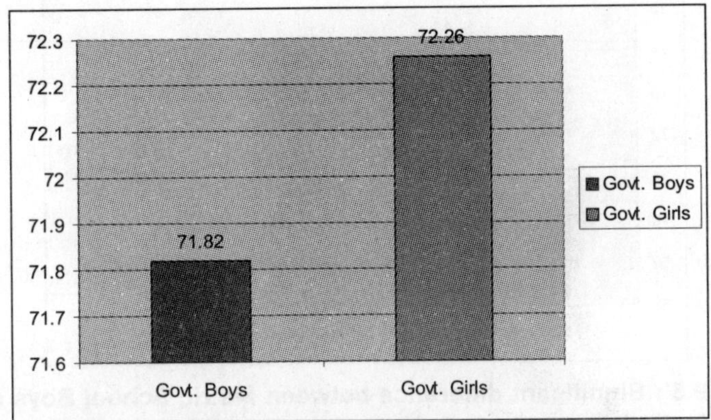

Fig. 19.4 : Significant difference between government school boys and girls towards awareness on yoga.

Table 19.5 : Significant difference between Metric School Boys and Girls Towards Awareness on Yoga

S.No.	Variables	N	Mean	Standard deviation	't' Value	Significant Level of 0.05
1.	Mat. Boys	43	70.67	5.53	2.54*	1. 97
2.	Mat. Girls	39	74.02	6.32		

*Significant **No Significant

In order to study the significant of the difference, the '*t*' value is calculated. It is 2.54 at 0.05 level and it is represented in table 19.5. The '*t*' value is higher than the table value. Hence it is concluded that, there is significant difference exists between boys and girls higher secondary school students in their yoga awareness. Thus, the framed hypothesis is rejected.

In order to study the significant of the difference, the 't' value is calculated. it is 1.97 at 0.05 level and it is represented in table 19.6. The 't' value is lower than the table value. Hence it is concluded that, there is significant difference exists between boys and girls higher secondary school students in their yoga awareness. Thus, the framed hypothesis is accepted.

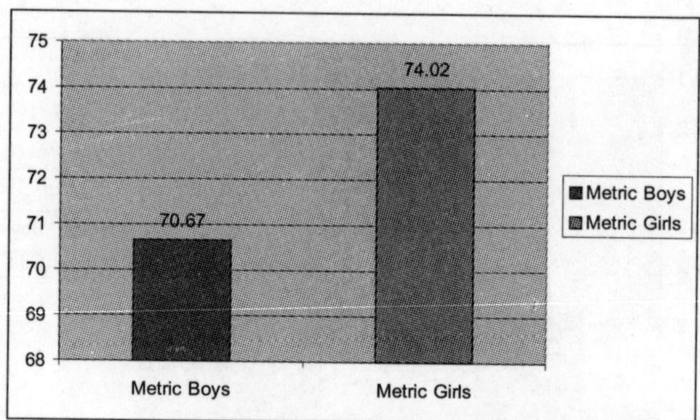

Fig. 19.5 : Significant difference between Metric School Boys and Girls Towards Awareness on Yoga.

Table 19.6 : Significant Difference between Government Occupation of Boys and Girls Parents Towards Awareness on Yoga

S.No.	Variables	N	Mean	Standard deviation	't' Value	Significant Level of 0.05
1.	Boys	31	70.90	6.19	1.97**	1.97
2.	Girls	34	74.02	6.618		

*Significant **No Significant

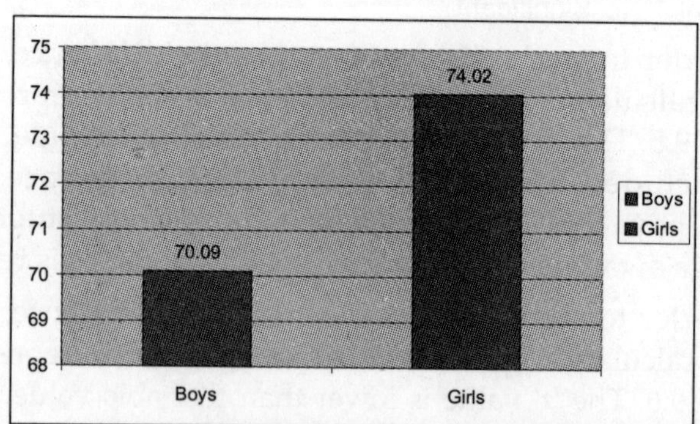

Fig. 19.6 : Significant Difference between Government Occupation of Boys and Girls Parents Towards Awareness on Yoga

Table 19.7 : Significant Difference between Private Occupation of Boys and Girls Parents Towards Awareness on Yoga

S.No.	Variables	N	Mean	Standard deviation	't' Value	Significant Level of 0.05
1.	Boys	46	71.47	5.312	2.332*	1. 97
2.	Girls	45	74.11	5.516		

*Significant **No Significant

In order to study the significant of the difference, the *'t'* value is calculated. It is 2.332 at 0.05 level and it is represented in table 19.7. The *'t'* value is higher than the table value. Hence it is concluded that, there is significant difference exists between boys and girls higher secondary school students in their yoga awareness. Thus, the framed hypothesis is rejected.

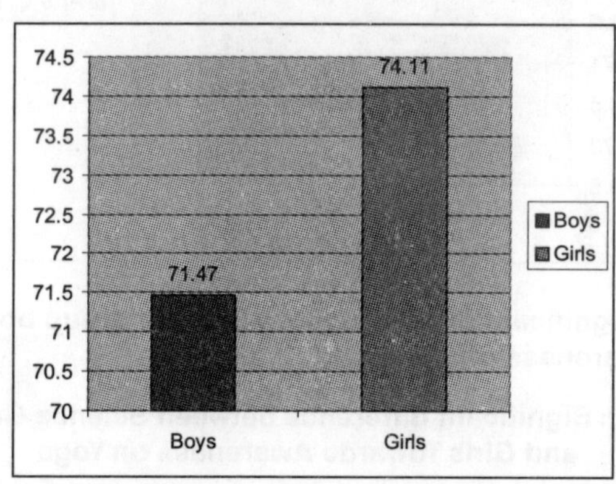

Fig. 19.7 : Significant difference between private occupation of boys and girls parents towards awareness on yoga

In order to study the significant of the difference, the *'t'* value is calculated. It is 1.914 at 0.05 level and it is represented in table 19.8. The *'t'* value is lower than the table value. Hence it is concluded that, there is significant difference exists between boys and girls higher secondary school students in their yoga awareness. Thus, the framed hypothesis is accepted.

Table 19.8 : Significant difference between Arts group Boys and Girls Towards Awareness on Yoga

S.No.	Variables	N	Mean	Standard deviation	't' Value	Significant Level of 0.05
1.	Arts Boys	42	71.33	6.23	1.914**	1.97
2.	Arts Girls	35	74.14	6.57		

*Significant **No Significant

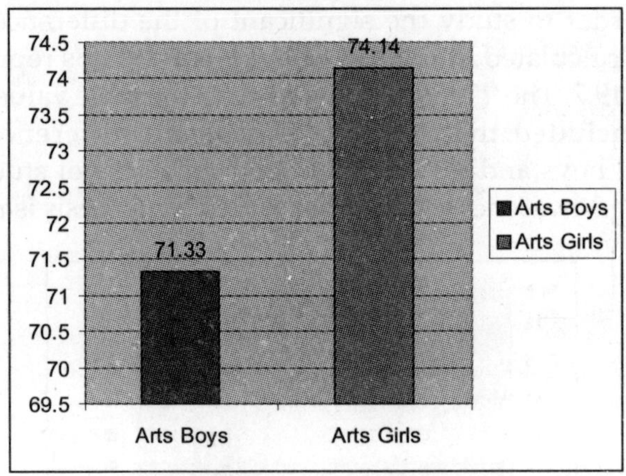

Fig. 19.8 : Significant difference between Arts group boys and girls towards awareness on yoga.

Table 19.9 : Significant difference between Science Group Boys and Girls Towards Awareness on Yoga

S.No.	Variables	N	Mean	Standard deviation	't' Value	Significant Level of 0.05
1.	Science Boys	35	71.42	4.87	2.064*	1.97
2.	Science Girls	38	74.18	6.528		

*Significant **No Significant

In order to study the significant of the difference, the '*t*' value is calculated. It is 2.064 at 0.05 level and it is represented in table 19.9. The '*t*' value is higher than the table value. Hence it is concluded that, there is significant difference exists between boys and girls higher secondary school students in their yoga awareness. Thus, the framed hypothesis is rejected.

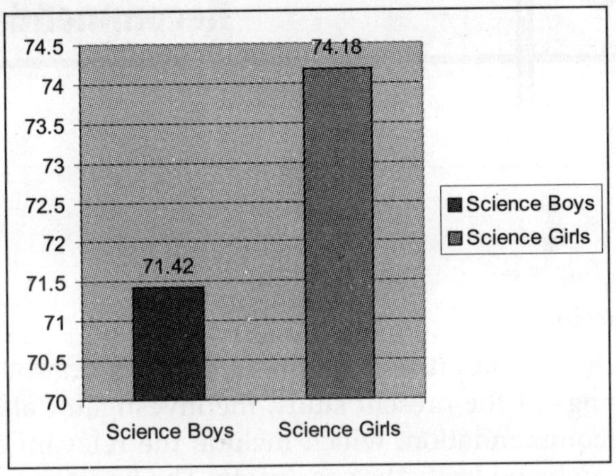

Fig. 19.9 : Significant difference between Science group boys and girls towards awareness on yoga.

Conclusion

Data analysis is ultimately necessary for any research. The obtained data was subjected to necessary statistical compotation the results these analyzed in terms of the corresponding table value are interpreted accordingly, he findings were calculated without any researchers bias which serves as a recommendation for further study.

Chapter

20

Findings, Conclusions and Recommendations

Introduction

In this chapter an attempt had been made to consolidate all the findings of the present study, the investigator also made some recommendation, which include the relevant area for this research and lastly the conclusion. The findings are based on the result collected from the opinioner.

The Study in Retrospect

The aim of the present investigation was to find out the awareness on yoga among higher secondary student at Namakkal District.

Methodology in Brief

For the present study normative survey method was adopted. For the sample of the study,150 students of Namakkal District were contacted. The tool used for the collection of data is yoga awareness scale

Restatement of the Problem

The problem under the study is entitled as awareness on yoga among higher secondary students at Namakkal district.

Objectives of the Study

The following objectives were formulated for the present study.

- To find out the yoga awareness of higher secondary school students in Namakkal Educational District.
- To find out the significance difference in the yoga awareness of:
  - Boys and girls (gender)
  - Locality of the student (Rural & Urban)
  - Types of the school (Government & Metric)
  - Parent's occupation (Government & Private)
  - Subjects. (Arts & science)

Major Finding of the Study

The following are the major findings of the present study:

1. Awareness on yoga among Higher secondary students is Dependent of their Gender.
2. Awareness on yoga among higher secondary students is Dependent of their rural area & Independent of their urban area
3. Awareness on yoga among higher secondary students is Independent of their Government School & Dependent of their Matriculation School
4. Awareness on yoga among higher secondary students is Independent of their parental occupation at government sector & Dependent of their private sector.
5. Awareness on yoga among higher secondary students is Independent to Arts group students & Dependent to science group students.

Conclusion of the Study

The present study concludes that the students adopt themselves to the changing word.

1. Yoga reducing the problem of unhappiness, restlessness, emotional-imbalance & hyperactivity towards school students.
2. Yoga is simply a means of maintaining health & well-being in an increasingly stressful society.
3. Yoga aims at bringing the different bodily functions into perfect co-ordination so that they were for the goad of the whole body.
4. Practice of yoga help to develop awareness regarding the interrelationship among the emotional mental & physical levels.
5. The specialty of the yogic process is that the faculties get sharpened in have with the spiritual process of man.
6. Finally, yoga should be included in the school curriculum as a compulsory subject for the harmonious development of all students (body, mind & soul)

So, the present study focused on Awareness on yoga among Higher Secondary students at Namakkal District.

Recommendations

The following recommendations are made:

1. Similar study can be conducted on wider samples.
2. A similar study may be undertaken by selecting different Districts of the same state.
3. A similar study may be conducted even in High school student.
4. A similar study may be conducted in various colleges and teacher training institutions.
5. Need of orientation program towards yoga, among teachers of different Group

Suggestions

1. Proper yoga study, training

2. Higher secondary students need proper counseling and guidance from the yoga teachers to create self - interest and motivation for better academic performance.
3. Parents should show satisfaction with their child's past and present performance in their academic.

Education Implication

The findings of the present investigation, are important for improving the awareness program of yoga, the following are the major recommendation that have been made from this study, the teach problem of discouraging attitude towards awareness programme.

The result of the study shows that the Awareness on yoga is high in general. Hence yoga must be introduced as a part of curriculum in school education. Proper orientation and refresher training must be provided periodically to the yoga teachers. The pray of yoga is very important in School hours.

Discussion

From the collected data the investigator found that this study reduces blood pressure and stress in their life activity. The investigator study on Awareness on yoga higher secondary schools students. The investigator study on various level schools children's and their Awareness programmed towards yoga. The investigation have no similar results has compare to collected review.

Areas of Research for the Future

Research is a chain activity their purpose of any research in education is 10 find solutions for problems related to teachers students, learning etc...but investigation on one problem always leaves many related research questions that can be investigated by other researchers: some of the areas for research in the future may be as follows:

- The present study can be repeated with wide sample.
- A similar study can be conducted on the professional college.
- A study can be conducted to find out the demographic and motivational variables associated with yoga activities.
- A similar study can be conducted on the high school students.
- The present study could be undertaken at various states in India.
- A study can be conducted on the primary, secondary and higher secondary school teachers.
- Development of CA, package on the awareness on yoga.
- A critical study on evolving strategies promoting the awareness on yoga among the arts and science college students.

Conclusion

The present study made on awareness of yoga among students the findings of the present study reveal that awareness among gender subjects locality types of school parents occupation with respect to the questionnaire.

Bibliography

Aditi Sharma. (2005). *"Environmental studies"*, New Delhi:Surjeet Publications.

Agarwal, V.K. and Usha Guota (2002). *"Ecology and Ethiology"*, New Delh, S. Chand and Co.

Agin, M.L. (1974). *"Educational for Scientific Literacy: A Conceptual Frame of Reference and Some Applications"*. Science Education. 58:403-415.

Alpem, Moris L. (1964, October). *"The Ability to Test Hypotheses"*. Science Education, 30: 220-229.

Amandeep Karu, *et.al.*, (2006). *"Scientific approach to Environmental Education"*, Ludihiana, Tandon Publications.

Ananthakrishnan, T.N. (1987). *"Bioresources Ecology"*, New Delhi: Oxford IBH Publishing Company Pvt Ltd.

Atkinson, J. Myron and R. Will Burnell, *" Science Education"*. Enclyclopedia of Educational Research, 4th ed. 1192-1205.

Bemal, J.D, (1970). *Science and Industry in the Nineteenth Century.* Bloomington: Indiana University press.

Best, John W. (1982). *Research in Education* , 4th ed. New Delhi , Prentice Hall of India Pvt. Ltd.

Bhandula, N., P.C. Chadha, S. Sharma and M.P. Bhasin (1985). Teaching of Science, Ludhiana, Prakash Brothers.

Bhaskara Rao, D. (1982). An Evaluative Studyof the New Science Curriculum at Upper Primary Level in Andhra Pradesh. Master of Education Dissertation, Nagarjuna University.

Bhaskara Rao, D. (1984, February). *"Private Educational Institutions"*. The Educational Review, XC: 35-36.

Bogerrider, A. and Klein, R. (1982). *"Does Solar UV influence the Competitive Relationship in Higher Plants"*, New York.

Boyce Ann. (1997). *"Introduction to Environmental Technology"*, New York: van Nostrand Reinhold International Thomson Pub.Inc.

Brown, Sandra, Iverson, L.R., Anantha Prasad and Logo, A.E. (1993) – Estimating Biomass and Biomass Change of Tropical Forests, CAIAC Communications, 18:7.

Caldwell, Otis W. and Francis D. Curtis (1943). Everydat Science. Boston: Ginn and Co.

Carleton, R. (1961). *"Editorial"*. The Science Teacher. 28:4.

Chandra Pal, *"Environmental Pollution and Development"*, Delhi, Mittal Publications.

Chikara, M.S. and S. Sharma (1985). Teaching of Biology Ludhiana: Prakash Brothers.

Collingwood, R.G. (1982). An Autobiography. Oxford: Clarendon Press.

Das, N.C. (1985). *"A Comparative Study of the Achievement in Science of High School Students of Urban and Rural Areas"*, Indan Journal of Community Guidance 2:83-86.

Das, R.C. (1985). *Science Teaching in Schools*. New Delhi, Sterling Publishers.

Despande, S.D. (1983). Modelling of the Atmospheric Minor constituents. Proc. Workship on Global Ozone Problem. National Physical Lab., New Delhi: 14-52.

Dewey, J. (1934). *"The Supreme Intellectual Obigation"*. Science Education. 18:1-4.

Downing, Elliot R. (1936, October). *"Some Results of a Test on Scientific Thinking"*. Science Education. 20:121.

Driver, R., E. Guesneandm A. Tiberghien, eds. (1985). Children's Ideas in Scinece, Milton Keyness: Open University Press.

English, H.B. and A.C. English (1958). A Comprehensive Dictionary of Psychoanalytical Terms. London; Longmans.

Eugence P.Odum. (1996). "Fundamental of Ecology (3rd Edn)", Dehradun: Nataraj Publications,

Fergusan, George A. (1981). *Statistical Analysis in Psychology and Education.* 5th ed. Tokyo: McGraw-Hill International Book Co.

Fox, F.M., and Caldwell, M.M. (1978). Competitive Interaction in Plants Populations Exposed to Supplementary UV-B radiations. Oecologia (Berl) 36:137-90

Freeman, Frank S. (1965). Theory and Practice of Psychological Testing, 3rd ed. Calcutta: Oxford & IBH Publishing Co.

Gadamer4, Hans-Georg (1981). Reason in the Age of Science. Cambridge: MIT Press.

Gage, N.L. (1966). Handbook of Research on Teaching. Chicago : Rand McNally & Co.

Ghai, Dharam (1995). Global Markets, Global Insecurity. Our planet, 7(3):6-8.

Ghanta, R.anmd Rao, D.B. (2001). *"Environmental Education, Problems and Prospects"*, New Delhi: Australia: Blackwell Publishing Company.

Goldstein, T. (1980). Dawn of Modern Science. Boston; Houghton Miffin Co.

Gravetter, Frederick J. and Larry B. Wallnau (1987). Statistics for the Behavioral Science New Delhi : MrGraw-Hill Pulishing Co. Ltd.

Gupta, Arun Kumar (1985), October). *"Differential Scientific Aptitude Abilities and Scholastic Achievement"*. Indian Educational Review XX: 151-157.

Hazen, R and J. Trefil (1991). Science Matters: Achieving Scientific Literacy. New York : Doubleday.

Heiss, Eldwood D., Ellsworth S. Obourn and Charless W. Hoffman (1950). Modern Science Teaching. New York: The MacMillan Co.

Henry, Nelson B., ed (1960). Rethinking Science Education. The fifty ninth Yearbook of the National Society for the Study of Education, Part-1 Distributed by the University of Chicago Press, Chicago, Illinois.

Hurd, P.D. (1970). *"Scientific Enlightenment for an Age of Science"*. The Science Teacher. 37 : 13-15.

Hutchings, Donal, ed. (1966, June). Towards More Creative Science. New College Conference. Oxford: Pegamon Press.

Jain, N.K. (1982). History of Science oand Scientific Method. New Delhi : Oxford & IBH Publishing Co.

Jocabson, Willard J. and Rodney L. Doran. (1988). Science Achievement in the United States and Sixteen Countries. The International Association for the Evaluation of Educational Research, Second IEA Science Study. Teachers College, Columbia University, New York.

Jose, K.M. (1987). A Comparative Study of the Biology achievement of High, Average, and Low Science Aptitude of Secondary School Pupils. M.Ed. Thesis, University of Calicut.

Kaela, R.M.(1976). Innovations in Science Teaching. New Delhi : Oxford & IBH Publishing Co.

Kerlinger, Fred N. (1964). Foundations of Behavioural Research. Holt, Rinehart & Winston.

Klopfer, L. (1969). *"The Teaching of Science and the History of Science"*. Journal of Research in Science Teaching. 6: 87-95.

Kumar, V.K. (1982). *"A study in Environmental Pollution"*, Varanasi:Tara Book Agency.

Lacey, A.L., (1966). Guide to Science Teaching. Belment, California: Wadsworth Publishing Co., Inc.

Link, F.(1967). *"An Approach to a more Adequate Systems of Evaluation in Science"*. The Science Teacher. 34:20-24.

Lowel, E.K. and J.W. Atkinson (1953). The Effect of Need for Achievement on Learning and Speed of Performance' Journal of Psychology 33: 31-40.

Maduraj, *"Emerging Trend in Environemntal Pollution"*, Delhi :IVY Publications, 2001.

Matyas, M.L., K.G. Dobbin and B.J. Fraser, eds. (1989). Looking into Window; Qualitative Research in Science Education. Washingron D.C.: American Association for the Advancement of Science.

Maybury, Robert H. and Adolph Y. Wilbrun, *"Science Education International"*. The Encyclopedia of Education, 8:107-117

Ministry of Human Resource Development, Department of Education, Government of India (1985). Challenges of Education—A Policy Perspective.

Mookerjee, Anjali (1983). Ultraviolet Effect on Unicellular Organisms in presence of drugs. proc.Indo-US Workshop on Global Ozone problem. Nat. Physical Lab., New Delhi-227-30.

Nair, A.S. and S. Joseph (1978). An Experimental Study of the overlap of Intelligence and Science Aptitude with Educational Outcomes in Biology Measured Using Host's Taxonomy. Department of Education, University of Kerala.

National Scheme of In-service Training of School Teachers (1987). Resource Material part II, Seondary. New Delhi: National Council of Educational Research and Training.

National Science Teacher Association (1962). " CurriculumDevelopment in Science ". The Science Teacher. 29:32-37.

Okey, James R. (1982). "The Scientific Attitude and Science Eucation : A Critical Reappraisal". Science Education. 66: 109-121.

Osbrone, R. and P. Freyberg. eds (1985). Learning in Science: The Implications of Children's Science. London; Heinemann.

Pal, G. (1982). An Enquiry into the factors involved in the Learning of Science by Adolescent Pupils.

O' Hearn and C. Gale (1966), *"Scientific Literacy—Its Referents"*. ...ence Tacher. 33:34.

Peterso..., ...ita W. and Gaylon R. Carlson (1979). *"A Summary of Research ihn Science Education 1977"*. Science Education. 63.

Radha, S.and Sankhyan, A.S. *"Environmental Challenges of the 21st Century"*, New Delhi, Deep and Deep Publications.

Rai, B.C.(1983). Methods of Teaching Science. Lucknow; Prakashan Kendra.

Reif, Frederick. (1986 , November). *"Scientific Approaches to Science Education"*. Physics Today. 38-44.

Rummel, J. francis (1958). An Introuduction to Research Procedures in Education. New York: Harper and Brothers.

Salmon, W.C. (1967). The Foundations of Scientific Influence. Pittsburgh; University of Pittsburgh.

Saxena, A.B. (1986). *"Environemntal Education"*, Agra: National Psychological Corporation

Saxena, K.N.A. (1963). *"A Comparative Study of the Achievement in Science of Urban and Rural Students"*. Journal of Education and Psychology, 21 : 38-44.

Sharma, B.K. *"Ecology and Environemnt"*, Meerut: Rastogi Publications.

Sharma, H.L. (1989). School Science Educational in India. New Delhi: Commonwealth Publishers.

Sharma, R.C. (1984). Modern Science Teaching. Delhi; Dhanpat Rai & Sons.

Sharma, Radha R (1985). Enhancing Academic Achievement—Role of Some Personality Factors. New Delhi: Concept Publishing Co.

Shukla R.s and Chandel, P.S. (1992). *"Plant Ecology"*, New Delhi, S. Chand and Co.

Shukla, S.K and Srivatava P.R. *"Evaluation of Environmentasl Noise Pollution"*, New Delhi, Commonwealth Publications.

Singh, S. (1995). *"Environmental Geography"*, Allahabad, Prayag Pustak Bhawan.

Singh, S. and Dubey. (1989). *"A Environemntal Management"*, Allahabad:Dept of geography, Allahabad Iniverstiy.

Sood, J.K., ed. (1978). Emerging Perspectives in Science Education Research. Ajmer : Regional College of Education.

Susils Appadurai. (2004). *"Environmental Studies"*, Chennai, New Century Book House.

Taylor, R.F. (1964). 'Personality Traits and Discreoant Achievement', Journal of Counseling Psychology. 11: 76-82

Teaching Life Sciences—A book of Methods. Chandigarh : Kohli Publishers.

Thampy, M.P. (1984). A study of the Interaction of Science Appitude and attitude towards Scienc on Biology Achievement of Secondary School Pupils. Master of Education thesis, University of Calicut.

Thangamani and Shymala Thangamani, *"A Text Book of Environmental Studies"*, Sivakasi, Pranav Syndicate Publications.

The Readers Digest (1962). Great Encyclopedic Dictionary, Vol. 1, A-L. London : The Reader's Digest Association.

Trivedi R.N. (1997). *"A Textbook of Environemntal Sciences"*, New Delhi, Anmol Publications Pvt. Ltd.

Underhill, O.E. (19441). The Origins and Development of Elementary School Science. New York : Scott Foresman and Company.

UNESCO (1974). Learning to be. New Delhi : National Council of Educational Research and Training.

Vaidya, Narendra (1976). Learning to be. New Delhi: National Council of Educational.

Venkara Rao, P. and D. Bhaskaran Rao. (1988). A Text Book of Zoology - Senior Intermediate, Revised Edition. Guntur: Vigyan Publishers.

Verma, P.S. and Agarwal, *"K. Environemntal Biology"* (Principles of Ecology), New Delhi:, S. Chand and Company.

Wanchoo, V.N., ed. (1982). World Views on Science Education. Oxford & IBH Pubklishing Co.

Washton, Nathan S. (1961). Science Teaching in the Secondary School. New York: Harper & Brothers.

Williams, S.S (1979). *"A Comparative Study of Pupils' Achievement in some of the Instructionjal Objectives in teaching General Science"*, Experiments in Education. XV: 67-73.

Williams, T. Mooon. A and Willians.M. (1991). *"Environment and Helath"*, Delhi, B.R. Publishing Corporation.

Yadav, M.S. (1992). Teaching of Science. New Delhi: Anmol Publishers.

Yadav. K. (1993). Teaching of Life Sciences. New Delhi: Anmol Publishers.

Young, Pauline V. and Calvin F. Schmid (1968). Scientific Social Surveys and Research. New Delhi, Prentice Hall of India Pvt. Ltd

Child Labour

Aggarwal, Y.P. Statistical Methods Concepts Application and Compotation, Sterling Publishers (P) Ltd., New Delhi-110016

Ahuja, Daman, *"Economics of Child Labour"*, In Tripathy, S.N., Exploitation of Child Labour in Tribal India, Daya Publishing House, New Delhi, 1991.

Ananda Kumar, N. (1986). A Way of Life. Catcutta:Vivekananda Kendra Yogas Publication.

Astrand and Kearl Rodhal, A.(1977). Text Book of Work Physiology. New York: McGraw Hill Book Co.,

Barik, B.C. (1994). Rural Migrant in An Urban Setting, Classical Publishing House, New Delhi, 1991.

Becker, Gary (1964). Human Captial—A Theoretical and Empirical Analysis with Special Reference to Education, New York: Columbia University Press.

Burra, Neera (1992). Child Labour in the Lock Industry of Aligarh, National Labour Institute, New Delhi.

Burra, Neera (1995). Born to Work: Child Labourin India, Oxford University Press, New Delhi.

Canagara, Sudharshan and Nielsen, Helena Skyt. (2001). *"Child Labour in Africa: A Comparative Study"*. The Annals of the American Academy, AAPSS, 575. May, p. 71-91.

Census of India (1991), Government of India, New Delhi.

Chakravarty, B. (1989), Education and Child Labour, Chugh Publication, Allahabad.

CHANDRASEKARAN, K.(1999). Sound Health Through Yoga. Madurai: Prem Kalyan Publication.

Chooudhury, D.P. (1996), A Dynamic Profile of Child Labour in India, 1951-1991. ILO, New Delhi.

Choudhury, Poul D. (1995), *"Girl Child and Gender Bias"*, Social Change, Vol. 25, No. 2-3, June-September, pp. 84-93.

Cockburn, John (2001). Child Work and Poverty in developing Countries Oxford: University of Oxford.

Cunningham, Hugh and Pier Paolo Viazzo (ed) (1996) Child Labour in Historical Perspective—1800-1985- Case Studies from Europe, Japan and Colombia, Florence, Unicef, International Child Development Centre.

Danielou, N and Alain, K.(1955). The Method of Reintegration. New York : The Murray Printing Company.

Delap, Emily (2001). " Economic and Cultural Forces in the Child Labour Debate": Evidence from Urban Bangladesh" Journal of Development Studies, 37 (4). 1-22.

Gangrade, K.D.(1995), *"Social Development and the Girl Child"*, Social Change, June-Septmber, Vol. 25, No. 2 and 3, pp. 71-83

GHAROTE, M.L. (1996). Applied yoga. Lonavala Kaivalyadhama, S.M.Y.M Samiti.

Good, Carter.V. (1959). Introduction of Educational Research, Appleton Century Crafts, IINC, New York.

Government of India (1975), Report of the Royal Labor Enquiry, The Controller of Publications, New Delhi

Gupta, C.B. (1972). An Introduction to Statistical Method, Vikas Publishing House, Delhi.

Gurupadaswamy, M.S. (1979) Report of Committee on Child Labour, Government of India, New Delhi. ILO(1991), Facts and Figures on Child Labour, ILO, Geneva.

Howley Edwar, T. and Dom Franks, B.(1997). Health Fitness Instructors Hand Book. Human Kinetics : Illinos.

ICCW. (1998). Poverty not Primary Reason for Child Labour—A Study. Indian Council for Child Welfare Journal Vol. V No. 1 & 2. April-June.

ILO (1993), World Labour Report, ILO Geneva.

ILO (1996), Child Labour : Targeting the Intolerable, ILO, Geneva.

ILO (1997), Yearbook of Labour Statistics, ILO, Geneva.

International Labour Organisation (1996). Child Labour targeting the Intolerable. Geneva: ILO.

Jain, Devaki (1990), *"Improving the Lot of Working Girl Child"*, Kurukshetra, No. 10-14.

Kitchulu, T.N. (1999). Child Labour Current Scenario, Yojana May.

Kothari, C.K. (1985). Research Methodology, Wiley Eastern Ltd., New Delhi.

Krishna, K.P. (1995). Girl Child and Sexual Victimization, Social Change, Vol. 25, No. 2-3, June-September, pp. 124-132.

Kuldip Nayar (1997). *"The Bane of Child Labour,"* The Hindu, 20 December.

LYENKAR, B.K.S. (2001). The path of Holistic Health. Great Britain : Darling Kindersley Limited.

MAZUMDAR, S. (1956). Yogic Exercise—Calcutta : Trichur Longman Limited.

MC ARDLE, AND WILLIAM, D. (1991). Exercise Physiology and Energy Nutrition and Human Performance. Philadelphia : Lea and Febiger publication.

MEHRA, B.K. AND LASHKARI, B.I . (1992). High Blood Pressure—Causes, Prevention and Tratment. Delhi, Orient Paperbacks.

Mishrsa, G.P. and Pandey, P.N. (1992). A Study in Child Labour in Glass Industry of Ferozavad, Giri Institute of Development Studies, Lucknow.

Mitra, Sujay, Combating Child Labour in India, Social Welfare, November, 2003.

Morehouse, and Lawrence, E.(1980). A New Light for Asthmatics. Calcutta: Vivekananda Kendra Yogas Publication.

Myron Weiner. (1991). The Child and the State in India. New York : Oxford University Prees.

Pichholia, K.R. (1993), Child Labour in Metropolitan City : A Case Study of Ahemdabad. Indian Journal of Labour Economics, Vol. 22.

Radha Krishna Rao. (1993). Child hood dreams in the dum. The Tribune, 7th January. Child Labour in Mechanical Workshops (A study of child workers in Urban centers of West Godavari District, A.P). Visakhapatnam : Andhra University (Unpublished Thesis).

Saini Debi, S. (1994). Children of a Lessor God, Child Labour Law and Compulsory Education : Social Action, Vol. 44, No. 3, July-September.

Sakshi Khattar,, Education is Key to Abolish Child Labour, Times of India, June 15, 2009.

Sathe, P. (1995). Child Labour Policy—Legal Perspectives. New Delhi: Asish Publishing House.

Sharma, R.A. (1980). Fundamentals of Educational Research, Loyal Book Dept., Meerut.

Simha, S. (1996). Child Labour and Education Policy in India. The Administrator. Vol. 41, No. 3. July-Sept.

Singh, I.S. (1992). Child Labour. New Delhi: Oxford & IBH Publishing Co.

Statistical Handbook (2005) Handbook of Department of Economics and Statistics. Government of Tamilnadu, Chennai. Retrieved on May 20, 2006, from http: / /www.tn.gov.in.

Suman Chandra. (1998). Problems and Issues of Child Labour. Social Action, Vol. 48, No. 1, Jan-March.

Toor, Sandia(2001). *"Child Labour in Pakistan: Coming of Age in the New World Order."* Annals of the American Academy of Political and Social Science. 575, p. 194-224.

Tripathy, S.n. (1989), *'Bonded Labour in India'*, Discovery Publishing House, New Delhi.

Tripathy, S.N. (2004), *Girl Child and Human Rights*, Anmol Publishing, New Delhi.

UNICEF (1997), Challenges Ahead UNICEF, Hyderabad.

UNICEF (2000), The State of World's Children, UNICEF, New York.

Usha Nair,(1991), *'Universal Primary Education of Rural Girls in India'*, National Council of Educational Research and Training, New Delhi.

Weiner, Myron (1988). Numble Little Fingers: The Making of Child Labour and Compulsory Education Policy in India. Madras: Centre for International Studies.

Widge. (1997). Child Welfare Programmes in the Five Year Plans. Social Welfare, Nov-Dec.

www.ilo.org/ipec, November 15, 2010

Zelizer, Viviana (1985) Pricing the Priceless Child. New York, Basic Books.

JOURNAL

Archanakual, Sinha, U.S., Pathak, Y.K., Aparajita Singh, Kapoor. A.K., Susheel Sharma & Sanju Singh. (2005). Factal Road Traffic Accidents, Study of Distribution, Nature and Type of Injury. JIAFM, Vol 27(2) ISSN 0971 – 0973, 71- 76.

Arvind Kumar Mavoori. (2005). An Activity Plan for Indian Road Safety. 1-90.

Gururaj, G. (2004). Alcohol and Road Traffic Injuries In South Asia: Challenges For Prevention. JCPSP, Vol. (14 (12), 713-718.

Gururaj, G. (2008). Road Traffic Deaths Injuries and Disabilities in India: Current scenario. The National Medical Journal of India, Vol. 21, No. 1, 14-26.

McKnight, AJ & McKnight, AS. (2003). Young Novice Drivers: Careless or Clueless? Accident Analysis and Prevention, Volume: 35 Issue: 6, pp. 921-925.

NAYAR, H.S (1975). Effects of Yogic Exercises on Human Physical Efficienty. India Journal of Medical Research, 63.

O'Flaherty. (1997). Transport Planning and Traffic Engineering. Arnold Publications, London.

POLLOCK, L (1971). Effects of Walking on Body Composition and Cardiovascular Function of Middle Aged Men. Jounal of Applied Physiology, 30:1

SAHAY, B.K. (1992). Biochemical Parameters Normal Volunteers Before and After Yogic Practices. Indian Journal of Medical Research, 76.

Swami, H.M, Puri, S, & Bhatia, V. (2006). Road Safety Awareness and practices Among School Children of Chandigarh. Indian Journal of community Medicine Vol. 31, No. 3, 199-200.

UDUPA, K.N.(1971). Study on pulse Rate and Metabolic Response to the Practice of Yoga in Young Normal Volunteers. Journal of Research in Indian Medicine, 75.

UPPAL, A.K. (1982). Effect of Endurance, Training of Resting and Exercise Blood pressure of secondary school Boys. SNIPES Journal, 5 No : 1

WARIS QIDWAI. K. (2000). Effect of Dietary Garlic on the Blood pressure in Humans. Journal of the Pakistan Medical Association, 50:6.

THESES

CHINNASAMY, R.(1992). Effects of Asanas and Physical Exercises on Selected Physiological and Biochemical Variable Among School Boys, Bharathidasan University, Trichy.

DHANARAJ, A.K. (1995). Effect of Selected Yogic and Physical Exercises on Flexibility and Cardio Respiratory Endurance of Madurai Kamarajar University Players, M.K. University,

KRISHNAN, ARUNAGIRI. (1990). Effect of Selected Yogic and Bharathiyam Exercises on Physiological Variables among School Boys, Alagappa University, Karaikudi.

MOORTHY, A.M Survey of Minimum Muscular Fitness of the school children of Age Group Influence of Selected Yogic Exercise and Physical Exercises on them, University of Pune, Pune.

RADHALAKSHMI, K. (1997). Effect of Selected Yogic and Physical Exercises on Physical Fitness of School Girls in Kerala, Alagappa University, Karaikudi.

VICTOR RONRCY, R. (1985). Comparative Study of the Pulse Rate and Systolic Blood Pressure of College Sprinters and Long Distance Runners, Alagappa University, Karaikudi.

WEBSITE

www education.nic.in

www.epa-govt.

www.eeweek.org

www. wwfechina.org.

www.wcs.org

Index